MONEY AND FINANCE IN THE ECONOMIC DEVELOPMENT OF TAIWAN

STUDIES IN THE ECONOMIES OF EAST AND SOUTH-EAST ASIA

General Editors: Peter Nolan, Lecturer in the Faculty of Economics and Politics, University of Cambridge, and Fellow and Director of Studies in Economics, Jesus College, Cambridge, England; and Malcolm Falkus, Professor of Economic History, University of New England, Armidale, New South Wales, Australia

In the last decades of the twentieth century the small- and medium-sized nations of East and South-East Asia have begun a process of potentially enormous political and economic transformation. Explosive growth has occurred already in many parts of the region and the more slowly growing countries are attempting to emulate this vanguard group. The impact of the region upon the world economy has increased rapidly and is likely to continue to do so in the future.

In order to understand better economic developments within this vast and diverse region, this series will aim to publish books on both contemporary and historical issues. It will include works both by Western scholars and by economists from countries within the region.

Melanie Beresford
NATIONAL UNIFICATION AND ECONOMIC DEVELOPMENT IN VIETNAM

Yin-Ping Ho
TRADE, INDUSTRIAL RESTRUCTURING AND DEVELOPMENT IN HONG KONG

Jomo K. S.
GROWTH AND STRUCTURAL CHANGE IN THE MALAYSIAN ECONOMY

Lee Sheng-Yi
MONEY AND FINANCE IN THE ECONOMIC DEVELOPMENT OF TAIWAN

Money and Finance in the Economic Development of Taiwan

Lee Sheng-Yi
Visiting Senior Research Fellow
Chung Hua Institution for Economic Research
Taipei, Taiwan, and
Associate Professor
Department of Economics and Statistics
National University of Singapore

M
MACMILLAN

First published 1990

Published by
THE MACMILLAN PRESS LTD
Houndmills, Basingstoke, Hampshire RG21 2XS
and London
Companies and representatives
throughout the world

Printed and bound in Great Britain by
WBC Ltd, Bristol and Maesteg

British Library Cataloguing in Publication Data
Lee, Sheng-Yi, *1922–*
Money and finance in the economic development of
Taiwan.—(Studies in the economies of East and
South-East Asia).
1. Taiwan. Economic development
I. Title II. Series
330.951'249
ISBN 0–333–51088–7

In happy memory of my visits to Chung Hua Institution for Economic Research, Taipei, 1984–90, and with profound gratitude

Contents

List of Figures

List of Tables

Preface

Although there are some articles and memorial books in the Chinese language published by banks on banking development in Taiwan, there are very few articles and books written in English on banking in Taiwan. Some notable economists such as Professor S. C. Tsiang, and Shirley W. Y. Kuo, have written on the monetary aspect, but not on banking. This book attempts to fill this gap. Hence, Part I gives a historical review of the banking system, different types of financial institutions and their statistics. Demand deposits of banks are the most important part of money. This leads to Part II which analyses the monetary policy in different periods.

The world has been amazed by the spectacular growth of the Taiwan economy. How did it come about in terms of agricultural development, industrialisation, and the financial and real sectors? What role did money and finance play in economic development of Taiwan? What development strategy was used? These questions are raised and in Part III (Chapter 7) an attempt is made to answer them.

The weakness of the financial system has been revealed in several crises. Liberalisation, internationalisation, and institutionalisation are now the key themes for the reform of the financial system.

I will take this opportunity to thank heartily the Chung Hua Institution for Economic Research, Taipei, which has given me the opportunity and facility for this research study for more than four years. Professor S. C. Tsiang, a monetary theorist, and the President of the Institution, has guided me in the monetary analysis. Dr Liang Kuo-Shu, formerly a professor and now the Chairman of Chang Hwa Commercial Bank, has gone through Chapter 2, and made valuable suggestions from his practical experience. Dr Lee Yung San, formerly the manager of the Research Department, Central Bank of China and now the Director of the Institute of Economics, Academia Sinica, has read Chapter 5 and suggested some corrections in statistical data. Mr Chen Mu-Tsai, the Deputy-Chief of the Banking and Finance Division, Ministry of Finance, Taiwan, has suggested some points in Chapter 7.

Dr Wayne S. Chow of the Chung Hua Institution for Economic Research advised me on the econometric analysis. Mr Po-Kuey Chen, Misses Shwu-Chyong Kuo, Judy Lo and Lydia Shian of the Data Processing Division of the Institution computed the statistics and drew the graphs in this book. Misses Chi-Jian Chien, Ling-Jung Chen, Jing-Yuan Huang and Shu-June Lin helped me to compile the data and type the manuscript. To all of them I owe a debt of gratitude.

LEE SHENG-YI

1 Introduction

Although Taiwan is poor in natural resources, her geographical position is a favourable factor for economic growth. This point is similar to Singapore and Hong Kong. Hence, the great trade flow of the western edge of the Pacific Basin has fostered the development of the three newly industrialising countries (NICs).

Second, the human factor has successfully exploited the geographical advantage. The people in the three countries are hard-working, well-educated and thrifty. In Taiwan, people had to work very hard in order to survive, particularly after the Nationalist Government retreated from mainland China to Taiwan, and in the difficult circumstances of losing international recognition, when Taiwan had to break off diplomatic relationship with the major countries in the world, culminating in Taiwan's withdrawal from the United Nations, World Bank, International Monetary Fund and other international agencies in 1971. Yet the country has achieved a high economic growth and tends to regain international recognition through economic achievement, and to re-enter international organisations, such as the Asian Development Bank, OECD, GATT etc.

The thriftiness of the people in Taiwan is well exemplified in the high savings ratio of 39 per cent in 1987 (see Chapter 5, Table 5.6). Education and technical training are very much emphasised in Taiwan, in order to foster a good labour force, and there has been industrial peace, with few strikes, since the 1950s. Those human factors have indeed contributed much to the economic growth of Taiwan.

Taiwan's real national income (at 1981 constant prices) had grown by 21.4 times from NT$115.4bn in 1951 to NT$2472.6bn in 1987.[1] The population growth rate was 2.59 per cent per annum on average in that long period of 36 years.[2] Hence, the real income per capita had multiplied by 9 from NT$13 976 in 1951 to NT$126 471 in 1987. This high income growth rate was achieved in spite of the heavy military commitment of manpower and resources.

The index of industrial production (1981 = 100) rose from 90.40 in 1979 to 166.63 in 1987, with an average annual increase of 10.5 percentage points.[3] The index of industrial labour productivity (1981 = 100) increased from 91.92 in 1979 to 153.14 in December 1987.

The high growth of GDP has been associated with a rapid change in industrial structure showing a marked shift from agriculture to manufacturing. Agriculture's share in net domestic product declined from 36 per cent in 1952, to 18 per cent in 1970, 9 per cent in 1980 and 6 per cent in 1987. Conversely manufacturing's share rose from 11 per cent in 1952, to 26 per cent in 1970, 34 per cent in 1980, and 39 per cent in 1987. The share of commerce, transport and communication declined marginally from 22 per cent in 1952, to 21 per cent between 1970 and 1987.

The composition of export commodities followed the pattern of change in industrial structure. In 1952, agricultural products constituted 22.1 per cent of total exports, processed agricultural products, 69.8 per cent and industrial products 8.1 per cent. Those respective percentages changed to 8.6, 12.8 and 78.6 in 1970; to 3.6, 5.6 and 90.8 in 1980; and to 1.2, 4.9 and 93.9 in 1987. Logically, bank finance also followed that pattern and its change (see Chapter 4, Table 4.9).

The high growth of GNP naturally reduced unemployment. The unemployment rate was as low as 1.2 per cent in 1979; it went up only slightly to 1.7 per cent in February 1988. Taiwan can be said to have achieved full employment in the 1980s.

Economic growth was successfully achieved with price stability. Apart from the high inflation rate in 1950–5 (the lagged effect of the civil war in China and the shortage of material supply when the nationalist government retreated to Taiwan) there was price stability thereafter, except for the effect of the two oil crises, i.e. consumer prices rose by 47 per cent in 1974, and 16–19 per cent in 1980 and 1981 (see Chapter 5, Table 5.2).

Taiwan also presents an example of growth without causing the income distribution to deteriorate.[4] Kuznets's generalisation that income inequality tends to widen in the early stage of economic development and then to narrow in the later stage,[5] is based on the past experience of Western economies and is not applicable to Taiwan. His contention is based on the observation that in those economies there is at work a disruptive force which arises from the deteriorating competitive position of the traditional modes of production relative to the new modern industries, resulting in a reduced income for many people. Taiwan succeeded in avoiding this pitfall because land reform in 1949–53 had the objective of land-to-the tiller, so that land was distributed to the poor farmers and farm-labourers. However, in the 1980s because of the various tax concessions to encourage exports and capital investment, and because of the fact that farmers' income would be driven lower than urban income by market forces, income distribution has become more unequal.[6]

The model of Taiwan development is unique in the sense that the real sector leads the financial sector. McKinnon and many theorists believe in financial liberalisation and financial deepening, and that the improvement of the financial sector should precede that of the real sector because economic growth would be suppressed if industries and economic activities cannot obtain adequate finance.[7] The experience of Taiwan shows that the informal money market can fill in the gap of the unsatisfied demand for funds to a certain extent, although it should be regarded as a temporary measure.

The financial crisis of the Tenth Credit Cooperative in 1985, and the financial trouble of several trust and investment companies and a small private bank in the late 1970s and 1980s (see Chapters 4 and 8) expose the weakness of the financial system, and call for reform. Thus the lagging behind of the financial sector to the real sector is demonstrated not so much in statistics but more importantly in organisations, and management.

With the spectacular growth of export trade, Taiwan is now ranked as the thirteenth largest exporting country in the world, in spite of her small population of only about 20 million and a small land area. With increasing export surplus, her international reserves have grown to US$76.7bn in February 1988; Taiwan has become the third largest reserve-holder in the world, ranking only after Japan and Germany.

Monetary and fiscal policies and various government measures have been playing an important role in stimulating this high growth. For example, the financial liberalisation and high interest rate policy in the early 1950s, the institution of preferential interest rate deposit to combat inflation (see Chapter 5), the preferential interest rate and re-discount facility for export financing the land reform in 1949–53 (see Chapter 7), the privatisation of four big public enterprises (namely paper, cement, mining and agro-industries) in 1955, and gradual shifting from import-substitution development strategy to one of export-orientation are the landmarks for progress.

The strategy of shifting the economic structure from labour-intensive industries to capital-and-technology-intensive industries and the increasing awareness of the need to reduce pollution are the two major issues of current development. Banking and finance have to support such efforts. Hence, the government has been encouraging banks to divert more loans to high-technology industries and to the instalment of equipment to control pollution.

It has been commented that because of the abnormally high

savings ratio and the decline of investment incentive in the 1980s, the savings ratio is almost twice the domestic investment ratio (see Chapter 5, Tables 5.9 and 5.12 and Figure 5.4). The resources which cannot be effectively invested at home have to be exported, causing a large export surplus, enhancing international reserves and putting pressure on NT dollars to appreciate. How to increase the investment incentive, or to bring the investment ratio closer to the savings ratio is an important problem.

Geographical position and political factors determine to a large extent the trade and investment of Taiwan. Taiwan is a small open economy, and is an island off the east coast of China. It lies on the main trade route between South-east Asia and Japan, and between the east rim and the west rim of the Pacific Basin. There is a great flow of trade for the exchange of Japanese manufactured and capital goods, and for industrial raw materials and foodstuffs from South-east Asia, although ships do not usually pass Taiwan, and Taiwan does not play a significant *entrepôt* trade function. Yet the trade flow between Taiwan and Japan is great and is increasing. Likewise, Taiwan exports much to the USA and Canada. The geographical position of Taiwan is a favourable factor for the growth of trade between Taiwan and Japan and between Taiwan and the USA and Canada.

As an illustration, in 1985 Taiwan exported 48.1 per cent of her products to the USA, 3.1 per cent to Canada, and 11.3 per cent to Japan. Most of her textile and textile-related products and electronic goods goes to the USA and Japan. Taiwan has a trade surplus with the USA and Canada but a trade deficit with Japan. Great effort has been made to diversify the export trade. Consequently, in 1987 these percentages were changed to 44.1 per cent to the USA, 2.9 per cent to Canada, and 13.0 per cent to Japan. In 1985, Taiwan imported 27.6 per cent of her total imports from Japan; 23.6 per cent from the USA, and 1.8 per cent from Canada. In 1987, these percentages changed to 34.3 per cent from Japan, 22.1 per cent from the USA and 1.9 per cent from Canada. Apparently, the policy of importing more from the USA than from Japan has not been successful.

On the other hand, trade between Taiwan and South-east Asia (except Hong Kong) is not great.[8] Apart from the fact, that Taiwan imports industrial raw materials (such as rubber, timber and logs) from the Asean countries, Taiwan exported only 6.5 per cent to the Asean countries and imported only 6.9 per cent from the Asean countries in 1985.

Historically, Taiwan has long been an integral part of China. Japan occupied the island for fifty years from 1895 to 1945, having some effect on the banking system (see Chapters 2 and 3), the cooperatives and the Farmers' Association, and the agricultural basis of the economy. After the Second World War Taiwan was returned to China by Japan and the Chinese Nationalist government retreated from the mainland to Taiwan. Since then, the growth of Taiwan has been quite distinct from the development of the People's Republic of China (PRC) on the mainland.

In the 1940s, 1950s and even 1960s Taiwan was basically an agricultural economy. The economy was gradually transformed into an industrial one around 1965, when the export of industrial goods began to surpass that of agricultural products (rice and sugar) and processed products. Monetary and financial development played a role in this crucial period by way of curbing inflation and reorganising the financial institutions, as expounded in Chapters 2, 5, 6 and 7. Land reform and agricultural development took the lead in the early 1950s, industrial development followed and financial development was stepped up in line with the growth of the real sector (see Figures 7.1, 7.2 and 7.3 in Chapter 7). Apparently, financial development seems to lag behind industrial development. Why? If there is a strong industrial growth with export surplus, how do the manufacturing firms obtain the supporting finance? The answer can only be sought in the informal money market (see Chapter 3). In spite of the gradual modernisation of the financial sector, the informal money market still plays a role in the financial system (see Tables 3.4 and 3.5 in Chapter 3).

The common restraints to the growth of developing countries are the savings gap and the foreign exchange gap, as expounded in many theories. The high savings and investment ratios in Taiwan have avoided these difficulties since the 1960s (see Figures 5.4 and 5.5 in Chapter 5).[9] This favourable factor has been translated into the real sector in terms of higher industrial growth and into the financial sector in terms of availability of investible funds, and the better development of financial instruments, markets and institutions, with the ultimate goal of financial liberalisation and internationalisation.

Hong Kong and Singapore as financial centres, and the Asian Dollar Market in Singapore may prompt the monetary authorities of Taiwan to establish offshore banking units (see Chapter 3) as a step towards internationalisation of banking. But the more important and immediate task ahead is to strengthen the domestic money and capital markets.

This book is divided into three parts. Part I deals with the study of banking, first because, commercial banks' deposits form the major part of money and it is useful to clarify the banking structure (which is unique in Taiwan) before analysing the monetary aspects. Second, there are very few articles (not to say, books) written on banking in Taiwan, except annual reports or memorial issues of some big banks. Chapter 2 traces the historical development of the banking system. Chapter 3 is a continuation of Chapter 2 and describes the present structure of the financial system, with the growth of money and capital markets and the offshore banking units. Chapter 3 also analyses the assets and liabilities of banks and financial institutions, their growth rates and their crucial ratios.

Part II deals with monetary analysis. Chapter 5 analyses the monetary system, including the currency issue, reserve requirements, the interrelationship of money, income and prices, demand and supply of money, income velocity of circulation and savings and investment ratios, which form the link between the financial and the real sectors. Chapter 6 analyses the objectives, instruments, and major issues of monetary policy. The appreciation of the new Taiwan dollar has become a great international issue, as well as a national one. It has a great effect on bank liquidity, money supply and international reserves of Taiwan.

Part III, especially Chapter 7, illustrates the link between financial development and economic growth. Land reform, agricultural development and industrial development are discussed. The strategy of import-substitution and export-orientation is evaluated to dispel some misunderstanding on Taiwan. Manufacturing and export growth go hand-in-hand. Chapter 8 focuses on the weakness of the financial system and discusses the reformation of the system. Chapter 9 summarises the major findings and issues and discusses the future prospect.

Generally speaking, it seems that Taiwan follows the classical model of economic development, stressing the importance of the aggregate supply function, real output, and productivity, rather than the Keynesian model focusing on the aggregate demand function; and on the monetary stimulation of the demand function. D. H. Robertson's theory has the following well-known equation:

Investment = voluntary saving + new money + dishoarding[10]

Robertson believes in voluntary saving rather than new money, in enhancing investment and consequently economic growth. The high savings ratio of Taiwan and the spectacular economic growth can be said to have a theoretical base in that equation.

K. Wicksell's famous equation:

Real interest rate = Nominal interest rate − inflation rate

also had important bearing on Taiwan interest rate policy, particularly in the early 1950s when Taiwan had a high inflation rate and when the current thinking was to have a low-interest-rate policy to stimulate investment following the Keynesian model. Taiwan was courageous enough to have a very high deposit rate (see preferential interest rate deposit in Chapter 5) in order to attract savings fund into the banking system and hence to combat inflation.

Robertson's and Wicksell's thinking on the classical model had much influence on Professor S. C. Tsiang who has been, *de facto*, adviser to the Government of the Republic of China on monetary matters. Perhaps partly because of the theoretical modelling, and partly because of the frightful experience of hyperinflation in mainland China, Taiwan has adopted a very conservative monetary policy, and does not believe in deficit financing in stimulating economic growth. Thus Taiwan has been able to achieve growth with price stability.

Solow presented the neoclassical model of growth and focused on the savings ratio, the capital/labour ratio and the growth of labour supply (or population);[11] he emphasised the aggregate supply function, rather than the Keynesian aggregate demand function.

Tsiang modified Solow's model and postulated the necessary condition for an economy to take-off as follows:[12]

$$S/Y > (I/\Delta Y)\Delta L/L$$

where S = savings
Y = national income or output
I = investment
$\Delta L/L$ = growth of labour supply (or population), which is assumed to be a function of the current real wage rate.

In other words, the savings ratio should be greater than the incremental capital/output ratio ($I/\Delta Y$), or the reciprocal of marginal productivity of investment multiplied by the growth of labour supply.

That implies that 'domestically generated savings would be enough to finance investment projects yielding an increase in national product more than proportionate to the increase in population'.[13]

On that basis, Tsiang presents statistics of many developing countries (including Taiwan, South Korea, Singapore, Hong Kong, India, Thailand, Philippines, Mexico, Brazil, Tanzania, Morocco, etc.) focusing on the finding

$$(S/Y) - (I/\Delta Y)(\Delta L/L)$$

which he considers to be the crucial indicator of take-off. He concludes that Taiwan's take-off period was around 1963 (the indicator being 6.10); since then the indicator has been rising continuously to the present (around 28.70 in 1984 (five-year moving average)).

The high and increasing savings ratio of Taiwan (see Chapter 5) has certainly contributed greatly to its growth. The steady or slightly declining, incremental capital/output ratio, $I/\Delta Y$ (see Table 5.7) is also a help because there is no need to have increasing capital investment to produce one unit of output. Population growth has been under control since the 1970s. Now the worry is the decline in the investment ratio since the 1980 (see Table 5.4) or the low investment incentive.

This major theme of the growth model should be borne in mind when reading the following chapters.

Part I
A Study of the Banking System

2 Historical Review of the Banking System

The banking system can be traced back to the period in China itself, when four major government banks – Central Bank of China, Bank of China, Bank of Communication, and Farmers' Bank of China – were predominant in the banking system. This framework still has a strong influence on the banking system of Taiwan today. All four big banks have moved their head offices to Taiwan (see Table 2.1). The Bank of China in the Taiwan district and jurisdiction was reorganised, and converted from government ownership into private ownership; and the name was changed to International Commercial Bank of China, immediately after Taiwan had withdrawn from the United Nations in 1971.[1] The Central Bank of China was rehabilitated in Taiwan in 1961. The Farmers' Bank of China was founded in 1933. Its head office was moved to Taipei in 1949, and resumed full operation in 1967. An important aspect is that its staff managed the Land Bank of Taiwan in order to carry out the land reform of China,[2] which success contributed significantly to the industrialisation of Taiwan. The Bank of Communication was established in Peking in 1907. Its head office was moved to Taipei in 1949 and resumed full operations in 1960.[3] It was then transformed into a development bank, a 'special purpose' bank. The four government banks remain the main structure of the banking system of Taiwan today, and the predominance of government banks has long been a tradition.

The influence of Japanese rule on banking in Taiwan is also great. The Bank of Taiwan today was reorganised from the old Bank of Taiwan. The new Bank of Taiwan, after its establishment in 1946 took over the old Taiwan Savings Bank and the three branch offices of Sanwa Bank.[4] The Land Bank of Taiwan was established in 1946, after taking over the assets of the branch office of Nippon Daiichi Kangyo Bank (old organisation). The Cooperative Bank of Taiwan (old organisation) was not listed as a bank during the Japanese occupation. It was reorganised in 1946 into the present Bank.[5]

The First Commercial Bank started as the Taiwan Savings Bank (1899–1902) and had gone through many phases of reorganisation and mergers with other banks; the name was changed first to Ka Yee Bank (1905–23), then successively to Sin Koh Bank (1916–23),

Table 2.1 Structures of various domestic banks, 1987 (end year) (in NT$ million)

Bank (year and month of incorporation/reorganisation)	*Organisation*	*Number of branches*	*Aggregate assets*	*Loans and discounts*	*Deposits*	*Capital, reserve and undistributed surplus*
1. Bank of Taiwan (1946.5)	Provincial government	63	614 590	225 448	466 210	19 153
2. First Commercial Bank (1947)	Provincial government	105	361 542	174 939	287 917	7 222
3. Hua Nam Commercial Bank (1949)	Provincial government	88	382 430	200 547	289 522	7 642
4. Chang Hwa Commercial Bank (1905)	Provincial government	104	349 039	184 862	263 987	6 802
5. City Bank of Taipei (1969.1)	Municipal government	26	182 902	94 575	145 316	7 558
6. City Bank of Kaohsiung (1982.1)	Municipal government	3	21 518	9 166	15 624	858
7. Bank of Communication (1960.10)	Central government, development bank	11	232 338	103 179	39 229	11 878
8. Farmers' Bank of China (1967.5)	Central government, agriculture bank	27	142 126	91 488	71 493	5 585
9. Land Bank of Taiwan (1946.9)	Provincial government	58	336 014	208 317	226 628	10 444
10. Cooperative Bank of Taiwan (1946.10)	Provincial government	87	561 654	268 323	447 153	3 709
11. Export–Import Bank of China (1979.11)	Central government	1	12 330	8 618	–	9 507
12. Central Trust of China (1935)	Central government	3	53 972	33 406	22 878	1 390

13. Medium and Small Business Bank of Taiwan (1976.7)	Provincial government	88	214 040	140 830	101 806	3 118
Sub-total for government banks		664	3 464 495	1 743 698	2 377 763	94 866
14. International Commercial Bank of China (1971.12)	Private bank	23	115 362	41 498	54 073	9 477
15. United World Chinese Commercial Bank (1975.5)	Private bank	8	77 988	45 993	50 067	2 931
16. Overseas Chinese Commercial Banking Corporation (1961.3)	Private bank	8	36 077	24 390	25 767	2 325
17. Shanghai Commercial and Savings Bank (1965.6)	Private bank	4	25 210	15 859	12 432	1 282
Sub-total for private banks		43	254 637	127 740	142 339	16 015
18. Medium and Small Business Bank of Taipei (1977.11)	Private bank	34	49 289	32 668	44 306	2 242
19. Medium and Small Business Bank of Hsinchu (1977.12)	Private bank	24	28 972	21 161	27 174	1 199
20. Medium and Small Business Bank of Taichung (1978.1)	Private bank	29	34 429	24 731	32 303	1 415
21. Medium and Small Business Bank of Tainan (1978.1)	Private bank	16	16 262	11 861	14 905	904

continued

Table 2.1 continued

Bank (year and month of incorporation/reorganisation)	*Organisation*	*Number of branches*	*Aggregate assets*	*Loans and discounts*	*Deposits*	*Capital, reserve and undistributed surplus*
22. Medium and Small Business Bank of Kaohsiung (1978.6)	Private bank	16	14 077	11 292	12 503	908
23. Medium and Small Business Bank of Hualian (1979.1)	Private bank	4	2 689	1 654	2 224	324
24. Medium and Small Business Bank of Taitung (1979.2)	Private bank	4	2 339	1 493	2 005	289
Sub-total for private medium and small business bank		127	148 057	104 860	135 420	7 281
25. Postal Remittance and Savings Bureau (1962.3)	Central government	1 157	373 913	719	791 590	12 196
Total (1–24)		834	367 189	1 976 298	2 655 522	118 162
Total (1–25)		1 991	441 102	1 977 017	3 447 112	130 358

Note: The organisation aspect should be read in conjunction with Chapter 2, 'Historical Review'. Perhaps the labels 'government banks' or 'private banks' are too general without reference to history and reality, e.g. International Commercial Bank of China.

Source: Supervision Department, CBC, *Annual Report of the Operation of Financial Institutions, Taiwan District*, 1987 and various issues.

Commercial and Industrial Bank (1910–47), Industrial and Commercial Bank (1947–9), Taiwan First Commercial Bank (1949–76) and finally to First Commercial Bank (1976 to the present).[6] The Hua Nam Commercial Bank was originally founded in 1919, specialising in international banking. It was reorganised in 1947. Chang Hwa Commercial Bank was established in 1905 in Chang Hwa, Taiwan; hence the name was adopted.

The eight Medium and Small Business Banks can also be regarded as a relic of Japanese organisation. During the Japanese occupation there were numerous 'savings societies', and these were reorganised into Taiwan Mutual Savings and Loan Company in September 1946, which was in turn reorganised to form the Medium and Small Business Bank of Taiwan in 1976.[7] The other seven medium and small business banks in different regions (see Table 2.1) were also reorganised from the mutual savings and loan companies in 1948–53 and finally in 1977–9 to form the Medium and Small Business Banks of Taipei, Hsinchu, Taichung, Tainan, Kaohsiung, Hualian, and Taitung respectively. They are privately owned by shareholders. They can only conduct banking business within their respective regions, with the main purpose of financing medium and small business.

After the Second World War, several new banks were set up. The Overseas Chinese Commercial Banking Corporation was established in 1961. It is a private bank owned mainly by overseas Chinese.

The City Bank of Taipei was established by the Taipei Municipal Government in 1969, and acts as the fiscal agent of the Taipei Municipal Government. The Shanghai Commercial and Savings Bank was established in Shanghai in 1915 and resumed business in Taipei in 1965; it was the only private bank that followed the Government from China to Taiwan. The United World Chinese Commercial Bank was established in 1975 to pool the financial resources of overseas Chinese (50 per cent shareholding), and domestic banking institutions (also 50 per cent shareholding) for the promotion of trade and investment between Taiwan and overseas Chinese. The Export–Import Bank of China was set up in 1979 for the primary purpose of promoting foreign trade, by supplying medium and long-term credit for exports of capital goods and imports of industrial raw materials or parts for the export products. It also provides export insurance to facilitate the export financing from banks. However, it is not allowed to accept deposits. It is regarded as a 'special purpose' bank. The City Bank of Kaohsiung, another municipal government bank was established in 1982.

Thus, there are three sets of banks:

1. those whose head offices were moved from China to Taiwan;
2. those which were a relic of Japanese organisation;
3. those which were set up after the Second World War.

From the standpoint of historical development, we can discuss the banking system in terms of four periods as follows:

1. When Taiwan was recovered from Japanese hands in 1945 there were seven banks operating in Taiwan: (i) the Bank of Taiwan (old organisation), (ii) Taiwan Savings Bank, (iii) Sanwa Bank, (iv) Daiichi Kangyo Bank, (v) Chang Hwa Commercial Bank (old organisation), (vi) Taiwan Commercial and Industrial Bank (old organisation) and (vii) Hua Nam Commercial Bank (old organisation).[8] It was obvious that during the Japanese occupation, Japanese capital had been predominant in those banks, particularly (i)–(iv).

The old Bank of Taiwan and Taiwan Savings Bank were established by the Japanese Government; indeed, the former was the central financial institution in Taiwan. Sanwa Bank and Daiichi Kangyo Bank were branches of Japanese banks. The old Chang Hwa Bank, Taiwan Commercial and Industrial Bank and Hua Nam Bank were Taiwanese enterprises, but with some Japanese capital. In fact, they were joint ventures of Taiwanese and Japanese capital.

In addition to the seven banks already mentioned, there was the Cooperative Bank of Taiwan.

2. The Period of Reconstruction, from Liberation, 1945, to the Rehabilitation of the Central Bank in 1961. Throughout this period, the Bank of Taiwan acted as the Central Bank.

In May 1946, the old Bank of Taiwan was reorganised to form the present Bank of Taiwan. In the same year, the Land Bank of Taiwan was formed and the Cooperative Bank of Taiwan (old organisation) was reorganised to form the present Cooperative Bank of Taiwan. The present First Commercial Bank came from the Taiwan Commercial and Industrial Bank. Hua Nam Commercial Bank and Chang Hwa Commercial Bank were also reorganised to their present form.

Thus in the reconstruction period, there were six banks in operation, with the Bank of Taiwan implicitly the central bank. It was entrusted by the Bank of China in 1947 to take care of the exchange and remittance business with respect to exports and imports; by the

Central Bank of China in 1948 to accept reserve deposits from other banks in Taiwan; and by the government to start issuing New Taiwan (NT) currency as from 17 August 1945 under the supervision of the Ministry of Finance. In the crucial period of currency reform in June 1949, it was entrusted with the custody of foreign exchange and assets of the country.

In 1959, the Daiichi Kangyo Bank re-established its branch in Taipei, which was then the first foreign bank after the war. In 1959, the Bank of Communication and the Bank of China resumed operation in Taiwan. The Overseas Chinese Commercial Bank opened in 1961. Thus by 1961 there were eleven banks including one foreign bank.

Immediately after the Second World War, government banks and organisations – but not their head offices – moved to Taiwan. It was not until 1948/9 that their head offices had to follow the government to Taiwan.

3. Rehabilitation of the Central Bank 1961 to the New Bank Act, 1975. With the re-establishment of the head offices of government banks and organisations, the banking structure had undergone big changes, necessitating the passing of the New Bank Act in 1975. Several new banks were established including the Overseas Chinese Commercial Bank in 1961, the City Bank of Taipei in 1969 and the United World Chinese Commercial Bank in 1975.[9] The Postal Remittance and Savings Bureau which had been established in 1930 in China resumed full operation in Taiwan in 1962.

The Stock Exchange of Taiwan was incorporated in 1961 and started operations in 1962. This was a step forward towards the formulation of a capital market.

4. The Modern Banking Period after the New Bank Act 1975. The Bank Act categorises banks in four main groups: (i) commercial banks; (ii) special purpose banks; (iii) savings banks, and (iv) trust and investment companies (clause 20). The Act opened a new epoch, e.g. the transformation of the Bank of Communication into a development bank, and the development of the money market and new financial instruments. Three bill finance companies were established following the promulgation of the 'Regulations Governing the Dealers of Short-Term Negotiable Instruments' – namely, Chung-Shing Bill Finance Company, (started or organised by the Bank of Taiwan in 1976), International Bill Finance Company (started by the Inter-

national Commercial Bank of China in 1977) and Chung-Hua Bill Finance Company (started by the Bank of Communication in 1978). The Ministry of Finance started issuing Treasury bills in November 1973. Bankers' Acceptance and Negotiable Certificates of Deposits started to be available in the money market in 1975.

The Fuh-Hua Securities Finance Company was established in 1980 to finance margin trading and advancing securities in the stock market, with a view to facilitating the orderly functioning of the market.

One important aspect to note in the modern period is that the Ministry of Finance promulgated the 'Rules Governing Trust and Investment Companies' and 'Criteria Governing Establishment of Trust and Investment Companies' on 30 November 1970, with the objective of raising long-term capital and channelling such funds into industrial investment.

The China Development Corporation, which is considered to be a trust company, started operation in May 1959. Seven other trust and investment companies were established in 1971 and 1972. They are akin to finance companies in Singapore and Malaysia.

Banks and trust and investment companies are chartered under the provisions of the Banking Law, although some of them are also governed by special statutes.

With financial liberalisation and internationalisation, one potential trend will be the growth of investment banking function along with commercial banking function, and the establishment of international investment houses. Domestic banks are beginning to adopt an outward-looking policy by establishing branch offices overseas, with the permission of the Ministry of Finance and the Central Bank. The monetary authorities too would be more prepared to grant licences to foreign financial institutions to operate in Taiwan. The Stock Market of Taiwan would be more willing to be closely associated with the overseas capital markets e.g. in New York and Chicago.

A study of the structure of domestic banks (Table 2.1) shows that the fourteen government-owned banks are dominant in the banking system in terms of aggregate assets, loans and deposits, and the four private commercial banks and seven private medium and small business banks play a much lesser role, while the Postal Remittance and Savings Bureau (PRSB) is the most active in collecting savings deposits. PRSB has as many as 1157 branches all over Taiwan, and the deposits are redeposited into the Central Bank and other banks.[10]

The government banks have 644 branches, whereas the private banks have only 169 branches. The aggregate assets of private banks are only 12 per cent of those of government banks; the loans and advances of the former are only 8 per cent of the latter; and deposits of the former are only 11 per cent of the latter.

The First Commercial Bank, Chang Hwa Commercial Bank, Hua Nam Commercial Bank and the Medium and Small Business Bank have the greatest number of branches (104, 105, 88, and 88 respectively), being engaged in wholesale and retail commercial banking. But in terms of aggregate assets the ranking is as follows:

1. Bank of Taiwan;
2. Cooperative Bank of Taiwan;
3. Land Bank of Taiwan;
4. Hua Nam Commercial Bank;
5. First Commercial Bank;
6. Chang Hwa Commercial Bank;
7. Bank of Communication;
8. Medium and Small Business Bank of Taiwan;
9. City Bank of Taipei;
10. International Commercial Bank of China.

One interesting problem in improving the banking system is the gradual conversion of some of the government-owned banks into private enterprises. It has been argued that government-owned banks are less efficient because of various regulations. As an example, the conversion of four public enterprises (paper, cement, mining and agro-industries – see Chapter 7) into private enterprises had stimulated the free enterprise spirit which has been the underlying force of industrialisation. It is hoped that by freeing government-owned banks from rigid regulations, the progress of the banking system can be accelerated.

Table 2.2 and 2.3 summarise the development of foreign banks in Taiwan. In 1959, the earliest foreign bank to start business in Taiwan was the Japanese Daiichi Kangyo Bank. In the 1950s because of the political uncertainty and the hyperinflation of 1949–52 most of the foreign banks adopted the wait-and-see attitude. Even foreign banks such as Hong Kong and Shanghai Banking Corporation and Chartered Bank, which were the most active in China did not establish branch offices in Taiwan until a much later date. From 1959 to 1975–7, the rate of increase in the number of foreign banks was very

Table 2.2 The development of foreign banks in Taiwan, 1961–87 (NT$ million)

Year	*Number of foreign banks*	*Number of representative offices*	*Aggregate assets*	*Loans*	*Deposits*	*Operation capital fund and undistributed surplus*
1959	1	0				
1961	1	0	231	70	6	↑
1962	1	0	179	60	23	
1963	1	0	267	91	16	
1964	2	0	462	111	11	
1965	4	0	1 151	326	71	
1966	4	0	1 286	507	114	
1967	5	0	1 362	721	99	
1968	5	0	1 820	1 268	81	n.a.
1969	5	0	2 832	2 179	106	
1970	6	0	4 022	2 979	120	
1971	6	0	6 066	4 733	157	
1972	9	0	8 473	6 761	105	
1973	9	0	14 954	11 982	991	
1974	12	0	27 658	23 900	1 038	
1975	12	0	31 567	27 589	1 210	↓
1976	12	2	40 441	36 406	1 380	1 414
1977	12	2	50 951	45 093	1 652	1 136
1978	13	2	51 505	45 159	1 904	1 511
1979	15	2	66 855	59 413	2 180	1 807
1980	22	3	93 415	85 286	3 229	3 292
1981	24	3	120 253	106 266	5 104	4 442
1982	25	5	117 167	98 093	7 659	5 187
1983	30	6	110 823	94 635	11 693	6 200
1984	31	7	114 218	91 078	18 342	6 997
1985	32	9	114 125	82 744	28 953	7 319
1986	33	9	142 449	101 154	26 120	7 560
1987	34	9	222 041	120 134	41 925	9 546
1988	35	9	193 437	137 789	52 428	n.a.

Source: Economic Research Department, Central Bank of China, *Financial Statistics Monthly, Taiwan District*, May 1988.

slow (see Table 2.2, 1–12). Reasons can be found in both the demand and supply sides. In the early period foreign banks were hesitating to enter Taiwan to do business. More important still, in the reconstruction period the domestic banks had not yet been rehabilitated in Taiwan and there were many banking, financial and fiscal problems waiting to be solved; Taiwan was not in a hurry to internationalise

Table 2.3 Aggregate assets, loans and deposits of foreign banks as at end of 1987 (NT$ million)

Bank (year and month of first opening)	*Country of incorporation*	*Aggregate assets*	*Loans and discounts*	*Deposits*
1. Nippon Daiichi Kangyo Bank (1959.8)	Japan	14 372	9 003	6 510
2. Citibank, North America (1964.8)	USA	25 107	13 963	6 482
3. Bank of America (1965.1)	USA	32 690	8 880	2 098
4. American Express International Banking Corporation (1967.6)	USA	5 626	4 100	645
5. Chase Manhattan Bank, N.A. (1972.7)	USA	12 924	7 266	1 548
6. Irving Trust Company (1972.9)	USA	9 792	4 942	907
7. Continental Bank (1972.10)	USA	17 485	9 659	1 377
8. Chemical Bank (1974.4)	USA	6 599	2 091	479
9. First Interstate Bank (1974.5)	USA	4 660	2 575	947
10. Rainier National Bank (1979.12)	USA	5 448	2 632	851
11. First National Bank of Boston (1980.1)	USA	6 515	3 306	2 628
12. Seattle – First National Bank* (1980.2)	USA	257	114	–
13. Morgan Guaranty Trust Company† (1981.3)	USA	–	–	–
14. Bankers Trust Company (1981.9)	USA	13 019	2 504	453
15. Manufacturer Hanover Trust Company (1982.5)	USA	5 592	3 115	329
16. Security Pacific National Bank (1987.2)	USA	5 407	1 494	373
17. Grindlays Bank Ltd. (1980.6)	UK	4 058	2 732	357
18. Lloyds Bank International Limited (1980.12)	UK	2 906	1 976	206
19. Hong Kong and Shanghai Banking Corp. (1985.4)	Hong Kong	5 782	2 896	1 756

continued

Table 2.3 continued

Bank (year and month of first opening)	*Country of incorporation*	*Aggregate assets*	*Loans and discounts*	*Deposits*
20. Standard Chartered Bank (1985.4)	UK	6 303	2 813	970
21. Hollandsche Bank-Unie NV (1980.8)	Netherlands	6 782	2 751	998
22. Amsterdam-Rotterdam Bank NV (1983.9)	Netherlands	4 717	2 064	1 738
23. Société Générale (1979.2)	France	10 891	5 234	869
24. Banque de Paris et des Pays-Ras (1980.8)	France	7 372	4 572	241
25. Crédit Lyonnais (1983.10)	France	18 063	8 550	2 806
26. Banque Nationale de Paris (1984.7)	France	5 797	2 019	515
27. Deutsche (Asia) Bank (1980.7)	West Germany	4 185	5 953	1 572
28. Toronto-Dominion Bank (1974.6)	Canada	6 117	2 385	446
29. Royal Bank of Canada (1983.7)	Canada	4 110	2 483	482
30. Bangkok Bank (1965.1)	Thailand	9 273	5 786	1 020
31. International Bank of Singapore (1978.7)	Singapore	1 292	535	472
32. Development Bank of Singapore Ltd (1983.3)	Singapore	3 470	1 639	921
33. Metropolitan Bank and Trust Company (1970.7)	Philippines	2 426	1 812	1 344
34. Westpac Banking Corporation (1986.7)	Australia	6 830	3 998	366

Notes: * Seattle – First National Bank sold the licence to Westpac Banking Corporation, Australia.
† The Branch of Morgan Guaranty Trust Company was changed to a representative office.

Source: Supervision Department, Central Bank of China, *Annual Report of the Operation of Financial Institutions, Taiwan District*, 1987, and *Statistics of the Business Operation of Financial Institutions in Taiwan* (confidential documents)

banking and finance, and hence was not well prepared to grant licences to foreign banks. In the world-wide period of prosperity, 1969–73, there were only between five and nine foreign banks in Taiwan . In the 1980s, amidst the officially declared policy of financial liberalisation, internationalisation and institutionalisation, the government started to liberalise the granting of licences to foreign banks. Thus the number of foreign banks was increased to thirty-five, and the number of representative offices of foreign banks to nine, as in 1988.

Table 2.3 analyses the nationality of foreign banks, the year of their first opening in Taipei, and their activity in Taiwan in terms of aggregate assets, loans and deposits. To date, there are only fourteen US banks, one Japanese bank, four British and Hong Kong banks,[11] two Dutch banks, four French banks, one German bank, two Canadian banks, one Australian bank and four Asian banks, totalling thirty-three. It is rather surprising that in spite of the close relationship in trade and investment between Japan and Taiwan, there is only one branch office of a Japanese bank. One plausible reason is that Japanese financial institutions pay attention to political factors, worrying that to establish more banking offices in Taiwan may adversely affect their business with Mainland China, which is their main interest.[12] Besides, they believe that their trade and investment with Taiwan would not be jeopardised because of the small number of banking offices.

In view of the very close economic relation between the USA and Taiwan, there are as many as fourteen US banks which have come to Taiwan at different times. They were not there in the 1950s. The earliest arrivals in the 1960s were Citibank, Bank of America and American Express International Banking Corporation. Six US banks opened their offices in the 1970s, and five in the 1980s.

The British banks were 'latecomers', also because of political consideration. The Hong Kong and Shanghai Banking Corporation came as late as in 1983 and the Chartered Bank in 1985. Their late arrival may unfavourably affect their business. Most of the EEC countries and Canada have a banking presence in Taiwan in the 1980s.

Among the Asian countries, the Bangkok Bank of Thailand and the Metropolitan Bank and Trust Company of the Philippines had established their branches as early as 1965 and 1970 respectively. Singapore has two banking offices, namely, the International Bank of Singapore (1978), and the Development Bank of Singapore (1983).

The latest foreign banks to settle in Taiwan are Westpac Banking Corporation (1986) from Australia,[13] and the Pacific Bank of America (1987). The former bought the banking licence from Seattle Bank of the USA, which withdrew its business from Taiwan.

Representative offices of foreign banks do only the liaison work for their banking corporations but cannot operate business such as lending and accepting deposits, in Taiwan. They began to be set up in 1976 and the number was increased from two to nine in 1986 (Table 2.2). The degree of activity of various foreign banks can be seen in Table 2.2, which shows the important items of a balance sheet – aggregate assets, loans and deposits in 1985.

Apparently US banks are very active in terms of those items, and Citibank and the Bank of America appear to be the leading foreign banks. Daiichi Kangyo Bank was ranked only fifteenth in terms of aggregate assets, eleventh in terms of lending, but third in terms of accepting deposits.

In reviewing the historical development of the financial system one would be impressed by (i) the rapid growth since 1961; (ii) the traditional dominance of government banks; (iii) the rather inward looking of the financial system resulting from the rather closed financial system (before the 1980s) without much international interaction. With respect to the last point, the adverse international factors have played a part.

The great export surplus and increasing international reserves in the 1980s together with US pressure have induced Taiwan to liberalise trade, investment and finance. More foreign banks are expected to be admitted, domestic banks are expected to establish more overseas branches and some of them to be converted gradually from government-ownership to private enterprise. The financial system will be more outward-looking to progress in step with the high economic growth. These expectations will be discussed in Chapter 7.

3 The Present Structure of the Financial System

The Ministry of Finance and the Central Bank are at the apex of the financial system regulating and supervising the financial system. The nucleus of the financial system is supplied by the banks, around which other financial institutions seem to revolve because demand deposits (or cheque accounts) of commercial banks are means of payment, or part of money supply.

In 1988 the financial institutions consisted of sixteen 'domestic' banks, eight 'medium and small business banks', the Postal Remittances and Savings Bureau (see Chapter 2, Table 2.1), thirty-four branches of foreign banks, nine representative offices of foreign banks (Chapter 2, Table 2.2); eight investment and trust companies (Table 3.1); seventy-four credit cooperatives; 285 credit departments of the Farmers' Association; nineteen credit departments of the Fishery Association; three bill finance companies (Table 3.7); one securities finance company; twenty-two insurance companies, totalling 472 financial institutions with 3163 offices (Table 3.6).

3.1 DOMESTIC BANKS

Although four banks (International Commercial Bank of China, Overseas Chinese Commercial Bank, Shanghai Commercial and Savings Bank and United World Chinese Commercial Bank) have some government shares, they are managed as private enterprises, i.e. they have independent boards of directors, and thus their managers have much more liberty in management, without the rigid restriction of government banks.

It should be noted that among the government banks there are some with private shares. For example, the Chang Hwa Commercial Bank has private shares of 43.75 per cent; the Hua Nam Commercial Bank has 41.86 per cent; and First Commercial Bank has 25.50 per cent. In this sense they are also joint ventures. But the law stipulates that if more than 50 per cent of a bank's shares are government-owned, it should be regarded as a government bank and should be subject to all sorts of government regulations; the management would not be run on the principle of private enterprise.

The Overseas Chinese Commercial Bank was founded by Overseas Chinese in March 1961. It faced a crisis in 1984 and was rescued by the government, which put up share capital of 18 per cent, and appointed the general manager. The United World Chinese Commercial Bank was established in 1975, at the time of world-wide recession. The Central Trust of China was established in 1935 in Mainland China. It has various departments to carry out its multiple functions, such as procurement, trading, banking and trust, life insurance, government employees' insurance, warehousing, transportation, and foreign-exchange operations, etc.[1]

The special purpose banks include the Bank of Communication (now a development bank), the Export–Import Bank of China, the Farmers' Bank of China (for providing rural credit),[2] the Land Bank of Taiwan (for financing hire-purchase of properties), and Medium and Small Business Banks (for financing medium and small enterprises).

3.2 FOREIGN BANKS

In going through Tables 2.2 and 2.3 (Chapter 2), one would naturally ask the following questions. Why were there so few foreign branches and why was the growth rather sluggish in the early period? The reason is that Taiwan traditionally adopted a protectionist policy in trade and finance because of the difficult circumstances, and the banks are predominantly government-owned. It was only in the 1980s, when the economy had become buoyant with rapid economic growth, that the financial system began to be gradually liberalised and open to international financial institutions, in order to absorb the skills of bank management, accounting and computerisation of modern banking.

3.3 INVESTMENT AND TRUST COMPANIES

With regard to the non-bank financial institutions, there are eight investment and trust companies with thirty offices (see Table 3.1). China Development Corporation was the earliest, established in 1959. Subsequently four others were established in 1971 and three in

Table 3.1 List of trust and investment companies in Taiwan

Company	*Date of establishment*
1. China Development Corporation	14 May 1959
2. Taiwan First Investment and Trust Company Ltd	22 June 1971
3. China Investment and Trust Company Ltd	1 July 1971
4. Overseas Trust Corporation	6 Aug 1971
5. China United Trust and Investment Corporation	12 Oct 1971
6. Taiwan Development and Trust Corporation	3 July 1972
7. Cathay Investment and Trust Company Ltd	28 July 1972
8. Asia Trust and Investment Corporation	7 July 1972

Source: Central Bank of China, *Financial Institutions in Taiwan*, February 1984, p. 18.

1972. Their main functions are to provide housing loans, to invest in properties and to accept trust funds, which are in effect a disguised way of taking fixed deposits because investment and trust companies are not allowed to accept deposits from the public.

They are instituted to finance industries in the form of (i) medium and long-term loans, (ii) equity investments, (iii) guarantees and (iv) trust and agency services. They are authorised to engage in investment in government bonds, treasury bills, company debentures and listed stocks and shares.

Their interest rates for loans and trust funds are higher than those of banks. Their operations are similar to the finance companies in Singapore, Malaysia and Hong Kong, but they are less active than the latter with respect to hire-purchase of consumer durables (such as motor vehicles, TV sets and household appliances). In view of the dull property market (1981–6), and the shaken confidence on the investment and trust companies, they face great difficulty in business.

A plan, which has been deliberated for some time, is to provide venture capital to small enterprises through China Investment Corporation. It has been recognised that this would stimulate new technology industries, but to participate in venture capital would involve much risk. To date, the idea has not yet been implemented, although efforts are being made in that direction.

There is no merchant bank yet in Taiwan, nor is any financial institution effectively operating the functions of corporate finance, underwriting new issues of shares, take-overs, or merger of companies etc.

In the capital market, there is the Stock Exchange of Taiwan which was incorporated in 1961 and commenced operation in February 1962.

The Fuh-Hua Securities Finance Company was established in 1980 to finance margin trading and other facilities in the stock market. Its primary business is:

1. to provide loan for the purchase of securities;
2. to provide accommodation for the sale of securities;
3. to serve as custodian of securities.

The first service was previously offered by the Bank of Communication, the Bank of Taiwan, and the Land Bank of Taiwan, and is now exclusively taken up by Fuh-Hua. The second and third services are authorised by the Securities and Exchange Commission, Ministry of Economic Affairs.

The Ministry of Finance started issuing Treasury bills in October 1973. Bankers' acceptance and negotiable certificates of deposits were introduced in 1975. The New Bank Act 1975 and the promulgation of the 'Regulations Governing the Dealers of Short-Term Negotiable Instruments' in December 1975 ushered in the money and discount market, with the establishment of three bill finance companies, as mentioned above.

3.4 CREDIT COOPERATIVES

Credit cooperatives in Taiwan were established as early as 1908, when Taiwan was under Japanese rule. After Taiwan was returned to China in 1945, all cooperative societies were reorganised according to Chinese law.[3] In 1949, the Provincial Government adopted the suggestion of the Joint Commission on Rural Reconstruction to combine all the rural credit cooperatives with the farmers' associations as credit departments in the farmers' associations. Hence, the present credit cooperatives consist of two categories, i.e. credit cooperatives of the cities and credit departments of farmers' associations. There are seventy-four credit cooperatives with 289 branches in Taiwan.

Credit cooperatives are regional institutions and are authorised to deal with their members only. They engage in all or some of the following activities:

1. acceptance of deposits;
2. extending loans and discounts;
3. acceptance of bills;
4. collection and disbursement of funds;
5. other operations licensed by the government.

In accordance with the principle of cooperatives, they are supposed to be managed in a democratic manner, i.e. one-member, one vote with respect to the sharing of profit and administrative matters. But in practice they tend to be controlled by families, who use the deposit funds to finance their own business. This weakness explains the Tenth Credit Crisis in 1985.

Credit cooperatives in Taiwan are quite active in collecting deposits and extending loans. As at the end of 1986 credit cooperatives accepted 10 per cent of total deposits in Taiwan (see Chapter 4, Table 4.1), and provided 7.3 per cent of total loans (see Chapter 4, Table 4.3). Their deposits and loans are even greater than those of trust and investment companies and those of credit departments of Farmers' Associations and Fishery Associations.

3.5 CREDIT DEPARTMENTS OF FARMERS' ASSOCIATIONS AND FISHERY ASSOCIATIONS

The Credit Departments of Farmers' Associations provide the base for agricultural credit in Taiwan. They are authorised to accept deposits from, and extend loans to, members; to handle remittances, and to serve as agent for the Land Bank of Taiwan, the Cooperative Bank of Taiwan, the Farmers' Bank of China and other government agencies in the provision of agricultural credit. They frequently make collections, keep custody and account for the township treasury.

They have some distinct characteristics. First, they differ from commercial bank credit in the sense that in order to facilitate small borrowers, collateral requirements are not so strictly enforced. Second, a package of service activities are coordinated with credit supply. Prior to credit extension, the loan application is investigated as to the feasibility of the investment plan, and the farmer is also advised of the improvement in farming techniques. Follow-up work is regularly carried out after the loan disbursement by the credit departments to assure proper use of the loan and to offer technical advice.

Marketing and purchasing functions of the farmers' associations are also related to the credit programmes.

In 1986, the township Farmers' Associations in Taiwan numbered 305. Of these associations, 283 had separate credit departments, with 523 branch offices or annexes.

The Farmers' Associations contributed much to the success of the agricultural reform in the 1950s. The effectiveness of agricultural credit had improved agricultural productivity tremendously. The high growth of agricultural productivity supplemented and stimulated the industrialisation of Taiwan. Financing agriculture is indeed a difficult task, because the farming unit is small, as compared with an industrial firm; the cost of administration for the bank is high; it is difficult to obtain proper collateral, apart from land deeds; and young and enterprising administrators are not keen to go to the countryside to manage agricultural credit. For these reasons, many developing agricultural countries, such as Malaysia, Indonesia, Philippines, and Thailand, cannot claim to be successful in their aspiration to agricultural reforms nor in their provision of rural credit. Taiwan is an exception in its outstanding success.

Agricultural finance in Taiwan has been well conducted through the Farmers' Bank of China, the Land Bank of Taiwan, the Cooperative Bank of Taiwan, credit departments of Farmers' Associations and other government agencies. Commercial banks also play a role in providing credit for export and import of farm products and for some investment projects in rural development.

The credit departments of Fishery Associations are similar to the credit departments of Farmers' Associations in their functions and regulations. There are sixteen credit departments which have two branch offices each.

3.6 INSURANCE COMPANIES

Up to 1961, there were only eight insurance companies in Taiwan, most of which were government-owned. After the Ministry of Finance lifted the restriction on the establishment of insurance companies in 1961, seventeen private companies were established and some old ones were merged. There are now fourteen fire and marine insurance companies with seventy-three branches in all; and eight life insurance companies with fifty-nine branches. All insurance companies are subject to government supervision, and their asset management subject to examination by the Central Bank of China.

A Government Reinsurance Fund was established in 1956; it was placed under the management of the Central Trust of China, under the supervision of the Ministry of Finance. A substantial amount of premium has already been retained in the Fund, as a result of its operation in the past two decades. The Central Reinsurance Corporation was then established in 1968, which is under the supervision of the Ministry of Finance. It also helps the Ministry to examine insurance business operations, financial conditions, and management of life and general insurance companies, and to compile insurance statistics.

3.7 OFFSHORE BANKING SYSTEM

A notable feature is that Taiwan started to develop an offshore banking system in July 1984, with total offshore banking assets of about US$439m, which rapidly increased to US$11 690m at the end of December 1987 – having multiplied by 26.6 (see Table 3.1).

By the end of April 1988, there were sixteen offshore banking units (OBU), which were approved by the Central Bank of China, namely:

1. International Commercial Bank of China;
2. the First Commercial Bank;
3. Hua-Nam Commercial Bank;
4. Bank of Taiwan;
5. Chang-Hwa Commercial Bank;
6. Bank of America;
7. Citibank, NA;
8. the First National Bank of Boston;
9. Chemical Bank;
10. Société Générale;
11. Banque Nationale de Paris;
12. Development Bank of Singapore;
13. Bangkok Bank;
14. City Bank of Taipei;
15. the Continental Bank;
16. Bank of Communication.

They include seven domestic banks and nine foreign banks. At the end of December 1987, loans to non-bank customers constituted only 5.2 per cent of total assets (see Table 3.2) of which loans to residents constituted about 0.6 per cent and to non-residents, 4.6 per cent.

Table 3.2 Assets and liabilities of offshore banking units (OBU), 1984–7 (US$ million)

	December 1984	*June 1985*	*December 1985*	*June 1986*	*December 1986*	*June 1987*	*December 1987*
Assets							
1. Loans to non-bank customers	118.9 (2.8)	135.4	173.2 (2.6)	788.9	693.6	651.0 (8.5)	611.1 (5.2)
1.1 Residents	54.0 (1.3)	73.9	113.5 (1.7)	92.6	89.9	80.6 (1.1)	72.2 (0.6)
1.2 Non-residents	64.9 (1.5)	6.5	59.7 (0.9)	696.3	603.7	570.4 (7.5)	538.9 (4.6)
2. Claims on financial institutions[1]	4 017.6 (94.3)	4 969.7	6 094.1 (92.7)	4 433.9	4 770.9	6 189.7 (81.1)	9 978.2 (85.4)
2.1 Domestic banks	410.8 (9.6)	323.7	442.3 (6.7)	700.0	2 356.2	4 591.4 (60.1)	7 854.4 (67.2)
2.2 Inter-OBU	522.8 (12.3)	180.3	168.2 (2.6)	46.7	272.9	188.2 (2.5)	590.8 (5.1)
2.3 Foreign banks	3 083.9 (72.4)	4 465.8	5 483.6 (83.4)	3 687.3	2 141.8	1 410.1 (18.5)	1 533.0 (13.1)
3. Securities investments	70.2 (1.6)	78.3	201.6 (3.1)	577.8	669.0	695.5 (9.1)	866.7 (7.4)
4. Other assets	55.2 (1.3)	78.8	102.9 (1.6)	104.7	74.8	96.0 (1.3)	233.7 (2.0)
Total assets/liabilities	4 261.9 (100)	5 262.1	6 571.8 (100)	5 905.4	6 208.2	7 632.1 (100)	11 689.7 (100)
Liabilities							
5. Deposits of non-bank customers	15.3 (0.4)	23.5	32.2 (0.5)	35.6	42.9	44.1 (0.6)	99.6 (0.9)
6. Funds due to financial institutions	4 215.7 (98.9)	5 179.4	6 473.7 (98.5)	5 769.3	6 099.1	7 489.6 (98.1)	11 411.0 (97.6)
6.1 Domestic banks	2 507.3 (58.8)	3 737.4	5 053.6 (76.9)	3 700.7	2 079.7	1 774.1 (23.2)	827.2 (7.1)
6.2 Inter-OBU	522.8 (12.3)	180.3	168.2 (2.6)	46.7	272.9	188.2 (2.5)	590.8 (5.0)
6.3 Foreign banks	1 185.7 (27.8)	1 261.7	1 252.0 (19.1)	2 021.9	3 746.5	5 527.3 (72.4)	9 993.0 (85.5)
7. Other liabilities	30.9 (0.7)	59.3	65.9 (1.0)	100.5	66.2	98.5 (1.3)	179.1 (1.5)

Note: [1] Include holdings of negotiable certificates of deposits and notes issued by banks.

Source: Central Bank of China, Economic Research Department, *Financial Statistics Monthly (Taiwan Districts)*, April 1988, pp. 129–30 and various issues.

Claims on financial institutions constituted 85.4 per cent, of which claims on domestic banks took up 67.2 per cent, whilst claims on foreign banks 13.1 per cent. There have been some changes in the structure of the offshore banking system. In the early phase, foreign banks played a more dominant role than domestic banks in borrowing from the system, but the reverse in the later phase (compare the relative percentages in December 1985 and December 1987). This implies that domestic banks have learned to draw finance from the system particularly under the circumstances of expected appreciation of NT dollars, when banks have to borrow US dollars in order to re-lend to business.

It should also be noted from Table 3.2 that the offshore banking system, along with the Asian Dollar Market in Singapore, and the offshore banking systems in the Philippines, London and elsewhere, is basically an inter-bank market, in view of the relative insignificance of lending and depositing by non-bank customers.

Likewise, deposits of non-bank customers constituted less than 1 per cent of total liabilities, whilst inter-bank deposits constituted 98 per cent. The share of domestic banks' deposits declined from 77 per cent in December 1985 to 7 per cent in December 1987, whilst the share of foreign banks' deposits was increased from 19 per cent to 86 per cent. In view of the expected appreciation of NT dollars, many foreign investment houses try to remit money into Taiwan. However, because of the difficulty of arranging deposits in NT dollars, they place the money in the offshore system through foreign banks as a temporary abode. This explains the sharp increase of deposits of foreign banks. The opposite is the attitude of domestic banks, which try to avoid depositing in foreign currencies.

Generally speaking, foreign banks play an active role in the system, because of their close connection with international financial centres. In the principle of the system, deposit funds are collected overseas and loans are extended overseas. Banking operations are related mainly to the overseas markets, and secondarily to the domestic market, as shown in the offshore banking systems of Singapore, Hong Kong, London, Frankfurt and Luxembourg. Lending and depositing are denominated in foreign currencies such as US dollars, Deutschmark, Japanese yen, pound sterling, Swiss franc, and French franc. But the US dollar is the most predominant currency used – about 80–90 per cent, because the US dollar – in spite of its depreciation – is still the most marketable currency in the world. It is a common practice for multinational corporations to borrow from an offshore banking system and re-lend overseas. In the case of Taiwan, such a phenomenon is beginning to take shape, as evidenced in the fact that loans to non-bank non-residents increased from 0.9 per cent in December 1985 to 4.6 per cent in December 1987. Loans to non-residents (4.6 per cent) were greater than loans to residents (0.6 per cent) in 1987, signifying the characteristic features of an offshore system.

After the introduction of the system, some of the foreign exchange held by domestic banks was shifted to the system, so that superficially in statistics the system appeared to the progressing very fast in the early phase. With the expectation of appreciation of the NT dollar, that type of shift no longer exists.

Like other financial centres the OBUs in Taiwan are primarily engaged in short-term finance. At the end of December 1987, 78 per cent of the loans were for six months or less; as were 96 per cent of the deposit liabilities (Table 3.3).

The establishment of the offshore banking system is a part of the strategy of financial liberalisation and internationalisations. In view of the growing strength of the Taiwan economy, and the increasing export surplus, it is expected that OBUs will progress by leaps and bounds in the next few years.

3.8 INFORMAL MONEY MARKET

The description of the financial structure in Taiwan would not be complete without discussing the informal money market, which is much more active than those in Singapore and Hong Kong. The informal money market includes borrowing from and depositing with friends, relatives and firms which are not authorised to accept deposits from the general public. Some corporations accept deposits from their employees, and therefore reduce the need to borrow from banks.[4]

Historically, Taiwan has had many private savings societies which constitute an important part of the informal money market. The Central Bank of Taiwan, in compiling the statistics of interest rates in the informal money market categorises the interest rates into three parts: (i) loans against post-dated cheques, (ii) unsecured loans, and (iii) deposits with firms.[5] For example the average interest rate in May 1986 in Taipei for loans against post-dated cheques was 1.85 per cent per month (or 22.2 per cent per annum); for unsecured loans,

Table 3.3 Maturities of assets and liabilities of offshore banking units, 1984–7 (US$ million)

	December 1984	*June 1985*	*December 1985*	*June 1986*	*December 1986*	*June 1987*	*December 1987*
Assets							
up to 1 month	1 024.7 (24.4)	1 238.3	1 548.8 (23.9)	1 078.9	1 167.7	1 594.2 (21.2)	3 008.3 (26.3)
1–3 months	1 079.2 (25.7)	1 065.8	1 126.3 (17.4)	777.5	1 494.2	1 803.0 (23.9)	1 911.9 (16.7)
3–6 months	1 556.7 (37.0)	2 223.0	2 460.2 (38.0)	1 763.3	1 303.0	2 048.2 (27.2)	3 984.1 (34.8)
	(87.1)		(79.3)			(72.3)	(77.8)
6–12 months	151.2 (3.6)	66.7	353.3 (5.5)	166.5	258.2	318.6 (4.2)	621.2 (5.4)
over 12 months	394.9 (9.4)	589.6	980.3 (15.2)	2 014.3	1 341.9	1 772.2 (23.5)	1 930.6 (16.8)
Total assets	4 206.7 (100)	5 183.4	6 468.9 (100)	5 800.5	5 565.1	7 536.1 (100)	11 456.0 (100)
Liabilities							
up to 1 month	1 983.5 (46.9)	2 366.8	2 346.0 (36.1)	2 055.0	2 275.9	2 187.7 (29.0)	2 485.2 (21.6)
1–3 months	755.7 (17.9)	846.1	1 212.1 (18.6)	911.3	2 048.2	2 644.4 (35.1)	2 744.7 (23.8)
3–6 months	1 395.3 (33.0)	1 940.1	2 825.7 (43.4)	2 687.3	1 576.9	2 622.1 (34.8)	5 798.7 (50.4)
	(97.8)		(98.1)			(98.9)	(95.8)
6–12 months	56.6 (1.3)	9.8	65.9 (1.0)	113.0	198.3	42.5 (0.6)	448.6 (3.9)
over 12 months	40.0 (0.9)	40.0	56.2 (0.9)	38.4	42.7	37.0 (0.5)	33.6 (0.3)
Total liabilities	4 231.0 (100)	5 202.9	6 505.9 (100)	5 800.5	6 142.0	7 533.6 (100)	11 510.8 (100)

Source: Same as Table 3.2.

1.93 per cent per month (or 23.16 per cent per annum); for deposits with firms, 1.37 per cent per month (or 16.44 per cent per annum), which were much higher than bank interest. The interest rate for unsecured loans is higher than that for loans against post-dated cheques, and that for deposits with firms. Apparently, employees favour – or have faith in – their employing firms. It should be noted that the interest rates in the informal money market varies slightly in different cities of Taipei, Kaohsiung and Taichung. The importance of the informal money market in the Taiwan economy can be realised in the following facts.

In 1986 domestic funds borrowed by business enterprises (including public and private ones), came from the informal money market to the extent of about 30 per cent; from banks and financial institutions (47 per cent); money market (7 per cent), and from the capital market (14 per cent) (Table 3.4). The 'Sino-American Development Funds and Government Agencies', which were related to the US Aid dropped from 26 per cent in 1964 to an insignificant share of 1.7 per cent in 1987.[6,7] In theory, as the money and capital markets become more developed, the informal money market should lose its significance. However, in spite of the falling interest rates in 1986 and 1987, the share of the informal money market was no lower (Table 3.5). Obviously, public enterprises borrow less from the informal money market than private enterprises, because the former, being government-owned, have the strong support of government banks.

With respect to the flow of savings fund into formal and informal money market (Table 3.5) we would note that the informal money market had a share of about 20 per cent in 1986; time and savings deposits with financial institutions, 67 per cent; money market, 5 per cent; and capital market, 9 per cent (Table 3.5).

In a way, the importance of the informal money market denotes the unsatisfied demand for funds and the underdevelopment of the banking and financial system. Some small enterprises, which do not yet have a properly audited account and cannot offer adequate collateral to banks, cannot borrow effectively from banks, and therefore have to borrow from the informal money market at a high rate of interest. There are about 70 000 exporting and importing firms, big and small, competing in the market. Moreover, there is a considerable number of small trading and manufacturing firms which are not registered at all, with the convenience of tax-evasion and freedom from all sorts of government regulations with respect to pollution control, fire precaution and other considerations. Naturally, an unregistered firm has to resort to the informal money market. The social and economic environment of Taiwan favours the development of the informal money market.

The underground, or subterranean, economy, which is closely related to the informal money market constitutes about 14 per cent of GNP of Taiwan according to a study in a direct method by a group of economists in Taiwan.[8]

In reviewing the economic growth of Taiwan since 1960, one would be impressed more by the high growth rates of her manufacturing industries, than by those of her financial sector.[9] Industrial development seems to outpace financial development.

The lagging behind of the financial sector can be explained in terms of the predominance of government bank bureaucracy, and the rigidity of the financial system. The spirit of free enterprise, which is prominent in industry is lacking in the financial sector, as we saw in Chapter 2. Most of the big banks are government-owned and controlled and there is much regulation on the financial system. Interest rates, foreign-exchange holding and other banking activities have long been regulated by the Central Bank and the Ministry of Finance. The government banks have to turn their profits back to the Treasury every year, and they cannot plough back their surplus to plan for future development, as can a private bank.

According to economic theories, as postulated by, say, McKinnon, Gurley and Shaw and others,[10] who emphasise the intermediate role of banks and financial institutions with respect to savings and investment, the financial sector must progress *pari passu* with the real sector, and the former must be strengthened in order to support the growth of the industrial sector. But in the case of Taiwan, the financial system is historically rigid, and inward-looking; yet both manufacturing industries, and exports, progress so fast. So how do the industries obtain their finance? The only answer is that the informal money market plays an important supplementary role. The small firms and those which are unable to obtain credit from banks turn to the informal money market for finance.

Although the informal money market can be said to make some contribution to economic growth under such peculiar circumstances, it can also be condemned as creating a disturbing effect on the monetary and financial system particularly in the long-run view, because it encourages the underground economy, and directs finance to the illegal channel. Interest rates are pushed up with all sorts of abuses, and the weight of finance is somewhat shifted from banks to the informal money market.

Let us exemplify this with a theoretical model. For the sake of

Table 3.4 Sources of domestic funds borrowed by business enterprises, 1964–87 (NT$ million)

From	Financial Institutions		Money market		Capital market				Informal money market		Sino-American development funds and government agencies		Total
	Amount	%	Amount	%	Debentures	Shares	Subtotal	%	Amount	%	Amount	%	Amount
1964	13 708	35.36	–	–	220	7 190	7 410	19.12	7 555	19.49	10 089	26.03	38 762
1965	16 940	37.56	–	–	240	8 950	9 190	20.38	8 922	19.78	10 044	22.27	45 096
1966	20 889	40.03	–	–	350	7 830	8 180	15.67	12 377	23.72	10 740	20.58	52 186
1967	27 869	47.09	–	–	400	5 530	5 930	10.02	13 467	22.75	11 917	20.14	59 183
1968	37 021	50.69	–	–	530	6 920	7 450	10.20	16 102	22.05	12 463	17.06	73 036
1969	43 929	52.83	–	–	480	7 670	8 150	9.80	19 067	22.93	11 998	14.43	83 144
1970	48 886	53.06	–	–	480	8 450	8 930	9.69	22 267	24.17	12 051	13.08	92 134
1971	69 628	57.45	–	–	580	8 520	9 100	7.51	30 081	24.82	12 396	10.23	121 205
1972	95 138	62.02	–	–	730	9 860	10 590	6.90	35 842	23.37	11 822	7.07	153 392
1973	134 724	65.60	–	–	663	16 180	16 843	8.20	42 204	20.55	11 606	5.65	205 377
1974	175 311	64.64	–	–	2 253	22 711	24 964	9.20	58 188	21.45	12 751	4.70	271 214
1975	217 858	65.36	–	–	3 728	29 069	32 797	9.84	68 449	20.53	14 235	4.27	333 339
1976	252 236	62.17	2 207	0.54	5 203	43 511	48 714	12.01	88 050	21.70	14 531	3.58	405 738
1977	281 041	58.72	9 949	2.08	7 142	55 943	63 085	13.18	107 502	22.46	17 016	3.56	478 593
1978	337 606	56.49	17 373	2.91	12 931	68 235	81 166	13.58	148 806	24.90	12 650	2.12	597 601
1979	425 321	53.35	46 417	5.82	19 087	85 702	104 789	13.14	189 495	23.77	31 184	3.91	797 206
1980	563 918	54.42	65 914	6.36	25 008	108 659	133 667	12.90	240 170	23.18	32 499	3.14	1 036 168
1981	650 168	51.67	109 769	8.72	29 682	128 398	158 080	12.56	305 304	24.26	34 975	2.78	1 258 296

1982	721 206	51.59	133 288	9.53	35 149	151 473	186 622	13.35	322 124	23.04	34 708	2.48	1 397 948
1983	818 964	53.15	159 425	10.35	34 836	167 163	201 999	13.11	323 985	21.03	36 419	2.36	1 540 792
1984	865 758	51.15	195 908	11.57	42 406	190 395	232 801	13.75	358 132	21.16	40 026	2.36	1 692 625
1985	886 810	49.61	195 423	10.93	39 087	213 449	252 536	14.13	412 578	23.08	40 352	2.26	1 787 699
1986	989 694	47.06	154 510	7.35	46 649	240 822	287 471	13.67	635 558	30.22	35 592	1.69	2 102 825
1987	..		138 066		51 730	287 346	339 076		..		..		..

Notes and Sources: [1] Funds borrowed from financial institutions, informal money market and Sino-American Development Fund and government agencies are taken from Economic Research Department, CBC, *Flow of Funds in Taiwan District*, December 1987, pp. 114–59. 'Informal money market' includes 'business borrowing from households' and 'mutual borrowing of business enterprises'.

[2] Funds from the money and capital markets are taken from Economic Research Department, CBC, *Financial Statistics Monthly, Taiwan*, June, 1988, pp. 97, 99–100 and 103. In the money market, commercial papers and bankers' acceptances outstanding (pp. 99–100) are added together. Total par value of listed stocks (p. 97) and outstanding debentures issued by government and private enterprises (p. 103) are added together. In fact, the listed stocks include those of business enterprises and financial institutions; strictly speaking, the latter should be excluded, because in this Table we are concerned only with the funds available to business enterprises. However, the listed stocks of private banks, investment and trust companies and other financial institutions are of a small proportion. Therefore, the figures would not be much distorted.

Table 3.5 The flow of savings funds into formal and informal money markets, 1964–87 (NT$ million)

From:	*Time and savings deposits with financial institutions*		*Money market*		*Capital market*				*Informal money market*		*Total*
	Amount	%	*Amount*	%	*Debentures*	*Shares*	*Subtotal*	%	*Amount*	%	*Amount*
1964	19 076	56.04	–	–	220	7 190	7 410	21.77	7 555	22.19	34 041
1965	22 210	55.08	–	–	240	8 950	9 190	22.79	8 922	22.13	40 322
1966	28 253	57.88	–	–	350	7 830	8 180	16.76	12 377	25.36	48 810
1967	33 737	63.49	–	–	400	5 530	5 930	11.16	13 467	25.35	53 134
1968	38 201	61.86	–	–	530	6 920	7 450	12.06	16 102	26.07	61 753
1969	46 958	63.31	–	–	480	7 670	8 150	10.99	19 067	25.71	74 175
1970	58 759	65.32	–	–	480	8 450	8 930	9.93	22 267	24.75	89 956
1971	74 424	65.51	–	–	580	8 520	9 100	8.01	30 081	26.48	113 605
1972	96 398	67.49	–	–	730	9 860	10 590	7.41	35 842	25.09	142 830
1973	111 630	65.40	–	–	663	16 180	16 843	9.87	42 204	24.73	170 677
1974	152 341	64.69	–	–	2 253	22 711	24 964	10.60	58 188	24.71	235 493
1975	193 777	65.68	–	–	3 728	29 069	32 797	11.12	68 449	23.20	295 023
1976	245 400	63.84	2 207	0.57	5 203	43 511	48 714	12.67	88 050	22.91	384 371
1977	323 326	64.17	9 949	1.97	7 142	55 943	63 085	12.52	107 502	21.34	503 862
1978	411 579	62.46	17 373	2.64	12 931	68 235	81 166	12.32	148 806	22.58	658 924
1979	455 686	57.22	46 417	5.83	19 087	85 702	104 789	13.16	189 495	23.79	796 387
1980	552 789	55.69	65 914	6.64	25 008	108 659	133 667	13.47	240 170	24.20	992 540
1981	674 084	54.05	109 769	8.80	29 682	128 398	158 080	12.67	305 304	24.48	1 247 237
1982	878 652	57.78	133 288	8.76	35 149	151 473	186 622	12.27	322 124	21.18	1 520 686
1983	1 151 537	62.69	159 425	8.68	34 836	167 163	201 999	11.00	323 985	17.64	1 836 946
1984	1 444 476	64.74	195 908	8.78	42 406	190 395	232 801	10.43	358 132	16.05	2 231 317
1985	1 836 128	68.09	195 423	7.25	39 087	213 449	252 536	9.36	412 578	15.30	2 696 665
1986	2 150 513	66.62	154 510	4.79	46 649	240 822	287 471	8.91	635 558	19.69	3 228 052
1987	2 593 409		138 066		51 730	287 346	339 076		..		..

Notes and Source: Same as Table 3.4.

simplicity, let us take one interest rate to represent the whole structure of interest rates, short and long term, and let it be either the deposit rate or lending rate of a financial institution.

Figure 3.1 shows the demand for loanable funds $D'D'$ and the supply of funds $S'S'$ which denotes savings of the community, flowing into banks and financial institutions. In equilibrium, the interest rate should be r_e and the amount of loanable funds demanded and supplied should be OE.

Suppose the interest rate is suppressed to r_1, the demand for funds would be OF, whilst the supply of funds would be OZ. The unsatisfied demand for funds is spilt over to the informal money market. Figure 3.2a integrates the formal with the informal money market.[11] Demand and supply of loanable funds in banks and financial institutions (formal money market) are denoted by DD and SS curves respectively. As the interest rate is controlled by the monetary authority at r_1 the supply is limited to OZ, and if the banking system allots funds to the most efficient borrowers, only those enterprises with the marginal rate of return, exceeding FZ, can obtain the funds. In other words, the effective demand and supply curves of the formal market are the segments of DF and SG (to the left of G).

The vertical line projected from Z, can be said to be the starting line of the informal money market. Its demand curve $D'D'$ has a steeper slope than that of the formal money market because the interest rate in the informal market is always higher than that of the formal market because of the risk premium. Given the demanded amount of loanable funds, OA, the demand curves of the informal and formal markets seem to converge at D', because that sets the limit or targeted amount.

The risk premium of the informal market is the vertical line $S'G'$, or the vertical difference between the supply curves of the informal and formal markets, i.e. $S'S'$ and SG. Again the supply curve of the informal market slopes up faster than that of the formal market.

Thus the demand and supply curves of the informal market are depicted as $D'D'$ and $S'S'$. The whole integrated demand curve would be DF (formal market), to be continued as $D'D'$ (informal market). Likewise, the whole integrated supply curve would be SG (formal market) to be continued as $S'S'$ (informal market). The equilibrium interest rate of the integrated market would be r_2, which is greater than the equilibrium interest rate of the formal market, r_e. The equilibrium amount of the former, OB is also lower than that of the latter, OE.

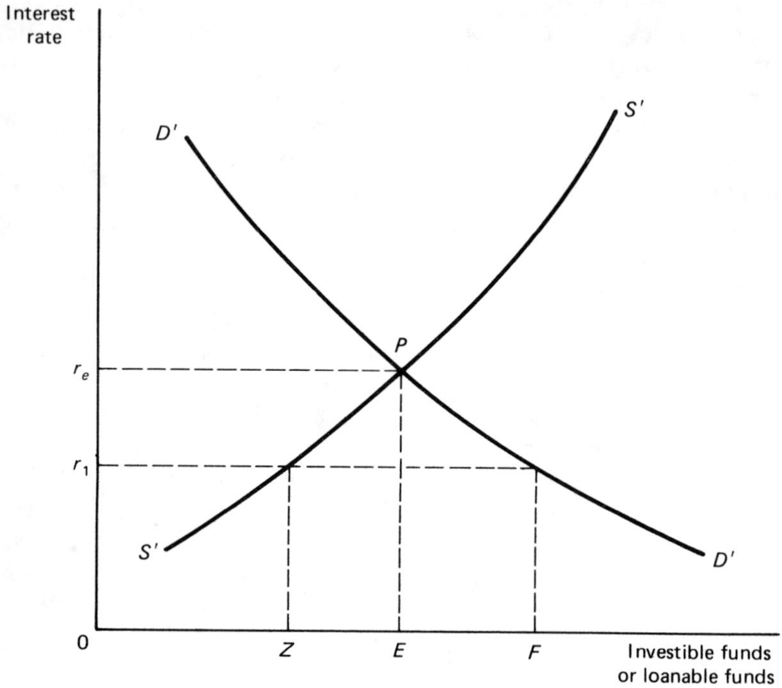

Figure 3.1 Demand and supply of loanable funds

The positive role of the informal market in terms of the supplementary financial function should be counterbalanced by the negative role in terms of the displacement effect on the intermediate function of the formal market. Because of the existence of the informal market offering higher interest rates to lenders or depositors, some funds are attracted away from the formal to the informal market. Thus in Figure 3.2b, the *ZZ* vertical line which is the starting-line of the informal market is shifted to the left to *Z′Z′* causing the volume of deposits or loanable funds in the formal market to contract. This poses a serious problem to the monetary authority in the management of monetary policy. The monetary and financial system would be distorted in the long run; interest rates would be higher than formal market equilibrium ($r_2 > r_e$ in Figure 3.2 a and b). The expansion of the informal market would accentuate the growth of the underground economy, with tax-evasion and all sorts of other abuses.

Indeed, in the case of Taiwan, the informal market has helped the growth of manufacturing industries and exports to surpass that of the

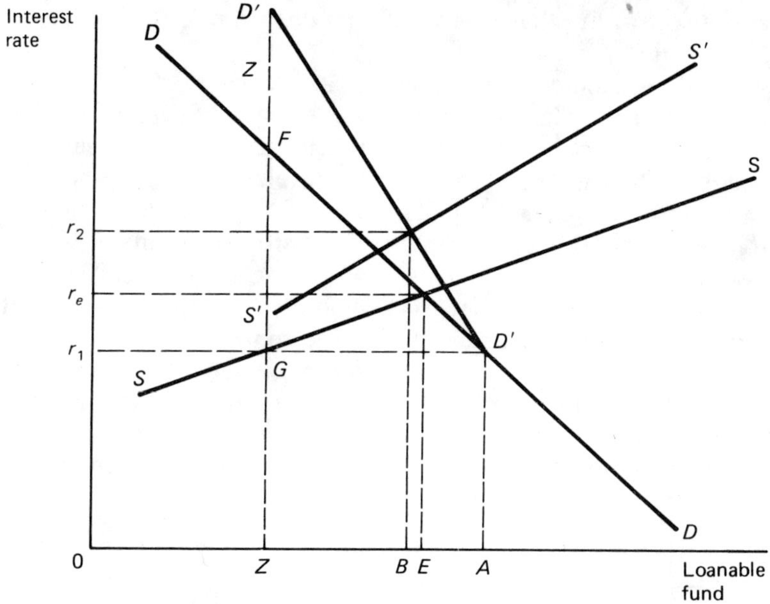

Figure 3.2 (a) Integration of the formal and informal money market

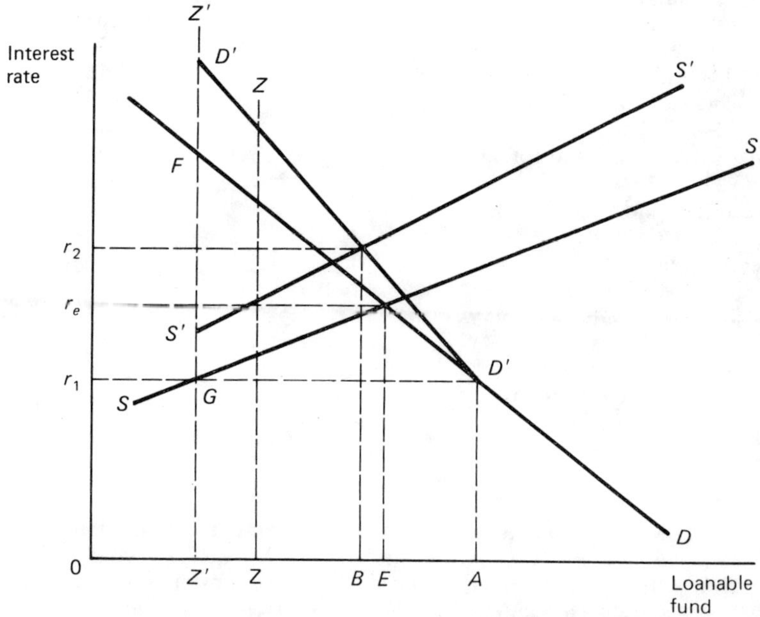

Figure 3.2 (b) Displacement effect of the informal money market on the intermediate function of the formal market

financial sector, but that gain would not compensate for the loss in the long run as aforesaid.

What then should be the appropriate policy to deal with the informal market? This cannot be done by merely suppressing the informal market by law, because there actually exists an unsatisfied demand for funds. The best way is to develop and strengthen the formal market by means of liberalisation of the financial system.

It has been estimated recently that there are as many as 200 underground investment companies, absorbing about NT$200 billion deposit funds in Taiwan. They pay high interest rates of 4–10 per cent per month! Their speculative activities had contributed to the abnormally rising stock market and property market. Recently, the New Bank Act 1989 caused a precipitous fall of the stock market, and the 'temporary' suspension of deposit withdrawal by the underground investment companies. There was a somewhat confusion in the financial market, with the worry of precipitating a crisis!

Table 3.6 Financial institutions in Taiwan in May 1988

	Number of institutions
Central bank	1 (1)
Domestic banks	16 (634)
Medium and small business banks	8 (235)
Postal Remittance and Savings Bureau	1 (1 164)
Branches of foreign banks	35 (35)
All banks (local and foreign)	61 (2 069)
Investment and trust companies (Table 3.1)	8 (34)
Credit cooperatives	74 (298)
Credit departments of Farmers' Associations	282 (607)
Credit departments of Fishery Associations	21 (11)
Bill finance companies (Table 3.7)	3 (11)
Securities finance company	1 (1)
Insurance companies	22 (132)
Total	472 (3 163)

Notes: 1. Domestic banks in this table, following the definition of the Economic Research Department of the Central Bank, exclude medium and small business banks and Postal Remittance and Savings Bureau.
2. Figures in parenthesis denote the number of offices.

Table 3.7 List of bill finance companies in Taiwan

Company	*Date of establishment*
1. The Chung-Shing Bill Finance Corporation	20 May 1976
2. The International Bill Finance Corporation	15 January 1977
3. Chung-Hua Bill Finance Corporation	1 December 1978

Source: Central Bank of China, *Financial Institutions in Taiwan*, February 1984, p. 22.

4 Assets and Liabilities of Financial Institutions and the Composition of Lending

Having described the financial structure in Chapters 2 and 3, let us analyse their assets and liabilities (which show the sources and uses of funds) and illustrate the relative importance of different categories of financial institutions in terms of deposits and loans.

4.1 DEPOSITS OF VARIOUS FINANCIAL INSTITUTIONS AND THEIR GROWTH RATES

Table 4.1 shows the deposits of various financial institutions from 1961 to 1987.[1] At the end of 1987, banks took the predominant share of 57.5 per cent of all deposits of the financial institutions; Postal Remittance and Savings Bureau, 19.8 per cent; investment and trust companies, 3.4 per cent; credit cooperatives, 10.3 per cent; credit departments of Farmers' Associations and Fishery Associations, about 9 per cent. From 1961 to 1987 the relative shares of deposits have undergone some changes. Domestic banks' share declined from 80.5 per cent to 56.5 per cent; foreign banks' share increased from 0.03 per cent to about 1 per cent; Postal Remittance and Savings Bureau's share increased substantially from 3 per cent to 19.8 per cent; credit cooperatives maintained their share of about 10 per cent; credit departments of Farmers' Associations and Fishery Associations increased their share from 6 per cent to 9 per cent.

Two departments of the Central Bank of China define 'domestic banks' in two different ways and hence present statistics differently. The Supervision Department taking a broad scope defines 'domestic banks' as inclusive of 'domestic general banks', medium and small business banks, and Postal Savings and Remittance Bureau.

The Economic Research Department defines domestic banks (DB_1) in a narrow way, exclusive of medium and small business banks and Postal Savings and Remittance Bureau. The medium and

Table 4.1 Deposits of various financial institutions in Taiwan, 1961–87 (NT$ million)

	Domestic banks[1]	*Foreign banks*	*All banks*	*Postal Remittance and Savings Bureau*	*Total*	*Investment and trust companies*[2]	*Credit cooperatives*	*Credit departments of Farmers' Associations and Fishery Associations*	*Total*
1961	15 035	6	15 041	632	15 673	–	1 892	1 105	18 670
	(80.53)	(0.03)	(80.56)	(3.39)	(83.95)		(10.13)	(5.92)	(100)
1965	26 586	71	26 657	2 438	29 095	–	5 341	2 894	37 330
1969	57 083	106	57 189	6 114	63 303	–	8 306	4 646	76 255
1971	82 146	157	82 303	11 812	94 115	768	12 983	6 557	114 423
1975	228 812	1 210	230 022	34 086	264 108	19 185	35 584	18 844	337 721
1979	509 306	2 180	511 486	100 680	612 166	53 081	89 800	53 305	808 352
1981	690 169	5 104	695 273	165 751	861 024	73 827	126 301	89 964	1 151 116
	(59.96)	(0.44)	(60.44)	(14.40)	(74.80)	(6.41)	(10.97)	(7.82)	(100)
1983	1 128 828	11 693	1 140 521	316 067	1 456 588	105 266	211 019	168 957	1 941 830
1984	1 373 106	18 342	1 391 448	392 572	1 784 020	136 884	260 021	214 011	2 394 936
1985	1 730 016	28 953	1 758 969	509 972	2 268 941	108 272	283 461	257 133	2 917 807
1986	1 799 862	26 120	1 825 982	660 716	2 486 698	117 331	324 202	306 855	3 235 086
1987	2 259 804	41 925	2 301 729	791 590	3 093 319	136 970	410 209	362 005	4 002 503
	(56.46)	(1.05)	(57.51)	(19.78)	(77.29)	(3.42)	(10.25)	(9.04)	(100)

Notes: [1] Include 'domestic general banks' and medium and small business banks (DB_1 plus DB_2).
[2] As investment and trust companies are not allowed to accept deposits from the public, those figures are in fact trust funds, or borrowed funds.
Figures in parenthesis are percentages.

Source: Economic Research Department, Central Bank of China, *Financial Statistics Monthly, Taiwan District*, June 1988 and various issues.

small business banks are designated as DB_2 in this book.

The growth rates of deposits of various financial institutions are presented in Table 4.2. The Postal Remittance and Savings Bureau consistently maintained the highest growth rate of 31.6 per cent in the long period. In the 26-year period 1961–87, domestic banks and 'all banks' also had a high growth rate of about 21 per cent. Foreign banks appeared to have a higher growth rate of 40.6 per cent. But in fact, they started with a very low level of only NT$6m in 1961 and with only one bank; it was only in the 1980s that more and more foreign banks opened their branches in Taipei. Yet in 1987, they collected only 1 per cent of the deposits of all financial institutions. Among the non-bank financial institutions the investment and trust companies appear to have a high growth rate of 38 per cent, which is rather a misleading figure, because they started from a low level and they are not allowed to accept deposits from the public; they do so in a disguised way through borrowed funds or trust funds. The credit cooperatives had a steady growth rate of 23 per cent.

The credit departments of Farmers' Associations and Fishery Associations had a growth rate of about 25 per cent, which reflected the prosperity and high savings ratio of the agricultural sector.

If we pay more attention to the recent period, 1980–7, we can note some interesting points:

(a) The medium and small business banks' (DB_2) deposits grew faster than those of other domestic banks, (DB_1).
(b) The deposits of foreign banks grew at a very fast rate of 45 per cent in the early 1980s because of the rapid increase of the number of foreign banks, and the gradual relaxation of regulation over foreign banks' deposits.
(c) The investment and trust companies had a set-back in the current period, 1980–7, with a lower growth rate of deposits of 12.6 per cent, as compared with the high growth rate of almost 70 per cent in the previous period 1970–9. In 1970–9, prices were rising, and the property and stock markets were booming. The investment and trust companies took advantage of the boom condition; some of them speculated in those markets. The falling property and stock markets in 1980–5 and the declining inflation rates in the 1980–5 had caused great difficulty to those companies. However in 1988, the property and stock markets rose again; that would give an impetus to the investment and trust companies.

Table 4.2 Growth rates (compound) of deposits of various financial institutions, 1961–87 (as percentages)

	1961–9	*1970–9*	*1980–7*	*1961–87*
Domestic banks exclusive of medium and small business banks (DB_1)	17.93	24.53	20.03	21.08
Medium and small business banks (DB_2)	21.16	23.59	25.48	23.41
Domestic banks	18.15	24.46	20.47	21.26
Foreign banks	43.18	35.31	44.71	40.56
All banks	18.17	24.50	20.68	21.35
Postal Remittance and Savings Bureau	32.80	32.33	29.40	31.57
Total of the above	19.06	25.47	22.45	22.54
Investment and trust companies	–	69.80	12.58	38.26 (1971–1987)
Credit cooperatives	20.31	26.88	20.91	22.98
Credit departments of Farmers' Associations and Fishery Associations	19.66	27.63	27.06	24.95
Total non-banks	20.08	31.23	21.13	24.58
Total financial institutions	19.23	26.63	22.14	22.93

Notes and Source: Same as Table 4.1.

The overall deposit growth rate was the highest at about 26.6 per cent in the period 1970–9, as compared with 19.2 per cent in 1961–9 and 22.1 per cent in 1980–7 (see Table 4.2).

4.2 LOANS OF VARIOUS FINANCIAL INSTITUTIONS AND THEIR GROWTH RATES

Similarly, Table 4.3 shows the loans of various financial institutions from 1961 to 1986. At the end of 1987, banks took the predominant share of about 81.5 per cent of all loans in the financial institutions. Postal Remittance and Savings Bureau took a very small share, as it is organised mainly for collecting savings deposits from the general public and redepositing the funds in the Central Bank, or government banks, or investing the funds in government securities rather than lending to the public.[2]

Table 4.3 Loans of various financial institutions in Taiwan, 1961–87 (NT$ million)

	Domestic Banks[1]	Foreign Banks	All Banks	Postal Remittance & Savings Bureau	Total	Investment & Trust Companies	Credit Cooperatives	Credit Depts of Farmers' Assn. & Fishery Assn.	Total
1961	13 593	70	13 663	56	13 719	237	1 212	788	15 956
	(85.19)	(0.44)	(85.63)	(0.35)	(85.98)	(1.49)	(7.60)	(4.94)	(100)
1965	27 369	326	27 695	41	27 736	791	3 052	2 456	34 035
1969	60 629	2 179	62 808	48	62 856	1 446	5 819	3 962	74 083
1971	91 186	4 733	95 919	112	96 031	2 833	8 270	4 881	112 015
1975	297 136	27 589	324 725	415	325 140	18 962	24 386	12 992	381 480
1979	584 730	59 413	644 143	1 369	645 512	40 875	65 031	40 833	792 251
1981	820 405	106 266	926 671	1 705	928 376	46 851	87 710	66 070	1 129 007
	(72.67)	(9.41)	(82.08)	(0.15)	(82.23)	(4.15)	(7.77)	(5.85)	(100)
1983	1 142 522	94 635	1 237 157	1 732	1 238 889	54 756	129 103	109 024	1 531 772
1984	1 280 936	91 078	1 372 014	2 344	1 374 358	57 647	148 484	128 851	1 709 340
1985	1 370 200	82 744	1 452 944	3 570	1 456 514	54 175	147 745	141 557	1 799 991
1986	1 525 039	101 154	1 626 193	4 140	1 630 333	48 961	144 107	146 991	1 970 392
1987	1 812 977	120 134	1 933 111	5 095	1 938 206	71 001	199 393	162 851	2 371 451
	(76.45)	(5.07)	(81.52)	(0.21)	(81.73)	(2.99)	(8.41)	(6.87)	(100)

Notes and Source: Same as Table 4.1.

Table 4.4 Growth rates (compound) of loans of various financial institutions, 1961–87 (as percentages)

	1961–9	*1970–9*	*1980–7*	*1961–87*
Domestic banks exclusive of medium and small business banks (DB_1)	20.27	25.35	14.35	20.31
Medium and small business banks (DB_2)	25.71	26.74	23.81	25.51
Domestic banks	20.55	25.44	15.19	20.71
Foreign banks	53.69	39.18	9.20	33.17
All banks	21.01	26.21	14.73	20.98
Postal Remittance and Savings Bureau	–1.91	39.80	17.85	18.94
Total of the above	20.96	26.23	14.73	20.97
Investment and trust companies	25.37	39.68	7.15	24.52
Credit cooperatives	21.67	27.30	15.03	21.69
Credit departments of Farmers' Associations and Fishery Associations	22.37	26.27	18.88	22.76
Total non-banks	22.34	29.31	14.49	22.45
Total financial institutions	21.16	26.74	14.69	21.21

Notes and Source: Same as Table 4.1.

The credit cooperatives had a share of 8.4 per cent; credit departments of Farmers' Associations and Fishery Associations, 6.9 per cent; and the investment and trust companies, about 3 per cent. The relative share of loans of domestic banks declined from 85 per cent while the share of foreign banks rose from about half per cent in 1961 to 5 per cent in 1961 to 76 per cent in 1987. The shares of lending of the investment and trust companies, the credit cooperatives and the credit departments of Farmers' Associations and Fishery Associations were increased.

Foreign banks' lending appeared to be at their height in 1981–3; thereafter the absolute amounts declined and the relative share declined from 9.4 per cent in 1981 to 5.1 per cent in 1987.

A striking feature in Table 4.4 is that loans of banks grew less than those of non-banks which is in fact a common phenomenon in many countries.

The total growth rates showed a decline from 26.7 per cent in 1970–9 to 14.7 per cent in 1980–7. The world recession in the early 1980s had an effect on the provision of credit. The worst hit were investment and trust companies, whose growth rates declined from 39.7 per cent in 1970–9 to 7.2 per cent in 1980–7; and also the credit cooperatives, whose growth rates declined from 27.3 per cent in 1970–9 to 15 per cent in 1980–7.

Foreign banks' growth rates declined sharply from 39.2 per cent in 1970–9 to 9.2 per cent in 1980–7. Among the domestic banks, DB_1's growth rates fell more than those of DB_2.

Although the overall growth rates of loans appeared to move in the same direction as those of deposits (compare the bottom lines of Tables 4.4 and 4.2), the times reflects more clearly the prosperity and recession of the economy.

4.3 AGGREGATE ASSETS OF VARIOUS FINANCIAL INSTITUTIONS

The aggregate assets of various financial institutions from 1961 to 1987 are presented in Table 4.5. As aggregate assets include loans, investments, liquid assets, fixed and other assets, they would naturally be strongly influenced by the loan structure. At the end of 1987, bank assets constituted 63 per cent of all assets of financial institutions.

The Postal Remittance and Savings Bureau had a big share of 16 per cent, as it could effectively mobilise savings of the community. The credit cooperatives had a share of 7.8 per cent. The credit departments of Farmers' Associations and Fishery Associations had a share of 6.8 per cent. The investment and trust companies had a share of 2.5 per cent, which was less than that of credit cooperatives and the credit departments of Associations.

As in the case of loans and deposits, the percentages for banks declined from 1961 to 1987, whilst those for Postal Remittance and Savings Bureau and non-bank financial institutions increased. The general pattern of the growth rates of the aggregate assets of various financial institutions is similar to that for loans (Table 4.4).

4.4 DOMESTIC BANKS (EXCLUSIVE OF MEDIUM AND SMALL BUSINESS BANKS), DB_1

The sources and uses of funds of various financial institutions can be discussed with reference to their assets and liabilities. As is common in commercial banking, deposits are the main source of funds (see Table 4.6). As at the end of 1987, 87 per cent of the sources of funds

Table 4.5 Aggregate assets of various financial institutions in Taiwan, 1961–87 (NT$ million)

	Domestic Banks[1]	*Foreign Banks*	*All Banks*	*Postal Remittance and Savings Bureau*	*Total*	*Trust and investment companies*[2]	*Credit Cooperatives*	*Credit departments of Farmers' Associations and Fishery Associations*	*Total*
1961	21 798	131	21 929	219	22 148	348	1 968	1 364	25 828
	(84.40)	(0.51)	(84.90)	(0.85)	(85.75)	(1.35)	(7.62)	(5.28)	(100)
1965	44 364	1 151	45 515	1 568	47 083	1 152	5 214	4 218	57 667
1969	87 722	2 832	90 554	4 293	94 847	1 813	9 633	6 503	131 787
1971	125 716	6 066	131 782	11 285	143 067	3 785	14 253	8 723	169 828
1975	401 226	31 567	432 793	36 861	469 654	26 661	42 634	23 497	562 446
1979	1 021 360	66 855	1 088 215	113 429	1 201 644	67 054	95 075	65 062	1 428 835
1981	1 217 224	120 253	1 337 477	182 812	1 520 289	81 513	136 619	105 926	1 844 347
	(66.00)	(6.52)	(72.52)	(9.91)	(82.43)	(4.42)	(7.41)	(5.74)	(100)
1983	1 742 719	110 823	1 853 542	342 768	2 196 310	107 355	224 166	189 868	2 717 699
1984	1 985 720	114 218	2 117 938	429 137	2 547 075	136 508	275 164	240 469	3 199 216
1985	2 337 008	114 125	2 451 133	566 426	3 017 559	130 840	298 363	283 020	3 729 782
1986	2 846 621	142 449	2 989 070	738 173	3 727 243	118 838	336 470	328 598	4 511 149
1987	3 503 649	222 041	3 725 690	884 348	4 610 038	137 897	432 180	380 304	5 560 419
	(63.01)	(3.99)	(67.00)	(15.91)	(82.91)	(2.48)	(7.77)	(6.84)	(100)

Notes: [1] Include 'domestic general banks' and medium and small business banks.
[2] Figures in parenthesis are percentages.

Source: Same as Table 4.1.

Table 4.6 Assets and liabilities of domestic banks (exclusive of medium and small business banks), DB_1 (NT$ million)

	1961	*1969*	*1975*	*1981*	*1983*	*1986*	*1987*
Assets							
Liquid assets							
1. Cash in vault	274	966	3 697	16 637 (1.46)	22 640	30 331 (1.17)	40 395 (1.27)
2. Deposit with CBC	2 623	7 476	32 242	79 601 (6.99)	92 168	315 781 (12.16)	374 613 (11.78)
3. Deposit with other monetary institutions	207	2 341	8 673	22 852 (2.00)	25 604	21 109 (0.81)	21 570 (0.68)
4. Deposit with other financial institutions	13	20	1 725	4 152 (0.36)	4 667	26 719 (1.03)	20 054 (0.63)
	3 117	10 803	46 337	123 242 (10.81)	145 079	393 940 (15.17)	456 632 (14.36)
Earning assets							
5. Loans and discounts	12 992	56 881	284 507	760 369 (66.78)	1 033 218	1 354 803 (52.18)	1 591 701 (50.06)
6. Investments	1 128	4 981	12 628	120 221 (10.56)	209 452	621 316 (23.93)	1 001 495 (31.50)
6.1 Government securities	288	2 487	3 409	17 698 (1.55)	33 357	29 270 (1.13)	29 809 (0.94)
6.2 Other securities	840	2 494	9 219	102 523 (9.00)	176 095	592 046 (22.80)	971 686 (30.56)
7. Foreign assets	3 515	8 942	39 144	130 337 (11.45)	211 359	221 573 (8.53)	125 129 (3.93)
	17 635	70 804	336 279	1 010 927 (88.79)	1 454 029	2 197 692 (84.65)	2 718 325 (85.49)
8. Real estates	238	647	2 464	4 445 (0.39)	4 319	4 652 (0.20)	4 636 (0.15)
Total assets	20 990	82 254	385 080	1 138 614 (100)	1 603 427	2 596 284 (100)	3 179 593 (100)
Liabilities							
9. Capital, reserves and undistributed profit	–	–	–	74 241 (6.52)	78 643	106 188 (4.09)	107 763 (3.39)
10. Other items in capital account	–	–	–	29 039 (2.55)	35 749	–25 449 (–0.98)	–8 697 (–0.27)
				103 280 (9.07)	114 392	80 739 (3.11)	99 066 (3.12)

11. Deposits	16 387	73 612	322 879	905 767 (79.55)	1 358 869	2 290 896 (88.24)	2 768 456 (87.07)
11.1 Deposits of business and individuals	9 846	43 883	188 279	555 869 (48.82)	810 997	1 495 192 (57.59)	1 833 658 (57.67)
11.2 Government deposits	4 274	8 951	29 278	77 587 (6.81)	98 133	145 533 (5.61)	208 913 (6.57)
11.3 CBC deposits	1 148	14 077	77 319	187 585 (16.47)	181 381	53 505 (2.06)	54 911 (1.73)
11.4 Other monetary institutions deposits	1 119	6 250	26 073	74 961 (6.58)	155 277	337 846 (13.01)	390 947 (12.29)
11.5 Other financial institutions deposits	285	451	1 930	9 765 (0.86)	18 581	25 739 (0.99)	28 346 (0.89)
11.6 Deposits replaced by PSS	–	–	–	–	94 500	233 081 (8.98)	251 681 (7.92)
12. Bank debentures issued	–	–	–	6 620 (0.58)	7 802	4 000 (0.15)	2 296 (0.07)
13. Other borrowings	–	368	1 004	1 985 (0.17)	3 978	11 327 (0.44)	13 152 (0.41)
14. Presettlement requirements for imports	939	1 726	9 351	14 582 (1.28)	18 421	23 653 (0.91)	26 459 (0.83)
15. Foreign liabilities	719	4 294	34 138	106 380 (9.34)	99 965	185 669 (7.15)	270 164 (8.50)
Total liabilities	18 045	80 000	367 372	1 138 614 (100)	1 603 427	2 596 284 (100)	3 179 593 (100)
Index	1.8	7.2	34	100	141	228	279

Note: Figures in parenthesis are percentages.
Source: Economic Research Dept. CBC, *Financial Statistics Monthly, Taiwan District, ROC*, May 1988 and various issues.

of domestic banks, DB_1 (exclusive of medium and small business banks), came from deposits, and only 3 per cent from the banks' shareholders' funds. Bank debentures issued, foreign and other borrowings constituted small percentages.

Deposits of non-bank customers (business and individuals) took up the major part (57.7 per cent). The government, apart from depositing in the Central Bank, also deposited some funds in commercial banks, particularly government banks; government deposits constituted 6.6 per cent. DB_1 deposited 11.8 per cent of the funds in the Central Bank,[3] which in turn deposited 1.7 per cent in the DB_1 so that DB_1 had a net deposit of about 10 per cent with the Central Bank. Other monetary institutions, such as the credit cooperatives, and credit departments of Farmers' Associations and Fishery Associations, had considerable amounts of deposits with DB_1 (12.3 per cent). As from 1982, the Postal Remittance and Savings Bureau was directed to redeposit some of its funds with four government banks (Bank of Communication, Farmers' Bank, Land Bank of Taiwan and Medium and Small Business Bank of Taiwan), instead of depositing with the Central Bank. This explains why 'deposits replaced by PSS' increased rapidly to NT$233bn (9 per cent) in 1986.

The composition of the source of funds had undergone some changes from 1981 to 1987, as the percentage figures in Table 4.6 show. Notably, CBC deposits declined absolutely from NT$188bn in 1981 to NT$55bn in 1987, and relatively from 16.5 per cent to 1.7 per cent.

Deposits of non-bank customers increased in both absolute and relative terms. The relative share of deposits of business and individuals was increased from 48.8 per cent in 1981 to 57.7 per cent in 1987.

With respect to the uses of funds, loans and discount took up 50 per cent in 1987; investment, 31.5 per cent; and foreign assets, about 4 per cent (see Table 4.6), totalling 85.5 per cent for earning assets. Liquid assets, consisting of cash, reserve deposits with CBC, and deposits with monetary and financial institutions constituted about 14.4 per cent of all assets (or use of funds). Through time (compare 1981 and 1987 in Table 4.6) and percentage wise, loans and discount had declined, and investments increased.

One important point to note is that in the portfolio of banks in Taiwan, banks hold very little in Treasury bills and government securities as we see in Table 4.6 – only 1.1 per cent in 1986, because the Government issued few Treasury bills and government securities and the money and discount market was not developed until 1973–5.[4]

For public borrowing in previous years the government had found it more convenient to borrow directly, and at a lower interest rate, from the Central Bank rather than to issue securities.

Furthermore, for maintaining liquidity, banks have to hold certain amounts of foreign liquid assets. The present policy of financial liberalisation and of introducing the offshore banking system has encouraged banks to hold more foreign assets.

The relation between one asset item and one liability item shows the bank policy; the crucial ratios are derived from Table 4.6 and are shown in Table 4.7. The cash/deposit ratio is affected directly by the statutory reserve requirement. In 1987, the ratio for domestic banks (exclusive of medium and small business banks), DB_1, stood at 0.15 (Table 4.7).[5] The cash/asset ratio signifies the proportion of fund without interest. Banks attempt to reduce this ratio as much as possible.

The loan/deposit ratio declined from 0.839 in 1981 to 0.575 in 1987; the growth rate of deposits in the 1980s which exceeded that of loans (see Tables 4.2 and 4.4) explained this phenomenon. The liquidity ratio, capital/loan ratio, capital/asset ratio and capital/risk-asset ratio also exhibited a decline.

The ratio of liquid assets to total assets showed a slight increase from 0.108 in 1981 to 0.144 in 1987. Loans and investment (earning assets) ratio increased from 0.773 in 1981 to 0.816 in 1987. The foreign asset ratio declined from 0.114 in 1981 to 0.039 in 1987, as banks anticipated the appreciation of the NT dollar. The risk asset ratio remained almost unchanged in the 1980s.

4.5 MEDIUM AND SMALL BUSINESS BANKS, DB_2

If we compare the consolidated balance sheet of DB_1 with that of the medium and small business banks, DB_2, we note that medium and small business banks hold more liquid assets, less government securities and less foreign assets than DB_1. This is because DB_2 specialise in financing small and medium business and are more inward-looking towards the domestic market, rather than towards foreign trade. There is less inclination to hold foreign assets. In their portfolio, loans and liquid assets constitute the predominant part, whilst investment in Treasury bills, government securities and foreign assets is relatively small.

Table 4.7 Crucial ratios of domestic banks (exclusive of medium and small business banks), DB_1, in 1961–87

	1961	*1969*	*1975*	*1981*	*1983*	*1985*	*1987*
1. Cash/deposit ratio	0.177	0.115	0.111	0.106	0.085	0.090	0.150
2. Liquid asset ratio[1]	0.190	0.147	0.144	0.136	0.107	0.126	0.165
3. Loan/deposit ratio	0.793	0.773	0.881	0.839	0.760	0.647	0.575
4. Capital/loan ratio	0.793	0.773	0.881	0.089	0.076	0.076	0.068
5. Cash/asset ratio	0.138	0.103	0.093	0.085	0.072	0.079	0.131
6. Capital/asset ratio	0.138	0.103	0.093	0.065	0.049	0.043	0.034
7. Capital/risk asset ratio[2]	0.138	0.103	0.093	0.073	0.054	0.048	0.039
8. Capital/deposit ratio	0.138	0.103	0.093	0.082	0.058	0.049	0.039
9. Liquid asset/ aggregate asset ratio	0.148	0.131	0.120	0.108	0.090	0.112	0.144
10. Loan and investment/ aggregate asset ratio	0.673	0.752	0.772	0.773	0.775	0.727	0.816
11. Overseas investment/ aggregate asset ratio	0.167	0.109	0.102	0.114	0.132	0.159	0.039
12. Risk asset/ aggregate asset ratio	0.848	0.867	0.898	0.892	0.908	0.905	0.860

Notes: [1] Liquid asset ratio = ratio of liquid assets (including cash in vault, reserve deposit with Central Bank and deposits with other monetary and financial institutions) to deposit

[2] Risk assets = aggregate assets *minus* cash, treasury bills and government securities

Capital/Risk Asset Ratio = ratio of capital and reserve to risk assets

Source: Economic Research Department, CBC, *Financial Statistics Monthly, Taiwan District*, May 1988 and various issues.

4.6 FOREIGN BANKS[6]

As in 1987, the source of funds came largely from foreign liabilities (69.4 per cent); deposits constituted only 23.6 per cent; operation capital funds and undistributed surplus constituted 43 per cent.[7] The large drawing of foreign funds stands in contrast to domestic banks.[8]

The relative importance of deposits had also been increased from 18.8 per cent in 1981 to 44.8 per cent in 1985 but declined to 23.6 per cent in 1987. The government had a more liberalised policy toward foreign banks in allowing them to accept fixed deposits.

Foreign banks were very active in extending loans in the early 1980s. The height of their lending activity appeared to be in the period 1981–3 when loans accounted for as much as 88 per cent of the use of fund in 1981. As some foreign banks got hurt, they reduced their lending in the subsequent period, 1984–6.[9] The decline in lending in 1984 and 1985 in absolute amounts as well as in percentage is clearly exhibited in statistics.

Generally speaking, the existing restrictions on foreign banks cannot be considered too severe in comparison with other developing countries, such as Indonesia, and Philippines.[10] The complaint on the restriction on foreign banks for accepting time deposits has been gradually liberalised. Some foreign banks interviewed also mentioned that the credit limit of NT$300m might impose a constraint on their lending to big projects.

Although there is restriction on multiple branches for foreign banks, (Article 8 of the Foreign Bank Criteria), amendment has been made to allow foreign banks to apply for another branch in Kaohsiung City.

It has often been commented by some people that foreign banks may have a negative effect, for example, in causing an over-expansion of credit in the early 1980s. Yet by and large in view of the need of adopting the policy of financial liberalisation and internationalisation, foreign banks should have a positive contribution in terms of helping to increase productivity, efficiency and flexibility in the banking system. They may introduce a more sophisticated system of bank management and accountancy. Computerisation and electronic banking can be accelerated, and may help both to induce foreign industrialists to invest in Taiwan, and to develop the offshore banking system.

4.7 COMPOSITION OF LENDING

Table 4.8 analyses the composition of bank lending to private enterprises, public enterprises, government organisations, financial institutions, social welfare organisations and individuals, for the period 1978–87.

Table 4.8 Bank lending to various organisations, 1978–87 (NT$ million)

	1978	*1981*	*1983*	*1985*	*1986*	*1987*
Domestic banks[1]	549 921 (100)	877 670 (100)	1 240 138 (100)	1 514 109 (100)	1 692 705 (100)	1 977 017 (100)
1. Private enterprises	75 629 (13.8)	506 310 (57.7)	658 502 (53.1)	750 696 (49.6)	802 964 (47.4)	931 329 (47.1)
2. Public enterprises	348 730 (63.4)	160 066 (18.2)	216 293 (17.4)	231 708 (15.3)	223 283 (13.2)	171 017 (8.7)
3. Government organisations	13 000 (2.4)	17 836 (2.0)	39 558 (3.2)	36 039 (2.4)	39 744 (2.4)	47 480 (2.4)
4. Financial institutions	21 271 (3.9)	14 599 (1.7)	21 723 (1.8)	27 635 (1.8)	21 068 (1.2)	30 448 (1.5)
5. Social welfare organisations	6 797 (1.2)	11 037 (1.3)	16 136 (1.3)	18 552 (1.2)	24 147 (1.4)	26 584 (1.3)
6. Individuals	84 494 (15.3)	167 822 (19.1)	287 926 (23.2)	449 479 (29.7)	581 499 (34.4)	770 159 (39.0)
Foreign banks	37 318 (100)	112 804 (100)	101 144 (100)	99 392 (100)	117 473 (100)	135 842 (100)
1. Private enterprises	32 296 (86.5)	87 653 (77.7)	84 945 (84.0)	90 643 (91.2)	108 537 (92.4)	121 546 (89.5)
2. Public enterprises	3 830 (10.3)	24 035 (21.3)	15 408 (15.2)	7 112 (7.2)	6 159 (5.2)	7 672 (5.6)
3. Government organisations	–	–	–	–	–	–
4. Financial institutions	1 056 (2.8)	834 (0.7)	239 (0.3)	129 (0.1)	472 (0.4)	424 (0.3)
5. Social welfare organisations	3	–	–	–	111 (0.1)	48 (0.1)
6. Individuals	133 (0.4)	282 (0.3)	522 (0.5)	1 508 (1.5)	2 194 (1.9)	6 152 (4.5)
All banks	587 239 (100)	990 474 (100)	1 341 282 (100)	1 613 501 (100)	1 810 178 (100)	2 112 859 (100)
1. Private enterprises	79 459 (13.5)	593 963 (60.0)	743 447 (55.4)	841 339 (52.1)	911 501 (50.4)	1 052 875 (49.8)
2. Public enterprises	381 026 (64.9)	184 101 (18.6)	231 701 (17.3)	238 820 (14.8)	229 442 (12.7)	178 689 (8.5)
3. Government organisations	13 000 (2.2)	17 836 (1.8)	39 558 (2.9)	36 039 (2.2)	39 744 (2.2)	47 480 (2.2)
4. Financial institutions	22 327 (3.8)	15 433 (1.6)	21 962 (1.6)	27 764 (1.7)	21 540 (1.2)	30 872 (1.5)
5. Social welfare organisations	6 800 (1.2)	11 037 (1.1)	16 136 (1.2)	18 552 (1.1)	24 258 (1.3)	26 632 (1.3)
6. Individuals	84 627 (14.4)	168 104 (17.0)	288 448 (21.5)	450 987 (28.0)	583 693 (32.3)	776 311 (36.7)
Index for all banks	59.3	100	135.4	162.9	182.8	213.3

Notes: [1] Include DB_1, DB_2 and Postal Remittance and Savings Bureau, according to the definition of the Supervision Department of CBC. Figures in parenthesis are percentages.

Source: Supervision Department, CBC, *Annual Report of the Operation of Financial Institutions*, 1978–87, p. 49.

Domestic banks, as defined by the Supervision Department CBC, include all 'domestic general' banks, medium and small business banks and Postal Remittance and Savings Bureau. In the early period, e.g. 1978, the major borrowers (63.4 per cent) were public enterprises as most of the important enterprises are public or government enterprises and the government banks (the most important ones in the banking system) tended naturally to lend to public enterprises. It was only in 1955 when the Government released the monopolistic control of paper-making, cement, mining and agricultural and forestry enterprises, and allowed private enterprises to take part in those activities that there was a great outburst of private entrepreneurship so that Taiwan was able to achieve a high economic growth. For the same reason domestic bank lending had begun to turn the focus toward private enterprises. Lending to private enterprises was increased from 13.8 per cent in 1978, to 57.7 per cent in 1981, but dropped to 47.1 per cent in 1987. Conversely, lending to public enterprises declined from 63.4 per cent in 1978 to 18.2 per cent in 1981 and to 8.7 per cent in 1987. Lending to government organisations, financial institutions, and social welfare organisations was steady at small percentages. Lending to individuals (including professionals, stock-market speculators, etc.) increased from 15.3 per cent in 1978 to 39 per cent in 1987. It should be noted that some of the lending to individuals is in fact business lending, because some of the proprietors wish to borrow in their own personal names for taxation and various reasons.

Similarly, foreign banks' lending to public enterprises declined from 10.3 per cent in 1978 to 5.6 per cent in 1987. Conversely, their lending to private enterprises rose from 86.5 per cent in 1978 to 89.5 per cent in 1987. The focus on lending to private enterprises is much more notable in foreign banks than in domestic banks.

The composition of lending for all banks is similar to that for domestic banks (see Table 4.8) because foreign banks' lending was, for example, only about 7 per cent of domestic banks' lending in 1987 and therefore the composition of domestic banks' lending was the predominant component.

For manufacturing production, public enterprises predominated over private enterprises in the early 1950s. The turning-point came in the period, 1953–8, when private enterprises began to predominate over public enterprises – the reverse. Accordingly, bank lending followed that general pattern.

The growth of lending of all banks is shown in the index at the bottom of Table 4.8. In nominal terms, the index stood at 59.3 in 1978 and 213.3 in 1987, the growth rates per annum being 19 per cent from 1978 to 1981, and 13.5 per cent from 1981 to 1987.

It should also be noted that the growth rates of foreign banks lending was 44.6 per cent from 1978 to 1981, but the growth rate was only 3 per cent from 1981 to 1987; whereas, the growth rates of domestic banks' lending was 16.9 per cent in 1978–81, and 14.5 per cent in 1981–7. Hence foreign banks' expansion of credit exceeded that of domestic banks in 1978–81, but was very much below that of domestic banks in 1981–7. The greatest downturn for foreign bank lending was in 1983–5.

Table 4.9 demonstrates the pattern of lending of domestic banks, DB_1. At the end 1987, bank lending to manufacturing constituted 28 per cent of the total bank loans, whilst that to commerce (wholesale and retail trade) was only 10.5 per cent and to individuals as much as 42.5 per cent. Loans to individuals include services, and personal and professional loans such as in the stock market. Hence such statistical classification of the Central Bank is not very clear.

From 1975 to 1987, the share of manufacturing seemed to decline from 60 per cent to 28 per cent. The share of commerce also declined from 12.6 per cent to 10.5 per cent. But in fact the manufacturing industries have continued to be strong in the 1980s. The sharp increase in the loans to 'individuals' from 8 per cent to 41.5 per cent has distorted the pattern of shares.

With respect to lending to manufacturing, metal goods (including electronic and electrical goods), chemical goods, textiles, garment- and food-manufacturing gain the most shares. Recently, the government has tried to encourage the development of strategic industries. So the Bank of Communication was principally entrusted with the task of financing these industries – for example, the electronic and information industries, chemical industries and metal industries, at low interest rates.[11]

Bank lending to agriculture, forestry and fishery declined from 3.5 per cent in 1975 to 1 per cent in 1987, reflecting the relative decline of the agricultural sector, which is also indicated in Chapter 7, Table 7.2. Let us compare Table 4.9 with Table 7.2. From 1975 to 1987, the contributive share of manufacturing to GDP increased from 37 per cent to 43 per cent, although the share of bank loans declined. The contributive share of commerce remained around the level of 13–14 per cent; and the share of bank loans to commerce remained almost unchanged. More attention should be given to Table 7.2 if we wish to have a general idea of the pattern of bank lending.

Finance for industries and trade is provided mainly by banks and other financial institutions and secondarily by the informal money market as discussed in Chapter 3. Finance for agriculture can be said to be quite successful in Taiwan, which is a good feature of the financial system.

The grass-root financial institutions include the credit cooperatives, credit departments of the Farmers' Associations and Fishery Associations, which specialise in providing rural credit and in financing small business in their own locality. The medium and small business banks also specialise in financing small business in their areas.

The Farmers' Bank of China, and the Land Bank of Taiwan finance agriculture and do land-mortgage business. The Cooperative Bank of Taiwan is the central banking institution for the credit cooperatives, which are categorised as rural and urban cooperative associations.

The investment and trust companies are supposed to provide medium- and long-term credit to industries, although they are actually interested in financing commercial credit, and in investment in the property market. They also provide housing loans.

4.8 INVESTMENT AND TRUST COMPANIES

In 1987 their lending, deposits, and aggregate assets were respectively about 3.0, 3.4 and 2.5 per cent of the financial system (see Tables 4.1, 4.3, 4.5). By law, they are not allowed to accept deposits from the public, but in fact they do so in a disguised way. Hence trust funds are the major source of funds (74 per cent) in 1986. They can also accept deposits from other financial institutions such as credit cooperatives (17 per cent in 1986), and the Central Bank of China.

With regard to the uses of funds, loans and investment each constitute about 33 per cent of the total usage. There is an increasing tendency to hold government securities, which have been issued in greater volume in recent years.

The progress of the investment and trust companies is not up to expectation. As the property market became dull in the 1980s, they found greater difficulty in their business operation.

Table 4.9 Outstanding loans of domestic banks, DB_1 in 1975–1987 (end of year) (NT$ million)

	1975	*1977*	*1981*	*1983*	*1985*	*1986*	*1987*
1. Agriculture, forestry and fishing	10 806	12 697	16 321	18 449	19 650	13 362	15 154
	(3.5)		(2.1)			(1.0)	(1.0)
2. Mining and quarrying	520	791	1 376	1 403	1 703	1 499	1 733
	(0.2)		(0.2)			(0.1)	(0.1)
3. Manufacturing	188 214	231 309	360 178	425 225	433 146	421 747	447 984
	(60.2)		(47.4)			(31.1)	(28.1)
Private enterprise	–	–	254 383	311 245	340 620	343 330	394 374
Public enterprise	–	–	105 795	113 980	92 526	78 417	53 610
4. Electricity, gas and water supply	10 953	14 470	51 009	66 122	62 783	65 842	57 977
	(3.5)		(6.7)			(4.9)	(3.6)
Private enterprise	–	–	1 595	2 503	2 109	2 477	2 525
Public enterprise	–	–	49 414	63 619	60 674	63 365	55 452
5. Construction	7 243	9 061	14 439	23 279	26 003	37 179	55 531
	(2.3)		(1.9)			(2.7)	(3.5)
Private enterprise	–	–	5 537	9 965	10 648	19 530	45 770
Public enterprise	–	–	8 902	13 314	15 355	17 649	9 761
6. Commerce (wholesale and retail trade)	39 408	53 278	82 539	118 340	131 964	137 404	166 891
	(12.6)		(10.9)			(10.1)	(10.5)

Private enterprise	–	–	77 559	100 122	110 788	113 429	142 988
Public enterprise	–	–	4 980	18 218	21 176	23 975	23 903
7. Transport, storage and communication	7 829	12 585	29 177	37 807	52 630	55 153	64 669
	(2.5)		(3.8)			(4.1)	(4.1)
Private enterprise	–	–	8 077	13 324	25 398	30 380	38 021
Public enterprise	–	–	21 100	24 483	27 232	24 773	26 648
8. Services	6 103	8 751	18 892	29 831	32 940	42 765	51 465
	(2.0)		(2.5)			(3.2)	(3.2)
Private enterprise	–	–	17 239	22 231	23 055	26 364	31 767
Public enterprise	–	–	1 653	7 600	9 885	16 401	19 698
9. Military and government agencies	12 995	13 089	19 466	41 059	37 679	42 371	28 596
	(4.2)		(2.6)			(3.1)	(1.8)
10. Educational and cultural institutions	1 345	1 725	2 948	4 591	4 627	6 863	8 708
	(0.4)		(0.4)			(0.5)	(0.5)
11. Non-profit institutions	2 909	4 279	7 696	10 833	13 014	13 962	16 760
	(0.9)		(1.0)			(1.0)	(1.1)
12. Individuals	24 341	50 601	156 328	258 395	318 638	516 656	676 233
	(7.8)		(20.6)			(38.1)	(42.5)
Total	312 666	412 636	760 369	1 035 334	1 134 777	1 354 803	1 591 701
	(100)		(100)			(100)	(100)

Source: Economic Research Dept, CBC, *Financial Statistics Monthly*, March 1988, p. 82.

In terms of lending, in 1985 the Cathay Investment and Trust Company, China Investment and Trust Company, Taiwan First Investment and Trust Company, Asia Trust and Investment Company ranked in that order with 32, 25, 13 and 10 per cent respectively.[12] Their lending includes principally housing loans, hire purchase of motor vehicles, TV sets and other consumer durables, and also business finance. The China Development Corporation (the earliest investment and trust company, established in 1959) was originally set up to provide venture capital. However, the objective has not yet been fulfilled. Its share of lending activity is only about 5 per cent.

With respect to borrowed fund, the Cathay Investment and Trust Company seemed to absorb more than 75 per cent of the borrowed fund in 1985. In 1979, they had taken only 17 per cent; Taiwan Development and Trust Corporation, 22 per cent; and China Development Corporation, 21 per cent.

There were four important cases in which the government had to intervene, and rescue the investment and trust companies – Wah Loong Company in 1977, Asia Trust and Investment Corporation in August 1982, Overseas Trust Corporation in August 1985, and the Cathay Investment and Trust Corporation in 1985. The Wah Loong Company had a big debt of about NT$750m to various banks. The Central Bank converted those debts into special shares of the Company and the Government appointed directors and supervisors for the Company.

The Asia Trust and Investment Corporation had a run in 1982, because the general public heard that the capital structure of the corporation had not been in good order and the net worth was very low. The cause of their trouble was that the Corporation had some mismanagement in violation of the Bank Act, i.e. (i) using the trust fund and own capital to speculate in the property market; and (ii) overtly financing their own related business. With the property market dropping in 1980–1, the Corporation was much shaken. There was a run on the corporation, totalling NT$2.6bn within a few days. The Ministry of Finance, the Central Bank and the Bank of Taiwan came to the rescue, providing finance of NT$4.3bn to tide over the crises. Then the monetary authorities arranged to let China International Commercial Banking Corporation invest NT$200m preferential shares in the Corporation and take over the management for two years.

The Overseas Trust Corporation had similar weakness in management, having much bad debt because of speculation in the property market. In early August 1985, the Ministry of Finance announced that it agreed to the investment of United World Chinese Commercial Bank of about NT$500m in the share capital of the Corporation, and that the Bank would take over the management of the Corporation.

The financial market was very disturbed on 9 February 1985, when the Ministry of Finance announced the suspension of operation of the Tenth Credit Cooperative for three days because of its blatant violation of the Banking Act. As long ago as 1974, the Central Bank had discovered that the Cooperative had given loans not in conformity with the Banking Act; in 1979, such 'illegal' loans were found to have increased to the extent of NT$1.1bn in 1979 which was internally recorded. Unfortunately the case was not brought up openly for correction until 1985. It was found that the Cooperative had diverted the deposit fund to the Taiwan Plastic Corporation and other related family business, and borrowed from the general public indirectly through their private organisations by issuing post-dated cheques, and that such borrowings and lendings were transacted by means of 'seals', instead of personal signatures. That means, persons (most of them employees of those related businesses) who entrusted the seals to the organisations were unaware that they themselves were legally committed to the post-dated cheques with their seals. When the case was blown open and the cheques could not be honoured, those who lent money to the private organisations of the Chua family at the high rates of interest lost their money. There was panic in the Cooperative and the related private organisations.

In March 1985, the Cooperative Bank of Taiwan (which is in a way a central bank for cooperatives) reported that the 'illegal' loans of the Tenth Credit Cooperative had been increased to over NT$3.5bn. Thereupon the Cooperative Bank took over the management of the Tenth Credit Cooperative.

Another important repercussion is that the Cathay Investment and Trust Company which is controlled by the Chua family had a run by depositors. It was rescued and taken over by a consortium of banks (consisting of the Bank of Communication, Farmers' Bank of China and Central Trust of China) with the approval of the Ministry of Finance. During the crisis, the Cathay Investment and Trust Company offered shares and properties as collateral to the banks. As the share and property markets went up to a high level in September 1987, the chairman of the Company – a member of the Chua family – desired to sell off the shares in order to pay off the debt. Since the reorganisation the Chua family has given up the holding or control of the company.

Part II
Monetary Analysis

5 Monetary System

5.1 HISTORICAL BACKGROUND OF CURRENCY ISSUE

There was hyperinflation during and immediately after the Second World War when the Nationalist Government retreated from China to Taiwan in 1949–50. As direct taxation was not established in war-torn China, the government had to rely upon indirect taxes as the major source of revenue.

The Japanese Occupation of the coast deprived the Chinese government of the revenue from custom duties. In order to finance the war, the government had to resort to the printing press, causing a progressive increase in money supply, and hence hyperinflation. It was practically impossible to talk of currency reserve in terms of gold and foreign exchange in the War against Japan, 1938–45, because exports had dropped to a tiny fraction, and hence gold and foreign exchange had declined to an insignificant amount.

Currency was issued in fact not against gold and foreign exchange, but against government securities – this is what is called fiduciary issue. The government simply deposited government securities (equivalent to an IOU) with the Central Bank, and currency was issued.

Currency issued in China had a profound effect on Taiwan; the hyperinflation by the end of the Second World War was then spread to Taiwan, in spite of the fact that Taiwan was supposed to be an 'Independent Currency Area'. In an attempt to curb the hyperinflation, on 19 August 1948 the government announced the so-called 'Currency Reform' by issuing the 'gold yuan notes' in Mainland China; one gold yuan was supposed to be equivalent to 0.2217 centigrams of pure gold and was equal to 3 million Chinese national currency (CNC). The idea was to encourage people to hold savings and not to rush to the market to purchase commodities or to acquire US dollars. By law, the issue of gold yuan notes was limited to 200 million gold yuan. All commodity prices were declared by the government to be frozen at the level of 19 August 1948 and any price change had to be sanctioned by the Authority. The private sector was not allowed to hold gold, silver or foreign exchange; holders had to surrender them to the government and to exchange for gold yuan notes.[1]

However, because of the progressive government deficit, the shortage of commodity supply, the contraction of production, and the civil war, the gold yuan notes could not stem the rising tide of hyperinflation. By the middle of October 1948 the big purchase-rush in Shanghai and subsequently in other places in China had rendered price-control a joke!

After the failure of the gold yuan episode, the government attempted to revive the silver standard by making use of the available stock of silver to issue silver dollar notes for circulation in China on 24 February 1949. By law, such notes had to have a minimum reserve of 50 per cent in silver. One silver dollar was equivalent to 320 gold yuan notes. The circulation of silver dollar notes was around $20m at its peak period. The general public had lost confidence in any paper currency in the heat of inflation.

By February 1949, the government had moved the gold stock to Taiwan. The failure of the 'gold yuan notes' and 'silver dollar notes' had conveyed an important message, i.e. it would be necessary for Taiwan to have an independent currency issue, different from the Chinese National Currency (CNC).

Hence the Bank of Taiwan was reorganised into its present form on 20 May 1946, to be free from the Japanese influence. On 22 May 1946, the Bank started to issue Taiwan dollar (afterwards called 'old Taiwan dollar' to be distinguished from 'new Taiwan (NT) dollar' in circulation today). The old Taiwan dollar was to replace the original plan of 'Central Bank notes for circulation in Taiwan'. The currency reserve of old Taiwan currency, kept in the custody of the Central Bank of China, included the following:[2]

1. national currency, not less than 40 per cent of the gross issue of the Taiwan dollar;
2. godown receipts of commodities;
3. approved short-term commercial papers;
4. government securities;
5. certificates of investment in productive enterprises.

These regulations aimed at linking the old Taiwan dollar with the national currency. The issue of the old Taiwan dollar was originally limited to 3 billion, but had to be progressively increased to 175 times by 14 June 1949 because of hyperinflation, and the fixed rate between OTD and National Currency (1.835 OTD = NC, after the issue of gold dollar notes).[3]

As hyperinflation was actually out of control, the Currency Reform was promulgated on 15 June 1949, and the NT dollar was issued to replace the old Taiwan dollar (NT$ = 40 000 OTD). Five NT dollars were to be exchanged for one US dollar (NT$5 = US$1). The new issue was limited to NT$200m. The currency reserve was based, 100 per cent, on gold, silver, foreign exchange and commodities which could be exchanged for foreign exchange. A New Issue Committee was formed to supervise the currency reserve. Furthermore, the NT dollar could be exchanged for gold in Taiwan by way of 'Gold Savings Deposit', which was started in May 1949 but ended on 27 December 1950 – a short period of only nineteen months. If people deposited NT$ into the Gold Savings Account, they could withdraw a limited amount of gold after a certain period (say, one year). Again, the idea was to encourage saving and discourage spending. The scheme had to be suspended because of the limitation of gold reserve and the continuation of hyperinflation. The new issue consisted of several devices as follows:

1. issue within the limit of NT$200m, which was obviously inadequate for the needs of trade and production;
2. issue outside the limit, which was promulgated on 7 July 1950 and subsequent dates as temporary devices. In principle, the backing of the currency issue was in terms of gold, foreign exchange and commodities which could be exchanged for foreign exchange. Currency issue was to be in a flexible, but not rigid, manner.
3. subsidiary issues such as coins.

After the Central Bank of China had resumed operation in Taiwan on 1 July 1961, it took over the work of currency issue and abolished what were called 'issues within and outside the limit'.

Because of the lack of effective monetary and fiscal measures, the continuing hyperinflation, the civil war and the adverse political and economic conditions, the reform of the NT dollar did not really help the situation. In the second half of 1949, prices rose again by more than 80 per cent, followed by another 34 per cent in the first quarter of 1950. The NT dollar simply changed the denomination of the old currency. A determined effort, however, was made to curb inflation by introducing the Preferential Interest Rates Savings Deposits in March 1950, which offered a very high nominal interest rate of 7 per cent per month for one-month savings deposits. This came to 125 per cent per annum when compounded! The high-interest deposit scheme obviously carried the risk of turning its own interest rate into an unbearable burden by its very success, when the inflation rate had slowed down. The PIR Scheme was abolished in March 1955. Nevertheless, the high-savings deposit rate, or high-interest-rate policy continued in Taiwan in the 1950's which was crucial in reversing the trend of inflation by encouraging saving and discouraging spending.

Another favourable factor for price-stabilisation was the resumption of US Aid to Free China (Taiwan) in July 1950 after the outbreak of the Korean War on 25 June 1950. That inspired confidence in people in Taiwan, and improved material supplies to Taiwan. The lessons from the failure of gold yuan notes and indeed from all other measures in the episode of hyperinflation point to the importance of the savings ratio and consequently the appropriateness of high-interest-rate policy or restrictive monetary policy in time of inflation.

5.2 CURRENCY ISSUE OF NEW TAIWAN DOLLARS (NT$)

The aforesaid historical background and the lesson from hyperinflation, should be borne in mind when we study the currency issue of the NT dollars. The Central Bank of China Act, promulgated on 23 May 1935 and amended on 8 November 1979 stipulated in Article 16, that '100 per cent reserve shall be kept, in equivalent, in gold and silver bullions, foreign exchange, and eligible bills and securities. The coins shall be exempt from reserves'. There is however an absence of the stipulation of the minimum proportion, or requirement of gold and foreign exchange. In theory, there are two types of currency issues – one is the issue backed by gold and foreign exchange, and the other is the issue backed by government securities, and called 'fiduciary issue'. It was precisely the excess amount of fiduciary issue in wartime that caused the inflation. Although under the present circumstances of huge and increasing international reserves the backing of the currency can rely entirely upon gold and foreign exchange without the need of using the government securities,[4] the fact remains that it is rather inappropriate to call it '100 per cent reserve',[5] because of the component elements of 'eligible bills and securities'. For the sake of argument, suppose one day in future Taiwan needs to issue currency beyond the limit of international reserves, she may have to resort to fiduciary issue, i.e. to issue against government securities.

This should not be construed as a criticism of Article 16 of the Central Bank of China Act. Modern thinking is that international reserves should be used not to back currency, but as a means of international payments. Therefore whether gold and foreign exchange, or international reserves, are adequate to cover currency issue is not as important as in the old concept; the crucial point is whether the country can maintain balance-of-payments equilibrium, and consequently foreign-exchange stability. In this respect, Taiwan can well fulfil the objective.

5.3 RESERVE REQUIREMENT OF DEPOSIT MONEY BANKS

Deposit money banks as defined in Taiwan include all banks (domestic and foreign), credit cooperative associations, and credit departments of the Farmers' and Fishery Associations. The relative importance of those institutions in the financial system is shown in Chapter 4, Tables 4.1, 4.3 and 4.5.

Reserve requirement (including cash in vault, and deposits with the Central Bank) is against deposit liabilities of banks; the deposits are subdivided into demand deposits and time and savings deposits.[6] Because of the higher rate of turnover demand deposits would naturally be subject to a higher reserve requirement than time and savings deposits. The Central Bank Act, Article 23, stipulates the legal requirement in terms of minimum and maximum as follows:

1. Cheque deposit: 15–40 per cent
2. Demand deposit: 10–35 per cent
3. Savings deposit: 5–20 per cent
4. Time deposit: 7–25 per cent

Hence, as effective from 11 July 1986, cheque accounts are required to maintain reserves of not less than 23 per cent; passbook demand deposits, 21 per cent; passbook savings deposits, 14 per cent; time deposits of savings account, 8 per cent; time deposits, 10 per cent; and certificate deposits of foreign currency, 7 per cent. The Central Bank may vary the reserve ratios from time to time in order to exercise credit expansion or contraction – an instrument of monetary policy.[7]

In addition to the cash-reserve ratio, there is also the requirement of minimum liquid assets, which include excess reserves, Treasury bills, trade bills, bankers' acceptances, commercial papers, government bonds, corporate bonds, bank debentures and other securities approved by the Central Bank of China. The required liquid asset ratio is 7 per cent of deposit liabilities as from 1978; hitherto, in 1977 it was 5 per cent. As Taiwan has had a big export surplus in the 1980s, international reserves are increasing and the banking system is in a liquid state; there is an excess of actual over required liquid assets, and an excess of actual over required reserves in the banking systems.

5.4 MONEY, INCOME AND PRICES

Because of the consistent export surplus and the active balance of payments, there has been a persistent pressure on both the monetary growth and income growth.

From 1961 to 1973 (the first oil crisis) money supply, M_{1B} grew at an annual rate (compound) of 23 per cent. The highest growth rate was 50.4 per cent in 1973. Consumer prices went up by 8.2 per cent in that year, 1973 but by 47.5 per cent in the subsequent year, 1974. If we take account of the time-lag of one year, the growth of M_{1B} had direct effect on prices. Consumer prices had an average increase of 7.25 per cent from 1962 to 1974. Hence, monetary growth did not have a proportional effect on prices, as is the usual case, unless at times of hyperinflation. In the period 1961–73 GNP grew at an annual rate (compound) of 15.87 per cent. Therefore monetary (M_{1B}) growth exceeded nominal income growth (see Table 5.1)

In 1961–73 M_2 grew at the annual rate of 23.24 per cent, which was similar to the M_{1B} growth rate. In the period 1973–1979 (the second oil crisis), M_{1B} grew at an annual rate of 23.25 per cent (more or less the same as the previous period, 1961–73). GNP grew at an annual rate of 19.41 per cent. Again monetary growth exceeded nominal income growth.

M_2 grew at the annual rate of 25 per cent, in 1973–9, which was greater than the M_{1B} growth rate and GNP growth rate. In the period 1974–80 (which was one-year lag of the period 1973–9) consumer prices went up at the high average growth rate of 13.83 per cent, mainly because of the effect of the two oil crises. In the period, 1979–87, M_{1B} grew at the annual rate of 21.8 per cent, which was lower than that in the previous periods, 1961–73 and 1973–9. GNP grew at the annual rate of 12.8 per cent. Monetary growth (M_{1B}) exceeded income growth.

A particularly interesting point to note is that because of the Central Bank's intervention in the foreign-exchange market to slow down the appreciation of the NT dollars, M_{1B} has been increasing at a fast rate; so much so that the annual M_{1B} growth rate was 51 per cent in 1986. From the end of 1986 to May 1987, the growth rate, however, slowed down to 12 per cent. The increase of M_{1B} was greater in 1986 than in 1987, because in 1986, the Central Bank tried very hard to slow down the rise of the NT dollar by active intervention in the foreign-exchange market, thereby issuing new money. In 1987, the NT dollar was allowed to float at a higher level, thereby reducing the pressure of new issue of money.

M_2 grew at the annual rate of 23.3 per cent in 1979–87 which was much higher than the growth rates of M_{1B}, and GNP. The increasingly high rate of savings, and the increasing flow of saving funds into banks and financial institutions explained why the growth rate of M_2 was higher than that of M_{1B}. The great increase of time and savings deposits, however, is a common phenomenon in most countries of the world.

Despite monetary (M_{1B}) growth being higher than income growth in all the aforesaid three periods, prices were steady except in 1974 and 1980, when the lag-effect of the two oil crises and world-wide shortage of food in 1973 were notably shown. As the monetisation process was under way, money supply could be increased without inducing price-increases to any considerable extent.

If we deflate the nominal M_{1B} growth with the consumer price index, we obtain the real M_{1B} growth, which is then compared with the 'real' GNP growth (Table 5.2). Again, the 'real' M_{1B} growth exceeded 'real' income growth.

From 1962 to 1973, the average 'real' M_{1B} growth rate was 20.3 per cent, as compared with its nominal growth rate of 23.6 per cent; in 1974–9, the percentages were 11.5 and 23.8 per cent respectively; in 1980–7, they were 17.5 and 22.5 per cent respectively (Table 5.2)

From 1962 to 1973, the average 'real' GNP growth rate was 11.2 per cent, as compared with its nominal growth rate of 16.0 per cent; in 1974–9, the percentages were 8.0 and 19.7 per cent respectively; in 1980–7, they were 7.4 and 12.9 respectively.

Table 5.1 Monetary and income growth and price change (NT$ million)

	M_{1B}	*Growth rate of M_{1B} (%)*	M_2	*Growth rate of M_2 (%)*	*GNP at current market prices*	*Growth rate of GNP (%)*	*Consumer price increase*[2] *(%)*
1951	658	–	838	–	12 252	–	–
1952	1 017	54.6	1 619	93.2	17 162	40.1	–
1953	1 364	34.1	2 124	31.2	22 859	33.2	18.8
1954	1 771	29.8	2 742	29.1	25 083	9.7	1.7
1955	2 140	20.8	3 216	17.3	29 835	18.9	9.9
1956	3 004	40.4	3 921	21.9	34 212	14.7	10.5
1957	3 417	13.7	4 776	21.8	39 881	16.6	7.5
1958	4 984	45.9	7 610	59.3	44 502	11.6	1.3
1959	5 399	8.3	8 886	16.8	51 369	15.4	10.6
1960	6 246	15.7	11 284	27.0	62 143	21.0	18.5
1961	7 699	23.3	16 718	48.2	69 594	12.0	7.8
1962	8 086	5.0	19 041	13.9	76 652	10.1	2.4
1963	10 355	28.1	24 843	30.5	86 710	13.1	2.2
1964	13 979	35.0	32 341	30.2	101 492	17.0	–.2
1965	16 194	15.8	37 350	15.5	111 895	10.3	–.1
1966	18 170	12.2	44 572	19.3	125 343	12.0	2.0
1967	23 637	30.1	54 875	23.1	144 839	15.6	3.4
1968	26 360	11.5	61 706	12.4	168 695	16.5	7.9
1969	30 472	15.6	75 068	21.7	195 693	16.0	5.1
1970	35 042	15.0	92 588	23.3	225 283	15.1	3.6
1971	45 756	30.6	119 331	28.9	262 125	16.4	2.9

1972	61 357	34.1	158 112	32.5	314 369	19.9	3.0
1973	92 268	50.4	205 157	29.8	407 419	29.6	8.2
1974	101 922	10.5	255 984	24.8	544 847	33.7	47.5
1975	131 227	28.8	327 711	28.0	581 150	6.7	5.2
1976	164 103	25.1	413 039	26.0	696 101	19.8	2.5
1977	219 188	33.6	545 213	32.0	815 349	17.1	7.0
1978	300 213	37.0	714 131	31.0	977 987	19.9	5.8
1979	323 417	7.7	782 285	9.5	1 180 952	20.8	9.8
1980	396 862	22.7	953 613	21.9	1 468 069	24.3	19.0
1981	451 560	13.8	1 131 401	18.6	1 739 794	18.5	16.3
1982	517 480	14.6	1 406 189	24.3	1 858 983	6.9	3.0
1983	612 902	18.4	1 777 608	26.4	2 044 090	10.0	1.4
1984	669 619	9.3	2 134 220	20.1	2 277 796	11.4	0.0
1985	751 469	12.2	2 633 142	23.4	2 398 369	5.3	0.2
1986	1 137 863	51.4	3 298 862	25.3	2 772 365	15.6	0.7
1987	1 568 225	37.8	4 175 021	26.6	3 090 792	11.5	0.4

Note: [1] M_{1A} = currency in active circulation + demand deposits (including cheque accounts and passbook deposits in Taiwan statistics)

$M_{1B} = M_{1A}$ + passbook savings deposits

We take M_{1B} as the money for transaction function, rather than M_{1A}, because people with passbook saving deposits can draw money out for spending freely.

$M_2 = M_{1B}$ + quasi-money (or time and savings deposits)

[2] The change of Consumer Price Index from the previous year.

Source: Council for Economic Planning and Development, *Taiwan Statistical Data Book, 1987*; and Economic Research Department, *Financial Statistics Monthly*, May 1988 and various issues.

Table 5.2 'Real' M_{1B} growth and 'real' GNP growth (shown as percentages)

End of period	M_{1B} *growth rate*	*Consumer price increase*	*'Real'* M_{1B} *growth rate*[1]	*'Real' GNP growth rate*[2]
1962	5.03	+2.35	2.68	9.0
1963	28.06	+2.22	25.84	12.0
1964	35.00	–0.19	35.19	13.8
1965	15.85	–0.08	15.93	7.6
1966	12.20	+2.02	10.18	9.5
1967	30.09	+3.35	26.74	11.1
1968	11.52	+7.91	3.61	9.7
1969	15.60	+5.05	10.55	10.8
1970	15.00	+3.57	11.43	12.2
1971	30.57	+2.82	27.75	13.0
1972	34.10	+2.99	31.11	13.8
1973	50.38	+8.17	42.21	12.0
1974	10.46	+47.48	–37.02	–2.4
1975	28.75	+5.23	23.52	4.2
1976	25.05	+2.50	22.55	16.6
1977	33.57	+7.04	26.53	9.7
1978	36.95	+5.77	31.18	12.0
1979	7.73	+9.76	2.03	8.1
1980	22.71	+19.01	3.70	4.2
1981	13.78	+16.33	–2.55	5.4
1982	14.60	+2.96	11.64	4.0
1983	18.44	+1.36	17.08	8.6
1984	9.25	–0.03	9.28	9.0
1985	12.22	–0.16	12.38	5.1
1986	51.42	+0.70	50.72	11.6
1987	37.82	+0.39	37.43	11.0

Notes: [1] 'Real' M_{1B} growth rate = M_{1B} growth rate *minus* consumer price increase.
[2] 'Real' GNP growth rate at constant 1981 prices after adjustment of terms of trade.

Source: Council for Economic Planning and Development, *Taiwan Statistical Data Book*, 1987.

5.5 DEMAND FOR MONEY IN TAIWAN

Demand for money is usually formulated in terms of three important determinants:

(i) income or wealth;
(ii) interest rate;

(iii) expected price change.

As people can substitute between money and goods (or real assets), as well as between money and financial assets, the relevant opportunity costs would be the expected rate of inflation and the rate of interest on financial assets. Theoretically speaking, the holding of money balance should be related to both income and wealth.[8] Because of a lack of wealth data, most empirical studies use income as the key variable. All analysts including the Keynesian School and 'monetarist' school agree that the income variable is the most important in the demand function.

The interest variable has been a subject of debate. The Keynesian liquidity preference theory postulates that the demand for money is inversely related to the rate of interest. Empirical studies by the post-Keynesian school of thought such as Latané, using the narrow definition of money, M_1 and long-term rate of interest, seem to support the Keynesian view.[9] They emphasise the importance of interest rate in the demand functions. The Radcliffe Report also believes that the interest-elasticity of the demand for money is relatively high.[10]

Milton Friedman, on the other hand, plays down the role of interest rate, and concludes that the interest-elasticity of the demand for money is zero. The different conclusion partly results from the definition of money, as he uses the broad definition of money, M_2; so the effect of the change in interest rate is partially 'absorbed' in the broad definition and would not be shown on the demand function.

The relative importance of the expected change in prices in the money demand function is also a subject of argument in different schools of thought. Milton Friedman regards it as the second most important determinant, next to income, but more important than interest rate. Keynes in his *General Theory* does not mention this variable in his liquidity preference function because he assumes a given wage unit, or a given price level, in his model. It can be argued in his defence that as prices and income go up, the liquidity preference schedule would be shifted upward; thus, expected price change would in fact enter into the demand function.

The expected change of price level is normally not an important determinant, unless the change is substantial, as in hyperinflation or deflation. It can be argued that demand for money is a demand for real balance, because people would try to maintain their average cash balance in real terms (i.e. taking into consideration the price change) to effect their transaction. But when the price change is not substantial, say a few per cent a year, people's desire to hold cash balance would not be much affected, as evidenced in statistical studies in many countries.

One more important consideration is to introduce the determinant of the ratio of foreign trade (exports *plus* imports) to GNP, which means in fact the degree of openness of the economy.[11] Taiwan is an increasingly open economy; the ratio of Trade/GNP was increased from 29.8 per cent in 1961 to 90.7 per cent in 1987. The export surplus would enhance the money supply and credit. Moreover, the ratio of *T/GNP* is to emphasise the transaction function of money, rather than the asset function (or store of value function) of money. The ratio would have an influence on the demand for money.

Thus the following model is based on the theory that the demand for money balance is a function of (i) national income; (ii) interest rate; (iii) expected change in prices, and (iv) Trade/GNP ratio (see Table 5.3).

The regression equation, 1961–88, can be formulated as follows:

$$\ln M_{1B} \text{ or } \ln M_2 = f(\overset{+}{\ln \text{GNP}}, \overset{-}{\ln r}, \overset{-}{\Delta\ln CPI}, \overset{+}{T/GNP})$$

where M_{1B} = money supply
= currency in active circulation + cheque account +passbook deposits + passbook savings deposits of banks (see Economic Research Department, CBC, *Financial Statistics Monthly*, June 1988, p. 60)

M_2 = M_{1B} + quasi-money (i.e. time and savings deposits + foreign currency deposits + deposits replaced by Postal Savings System)

GNP = GNP at current prices (see Council for Economic Planning and Development, *Taiwan Statistical Data Book*, 1988)

GNP' = *GNP* at constant (1981) prices

r_1 = one year deposit rate (see *Financial Statistics Monthly*)

r_2 = Central Bank rediscount rate. It is more responsive to market forces. It is used as an alternative to r_1 in the regression equations.

P = *GNP* deflator. It is estimated by deflating the series of *GNP* at current prices, by the series of *GNP* at constant (1981) prices.

We take natural logarithm, as the estimated coefficients of explanatory variables would give the elasticities of those variables. $\Delta \ln P$ can be used as the proxy for the expected change in prices, on the assumption that the expected change is equal to the actual change in the immediate past; this is a sort of 'adaptive expectation'.

$$\Delta \ln P = \ln P_t - \ln P_{t-1}$$

or

$$\ln \frac{P_t}{P_{t-1}} \text{ (ln of the price relatives)}$$

Demand for money balance (Table 5.3, Equations 1.1, 1.2, 1.3, and 1.4) is positively correlated to GNP. The income-elasticity of the demand for M_{1B} is about 1.3, i.e. 1 per cent increase in GNP would lead to about 1.3 per cent increase in holding cash balance. The income elasticity of the demand for M_2 is slightly higher, being higher than 1.3 in Equations 2.1 and 2.2 because M_2 includes time and savings deposits denoting the store of value function. The high income-elasticity of the demand for money is common in many countries, such as the USA, UK and Singapore.[12]

The interest rate variable, either r_1 or r_2, has the correct negative sign, i.e. an increase in interest rate would lead to a decline in holding money balance. For example, in Equations 1.1 and 1.2, 1 per cent increase in deposit rate would lead to about 0.6 per cent decline in holding money balance. In Equations 1.3 and 1.4, 1 per cent increase in Central Bank rediscount rate would lead to about 0.3 per cent decline in holding money balance. Similarly, in Equations 2.3 and 2.4, 1 per cent increase in rediscount rate would lead to about 0.5 per cent decline in holding M_2. Generally speaking, Central Bank's rediscount rate is more sensitive to market forces than the deposit rate.

The t-values of the income variables and interest-rate variables are all statistically significant at the 5 per cent level. The good performance of the interest-rate variable is rather surprising, as the interest rate has long been under the rigid control of the Central Bank and market forces did not have much influence on the interest rate until recently. As a comparison, in Singapore, where there is much more financial liberalisation, the interest rate variable did not perform so well.[13]

Table 5.3 Demand for nominal money function (M_{1B} and M_2), 1961–88 (annual data)

Dependent variable	*Estimated coefficients for explanatory variables*						*R^2 adjusted*	*DW*
	Constant	*lnGNP*	*lnr_1*	*lnr_2*	*ΔlnP*	*lnT/GNP*		
1.1 $\ln M_{1B}$	–15.329	1.263	–0.580		–0.157	0.147	0.961	1.057
	(–2.88)	(15.86)	(–4.13)		(–0.52)*	(0.55)*		
1.2 $\ln M_{1B}$	–14.652	1.288	–0.568		–0.072		0.972	1.022
	(–5.16)	(26.91)	(–4.12)		(–0.27)*			
1.3 $\ln M_{1B}$	–7.895	1.238		–0.338	–0.297	0.049	0.985	1.348
	(–2.63)	(14.07)		(–2.16)	(–0.75)*	(0.19)*		
1.4 $\ln M_{1B}$	–7.843	1.251		–0.338	–0.246		0.987	1.319
	(–4.86)	(28.74)		(–2.27)	(–0.69)*			
2.1 $\ln M_2$	–9.746	1.322	–0.462		–0.333	0.031	0.995	1.566
	(–5.66)	(33.20)	(–5.82)		(–1.89)	(0.23)*		
2.2 $\ln M_2$	–10.149	1.330	–0.457		–0.317		0.998	1.560
	(–10.81)	(66.99)	(–6.02)		(–2.02)			
2.3 $\ln M_2$	–4.577	1.259		–0.480	–0.274	0.036	0.998	1.388
	(–4.82)	(35.51)		(–7.17)	(–1.50)*	(0.35)*		
2.4 $\ln M_2$	–4.809	1.270		–0.474	–0.245		0.998	1.354
	(9.11)	(74.95)		(–7.49)	(–1.49)*			

Notes: All equations are to use the Cochrane–Orcutt First Order Autoregression Method, because their DWs by OLS Method are too low.

r_1 = one year deposit rate. In Taiwan, the predominant part of fixed deposits is for one year. Therefore we use the one-year deposit rate.

r_2 = Central Bank rediscount rate

$GNP = GNP$ at current prices. $GNP' = GNP$ at constant (1981) prices.

$P = GNP$ deflator; $\triangle \ln \mathrm{P} = \ln \dfrac{P_t}{P_{t-1}} = \ln P_t - \ln P_{t-1}$

T/GNP = Total trade (imports plus exports) ÷ GNP at current prices

Figures in parenthesis are t-values.

*t-values are not statistically significant. With $n = 27$, the significant value at 5 per cent level should be about 1.7.

Source: Economic Research Department, CBC, *Financial Statistics Monthly*, January 1989 and various issues; and Council for Economic Planning and Development, *Taiwan Statistical Data Book*, 1988.

The variable, $\Delta \ln P$, has the correct negative sign for all eight equations, as an expected increase in prices would induce people to reduce the holding of money balance, M_{1B} or M_2. For example, in Equation 1.1, 1 per cent increase in expected price-change would induce people to hold less cash balance M_{1B} by 0.16 per cent. With respect to M_2, the elasticity of the variable of expected price-change is about 0.3 (see Equations 2.1, 2.2 and 2.3). However, their *t*-values in six equations are statistically insignificant; the only significant *t*-values are in Equations 2.1 and 2.3.

The variable, *T/GNP*, shows a correct positive sign in all the four equations, as an expansion of foreign trade relative to GNP implies an increasing demand for money balance for transaction purpose. Unfortunately, the four equations 1.1, 1.3, 2.1 and 2.3 have the statistically insignificant *t*-values. This statistical finding gives evidence that the variable, *T/GNP*, has an influence on the money demand function.

For all the eight equations the R^2 coefficients of determination are very high, being almost approaching one, and the *DW*s are within acceptable limit. However by using the Ordinary Least Squares (OLS) Method, some equations have rather low *DW*s. So we have to re-estimate those equations with Cochrane–Orcutt First Order Auto-Regression Method (two stages) as reported in Table 5.3.

The expanding foreign trade, the rising income and the development of the financial system in a progressive economy would naturally contribute to the high R^2 in the equations.

It should be noted that some equations (1.2, 1.4, 2.2 and 2.4) do not include the variable, $\ln T/GNP$, and yet their R^2 are also very high and their *DW*s are within acceptable limit after auto-regression. The addition of the variable, $\ln T/GNP$, does not greatly affect the structure of the equations, nor does it alter much the income elasticity, and interest-rate elasticity. The introduction of $\ln T/GNP$ does not cause the problem of multicollinearity in statistics, as some people may erroneously argue.

By and large, the demand for nominal money function is in conformity with the aforesaid theoretical model. Income is apparently the most important determinant of the demand for money balance. Interest rate is the second important determinant, which is close to the Keynesian thinking. Expected price-change is a rather weak determinant. Similarly, the *T/GNP* ratio needs cautious interpretation.

Table 5.4 presents the model for the demand for money function, real terms, on the following formulation:

$$\ln \frac{M_{1B}}{P} \text{ or } \ln \frac{M_2}{P} = f(\ln GNP', \ln r, \Delta \ln P, \ln T/GNP)$$

where GNP' = *GNP* at constant (1981) prices after adjustment of the terms of trade (see *Taiwan Statistical Data Book*, 1988. The Quarterly GNP at current prices and at constant prices is published in DGBAS, *Quarterly National Economic Trends, Taiwan Area*, various issues.)

Both demand for nominal money function (Table 5.3) and demand for money function real terms (Table 5.4) are acceptable statistically, but the nominal function seems to be slightly better, because:

1. the income-elasticity of the real function seems to be unrealistically high, being about 1.6–1.7 in Table 5.4;
2. the variable $\ln T/GNP$ in Table 5.3 shows better performance because the coefficients of the four equations (1.1, 1.3, 2.1 and 2.3) have the correct positive sign, whereas those four relevant coefficients in Table 5.4 have the wrong negative signs. Nevertheless all the relevant *t*-value in both tables turn out to be statistically insignificant;
3. the interest-rate variables in Table 5.3 appear to be flawless with all negative signs of coefficient and with all the *t*-values to be statistically significant at the 5 per cent level whereas in Table 5.4, two *t*-values with respect to r_2 in Eqs 1.3 and 1.4 are statistically insignificant. The relative coefficients with respect to r_1 and r_2 in Table 5.3 are also higher than those in Table 5.4.
4. the variable of $\Delta \ln P$ in Table 5.3 has fewer statistically insignificant *t*-values (Equations 2.1 and 2.2) and has slightly higher coefficients.

In literature, demand for money function is usually presented in real terms. But in the case of Taiwan, the demand for money function in nominal terms shows even better performance. Generally speaking, the stability of prices in 1961–88 (except for the effect of the two oil crises in 1973 and 1978/9), implies that the demand for nominal

Table 5.4 Demand for money function, real terms, 1961–88 (annual data)

Dependent variable	*Estimated coefficients for explanatory variables*						R^2 *adjusted*	*DW*
	Constant	*lnGNP′*	lnr_1	lnr_2	ΔlnP	*lnT/GNP*		
1.1 $\ln \frac{M_{1B}}{P}$	–50.934 (–5.16)	1.610 (9.53)	–0.403 (–2.60)		–0.056 (–0.18)*	–0.052 (0.18)*	0.941	1.192
1.2 $\ln \frac{M_{1B}}{P}$	–56.512 (–8.37)	1.598 (15.36)	–0.413 (–2.95)		–0.085 (–0.33)*		0.932	1.220
1.3 $\ln \frac{M_{1B}}{P}$	–37.936 (–5.60)	1.696 (9.62)		–0.165 (–1.08)*	–0.124 (–0.36)*	–0.274 (–0.99)*	0.964	1.347
1.4 $\ln \frac{M_{1B}}{P}$	–32.690 (–8.95)	1.545 (17.30)		–0.212 (–1.47)*	–0.300 (–1.00)*		0.963	1.368
2.1 $\ln \frac{M_2}{P}$	–38.119 (–9.63)	1.729 (18.04)	–0.251 (–2.61)		–0.252 (–1.34)*	–0.163 (–1.00)*	0.989	1.701
2.2 $\ln \frac{M_2}{P}$	–35.857 (–19.34)	1.644 (38.85)	–0.293 (–3.43)		–0.333 (–1.98)*		0.988	1.682
2.3 $\ln \frac{M_2}{P}$	–32.600 (–11.95)	1.648 (22.90)		–0.330 (–5.30)	–0.177 (–1.24)*	–0.176 (–1.57)*	0.995	1.230
2.4 $\ln \frac{M_2}{P}$	–29.660 (–19.30)	1.551 (41.16)		–0.359 (–5.90)	–0.290 (–2.27)		0.994	1.324

Notes and Source: Same as Table 5.3.

money balance is close to that for real balance. Furthermore, if we consider that the transaction function of money is more important than the asset function of money, there is a good theoretical reason for emphasising the demand for money function in nominal terms, rather than on real terms. Monetary economists in modern times including James Tobin and Milton Friedman, however, tend to over-emphasise the asset function of money. In reality, the transaction function of money constitutes the major part of the demand for money.

For the sake of verification or refinement, quarterly data analysis is presented in Tables 5.5 and 5.6. The whole long period, 1961–88, and the two subperiods 1961–73 and 1974–88 are shown simultaneously for comparison. The year 1974 is chosen to be the demarcation line, because the first oil crisis occurred in 1973 and the money and capital markets were developed in an accelerated rate with passing of the New Bank Act, 1975 and the emergence of the big export surplus in 1985–8. The rapid development in later year would certainly affect the structure of the money demand functions as shown in Tables 5.5 and 5.6.

Thus the income-elasticity in the early period, 1961–73 is lower than that in the later period, 1974–88 in all sets of equations; this is true in nominal money functions (Table 5.5) as well as in real money function (Table 5.6). The income-elasticity in the real money function is greater than that in the nominal money function; that is also evident in both annual data analysis (Tables 5.3 and 5.4) and quarterly data analysis (Tables 5.5 and 5.6).

By and large, the structures of the equations of annual data analysis are in congruence with those of the quarterly data analysis. The general conclusion from one analysis would not contradict that from the other.

Similarly the interest-rate (r_1 and r_2) elasticities show remarkably well in statistics in both nominal and real money functions, in spite of the fact that the money and capital markets have not yet been well established.

The expected price-change elasticity and the variable of $\ln T/GNP$ exhibit some difficulty with respect to the wrong signs of some coefficients and the statistically insignificant t-value.

Attempts have been made to go further into the quarterly data analysis by introducing the lagged variable, such as:

$$\ln M_{1B} = f(\ln GNP, \ln M_{1B-1}, \ln r, \Delta \ln P, \ln T/GNP)$$

Table 5.5 Demand for nominal money function (M_{1B} and M_2), 1961–88 (quarterly data)

Dependent variables	Estimated coefficients for explanatory variables						R^2 adjusted	DW
	Constant	*lnGNP*	*lnr*$_1$	*lnr*$_2$	Δ*lnP*	*lnT/GNP*		
1.1.1 lnM_{1B}	–14.432	1.268	–0.437		–0.455	0.046	0.949	1.949
	(–3.62)	(28.76)	(–4.05)		(–2.35)	(0.38)*		
1.1.a lnM_{1B}	1.015	1.066	–0.767		0.097	0.291	0.976	1.679
	(0.43)	(9.62)	(–3.33)		(0.24)*	(1.61)*		
1.1.b lnM_{1B}	–30.382	1.271	–0.246		–0.293	–0.131	0.729	1.878
	(–1.70)	(10.88)	(–2.25)		(–1.48)*	(–0.78)*		
1.2.1 lnM_{1B}	–10.460	1.196		–0.367	–0.480	0.082	0.946	1.956
	(2.21)	(23.83)		(–4.23)	(–2.51)	(0.67)*		
1.2.a lnM_{1B}	2.401	1.012		–0.714	0.104	0.238	0.965	1.552
	(0.78)*	(8.83)		(–2.80)	(0.27)*	(1.23)*		
1.2.b lnM_{1B}	–37.704	1.272		–0.129	–0.353	–0.041	0.667	1.952
	(–1.69)	(9.68)		(–1.49)*	(–1.72)	(–0.23)*		
2.1.1 lnM_2	–4.223	1.320	–0.547		–0.667	0.092	0.994	1.823
	(–4.39)	(52.27)	(–8.69)		(–3.46)	(1.22)*		
2.1.a lnM_2	2.807	1.046	–0.858		–0.400	0.417	0.989	1.640
	(1.73)	(11.48)	(–5.08)		(–1.15)*	(2.83)		
2.1.b lnM_2	–5.805	1.298	–0.517		–0.076	–0.296	0.978	1.589
	(–2.49)	(31.82)	(–7.19)		(–0.43)*	(–2.20)		
2.2.1 lnM_2	–1.492	1.222		–0.522	–0.678	0.125	0.996	1.817
	(1.64)*	(46.18)		(–11.11)	(–3.83)	(1.90)		
2.2.a lnM_2	4.289	1.005		–0.923	–0.362	0.282	0.985	1.373
	(2.19)	(10.71)		(–4.57)	(–1.06)*	(1.74)		
2.2.b lnM_2	–5.971	1.280		–0.390	–0.303	–0.037	0.978	1.749
	(–2.60)	(29.56)		(–7.01)	(–1.66)*	(–0.25)*		

Notes: 1.1.1 refers to the whole period, 1961. II – 1988. IV
1.1.a refers to the early period, 1961. II – 1973. IV
1.1.b refers to the later period, 1974. I – 1988. IV
Similarly .1, .a, and .b in other sets of equations
Other notes and source: Same as Table 5.3.

Table 5.6 Demand for money function, real terms, 1961–88 (quarterly data)

Dependent variables	*Constant*	ln *GNP'*	ln r_1	ln r_2	Δln *P*	ln *T/GNP*	R^2 *adjusted*	*DW*
1.1.1 $\ln \frac{M_{1B}}{P}$	–38.967 (–8.86)	1.428 (20.15)	–0.377 (–3.55)		–0.316 (–1.50)*	0.157 (1.34)*	0.939	1.855
1.1.a $\ln \frac{M_{1B}}{P}$	–5.573 (–1.76)	1.014 (7.18)	–0.770 (–3.33)		0.206 (0.56)*	0.378 (2.37)	0.961	1.670
1.1.b $\ln \frac{M_{1B}}{P}$	–107.298 (–3.71)	1.357 (8.12)	–0.197 (–1.73)		–0.142 (–0.69)*	–0.130 (–0.79)*	0.650	1.989
1.2.1 $\ln \frac{M_{1B}}{P}$	–33.688 (–6.61)	1.306 (16.22)		–0.376 (–4.41)	–0.367 (–1.81)	0.178 (1.58)*	0.938	1.843
1.2.a $\ln \frac{M_{1B}}{P}$	–5.559 (–1.47)	0.973 (6.67)		–0.710 (–2.78)	0.167 (0.46)*	0.288 (1.65)*	0.947	1.477
1.2.b $\ln \frac{M_{1B}}{P}$	–131.287 (–3.61)	1.346 (7.63)		–0.099 (–1.13)*	–0.195 (–0.90)*	–0.063 (–0.36)*	0.590	2.068
2.1.1 $\ln \frac{M_2}{P}$	–18.865 (–15.03)	1.625 (34.42)	–0.397 (–6.20)		–0.617 (–2.68)	0.000 (0.00)*	0.991	1.748
2.1.a $\ln \frac{M_2}{P}$	–4.235 (–2.85)	1.168 (10.89)	–0.823 (–6.43)		–0.266 (–0.74)*	0.312 (2.65)	0.990	1.518
2.1.b $\ln \frac{M_2}{P}$	–20.255 (–12.15)	1.547 (30.27)	–0.498 (–8.16)		0.264 (1.36)*	–0.352 (–2.77)*	0.988	1.667
2.2.1 $\ln \frac{M_2}{P}$	–13.799 (–11.74)	1.457 (29.46)		–0.445 (–9.27)	–0.632 (–3.08)	0.060 (0.91)*	0.994	1.697
2.2.a $\ln \frac{M_2}{P}$	–3.642 (–1.58)	1.054 (8.87)		–0.905 (–4.51)	–0.369 (–1.11)*	0.239 (1.66)*	0.980	1.293
2.2.b $\ln \frac{M_2}{P}$	–21.160 (–10.97)	1.511 (25.84)		–0.371 (–7.54)	–0.022 (–0.11)*	–0.113 (–0.79)*	0.985	1.818

Notes and Source: Same as Tables 5.3 and 5.5.

The structure of the equations has been so much disrupted, and some of the estimated long-run elasticities with respect to income, interest rates and price change have become so unrealistic that we have abandoned such a presentation.

An analysis has also been made to insert some dummy variables Q_1, Q_2, and Q_3 for the first, second and third quarters, such as the following:

$$\ln M_{1B} = f(\ln GNP, \ln r_1, Q_1, Q_2, Q_3)$$

The results show a seasonal variation. At the close of a year, when firms have to close their accounts, or in New Year festive season people tend to hold a greater money balance. However, for economy of space, such results are not presented here.

5.6 DETERMINANTS OF MONEY SUPPLY, M_{1B}

There are three important determinants of money supply, M_{1B} – (i) external sector – net foreign assets; (ii) private sector – net claims or deposits (−); and (iii) government sector – net claims or deposits (−). The increase in net foreign assets has been the major factor in determining the increase in money supply. The change in net claims on the private sector and government sector (loans minus deposits) is the secondary factor.

Table 5.7 shows clearly the very close correlation between the change in net foreign assets and that in money supply, M_{1B}. For example, in 1987, when the net foreign assets were increased by NT\$694bn, the money supply, M_{1B}, was increased by NT\$430bn. From 1976 to 1987, net foreign assets declined only in 1979 and 1980 after the second oil crisis, 1978–1979. From 1982 to 1986, the increase was accelerated.

The net claim on the private sector as contributing to the increase in money supply exhibited positive signs in only four years (1977–1980), but negative signs in 1976 and 1981–7 (Table 5.7). Quasi-money or time and savings deposits, which contribute to a decrease in money supply, have increased rapidly in the 1980s thus causing the negative claim on the private sector in the recent years.

The net claim on the government sector also shows negative signs in 1983–7 (Table 5.7). The claims on government enterprises show negative signs in 1983–7. Government deposits, which cause a de-

Table 5.7 Determinants of money supply, M_{1B}, changes (NT$ million)

	1976	*1979*	*1980*	*1981*	*1982*	*1983*	*1984*	*1985*	*1986*	*1987*
Money supply, M_{1B}	+32 876	+23 204	+73 445	+54 698	+65 920	+95 422	+56 717	+81 850	+386 394	+430 362
Determinants										
1. External sector: Net foreign assets	+35 833	–6 397	–18 394	+43 699	+100 870	+198 004	+235 841	+375 303	+626 149	+693 966
2. Private sector: Net claims or deposits (–)	–8 361	+56 219	+52 699	–7 498	–54 553	–51 805	–88 960	–298 797	–172 582	–67 838
2.1 Claims on private enterprises & others	+44 091	+101 169	+150 582	+115 592	+154 315	+224 192	+210 935	+118 275	+106 744	+377 959
2.2 Quasi-money	–52 452	–44 950	–97 883	–123 090	–208 868	–275 997	–299 895	–417 072	–279 326	–445 797
3. Government sector: Net claims or deposits (–)	+8 644	+2 724	+73 961	+75 888	+63 721	–21 897	–33 469	–12 975	–33 600	–139 184
3.1 Claims on government	+7 086	+3 144	+940	+13 337	+28 173	+5 586	–12 431	+8 981	+7 578	+5 773
3.2 Claims on government enterprises	+10 973	+33 696	+67 784	+43 516	+44 300	–3 631	–445	–8 289	–1 614	–41 375
3.3 Government deposits	–9 415	–34 116	+5 237	+19 035	–8 752	–23 852	–20 593	–13 667	–39 564	–103 582
4. Pre-settlement requirements for imports	+450	–2 278	–3 548	+6 006	–790	–4 156	+380	–6 248	+231	–4 197
5. Other items	–3 690	–27 064	–31 273	–63 397	–43 328	–24 724	–57 075	+24 567	–33 804	–52 385

Source: Economic Research Department, CBC, *Financial Statistics Monthly*, May 1988 and various issues.

crease in money supply (negative signs in Table 5.7, Item 3.3), have also been increasing in 1982–7. Pre-settlement requirements for imports (mainly deposits for opening letters of credit) are only a minor factor in Table 5.7.

In 1986 and 1987 because of the lack of investment incentive (and hence the demand for loans) and the sharp increase in deposits (resulting from the great export surplus and the inflow of foreign funds in anticipation of the appreciation of the NT dollar), the growth rate of deposits was almost five times that of bank lending, causing an imbalance in bank management.

Deposit funds cannot be effectively lent out. At the same time, the net claim of the banking system on both the public and private sectors would be much reduced because of the large amounts of deposits.

In order to slow down the appreciation of the NT dollar the Central Bank had to be persistent in purchasing US dollars in the exchange market. Thus NT dollar is issued in exchange, causing an increase in M_{1B}. It has been a worry that inflation may follow, after a time-lag of a few months or a year. So the Central Bank issues Certificates of Deposits, Savings Bonds and Treasury Bills-B, in order to absorb liquidity in the market,[14] or to reduce the effect of the increase of money supply on prices. The Ministry of Finance has also stepped up the issue of Government bonds.

To what extent would the increase in money supply affect prices? According to '*Monetary Theory*', the consistent increase in money supply would cause an increase in prices, although with a time-lag. However in the experience of Taiwan, the sharp increase in prices was associated with the world-wide increase in prices of commodities such as petroleum, and food. The increase of 47.5 per cent on consumer prices in 1974 after the first oil crisis and the world food shortage in 1972 and 1973, and the increases of 19.0 per cent and 16.3 per cent in 1980 and 1981 respectively, after the second oil crisis, could well be explained by the sharp rise in commodity prices. Perhaps a combination of an increase in money supply and in commodity prices may present a more comprehensive picture of the price increase.

In the present case, the appreciation of the NT dollar has caused a sharp decline in import prices, including particularly those of industrial raw materials. Import prices of daily necessities and the cost of living have not been increased, so that prices were rather stabilised in 1987. Hence, whether consumer prices would go up or not after a time-lag would remain to be seen.

5.7 THE MONETARY IDENTITY AS APPLIED TO TAIWAN

A theoretical approach to the analysis of the determinants of the money supply is to make use of the 'monetary identity' devised by Milton Friedman and Anna Schwartz:[15]

$$\text{Money supply, } M_2 = H \cdot \frac{D/R(1 + D/C)}{D/R + D/C}$$

where H = Monetary base, or High-power money,
= Currency in active circulation plus bank reserves $(C + R)$
D = Total deposits
R = Bank reserves
C = Currency in active circulation
Hence D/R = Banks' cash ratio, which exhibits the behaviour of banks
D/C = Public's cash ratio, which exhibits the behaviour of the general public
Money supply, $M_2 = C + D$

Although the interest rate is not explicitly stated in the equation, the D/R and D/C ratios are related to the interest rate because a higher (lower) interest rate will induce banks to reduce (increase) the level of reserves (or excess reserves to be precise), and interest-rate change may affect the public's choice between petty cash and bank deposits.

It is important to note that what Friedman calls 'money supply' is M_2 because he emphasises the importance of M_2, rather than M_1, as the objective of monetary policy; he argues that since funds flow flexibly between demand deposits and time and savings deposits, it is better to direct attention to M_2 in monetary control. Hence D in Friedman's monetary identity denotes all deposits, including demand, time, and savings deposits.

A study of the D/R (or D_2/R in Figure 5.1) ratio shows that it had an upward trend from 1978 to 1984 and then stabilised thereafter. Bank reserves grew faster than currency in active circulation from 1984 to 1987; this is a factor contributing to the steadiness of the D/R ratio.

The D/C (or D_2/C in Figure 5.1) ratio shows a continuously rising trend from 1973 to 1986, particularly in the 1980s. The high growth

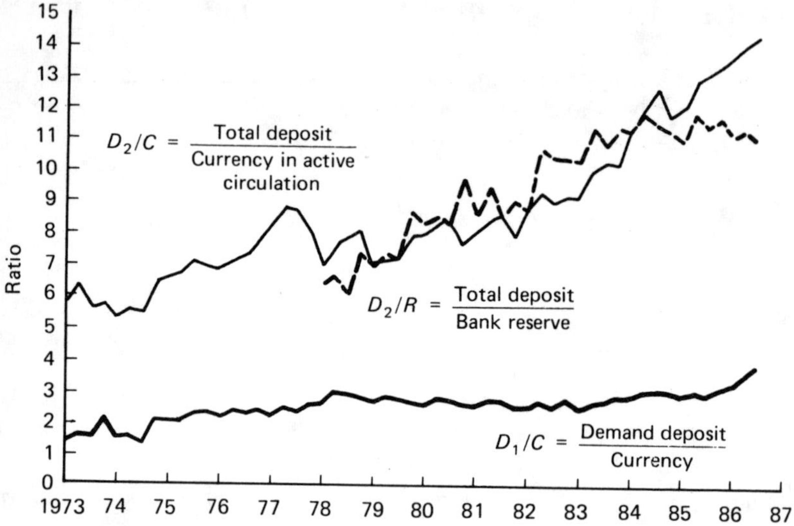

Figure 5.1 D_2/C, D_2/R and D_1/C ratios, 1973–87

rate of time and savings deposits, relative to that of currency in active circulation explains the rising trend of the D/C ratio.

The demand deposits to currency ratio (D_1/C in Figure 5.1) however exhibits a high degree of stability around 2 in 1973–7, and around 3 in 1978–86.

The social habit of alternative payment by cheques or passbook deposits, or by cash (notes) would usually remain unchanged for some time; nevertheless the slightly higher ratio in the latter period than in the former period may suggest the gradual monetisation of the economy.

5.8 MONEY MULTIPLIER

The analysis of the money supply is usually presented as follows:

$$\text{Money supply} = \text{monetary base} \times \text{money multiplier}$$

Harry Johnson put forward the following equation which is similar to Friedman and Schwartz's 'monetary identity':[16]

$$\text{Money supply, } M_2 = B \cdot m_2$$

$$= B \cdot \frac{1}{c + r(1 - c)}$$

where B = monetary base = $C + R$
C = currency held by the public, i.e., $C = cM_2$
c = ratio of currency held by the public to the total quantity of money
D = total deposits = $(1 - c)M_2$
r = ratio of reserves to deposits of commercial banks

Note that r and c are alternative ways of expressing the D/R and D/C ratios.

Abrendorf and Kanesathasan define money supply as M_1 and present the following equation.[17]

$$\text{Money supply, } M_1 = B \cdot m_1$$

$$= B \cdot \frac{d}{(1 - c)\, r + cd}$$

where d = ratio of demand deposits to total deposits

This d is the additional element which they introduce into the equation; it denotes the changing structure of deposits, or the shift between demand and time deposits.

The ratio of M_{1B} to reserve money ($m_1 = M_{1B}$/Reserve money) has remained very stable at around 2 since 1978 (Figure 5.2 and Table 5.8). However, the ratio of M_2 to reserve money ($m_2 = M_2$/Reserve money) has been rising in the 1980s; the progressive increase in time and savings deposits is the main reason.

The ratio of bank reserves to reserve money has been quite stable at around 0.5 level (Figure 5.3) from 1978 to 1987; that means reserve money consisting of bank reserves and currency in active circulation in about equal proportion.

5.9 INCOME VELOCITIES OF CIRCULATION

The concept of income velocity has long been a subject of debate in monetary theory. Irving Fisher introduced transaction velocity in his

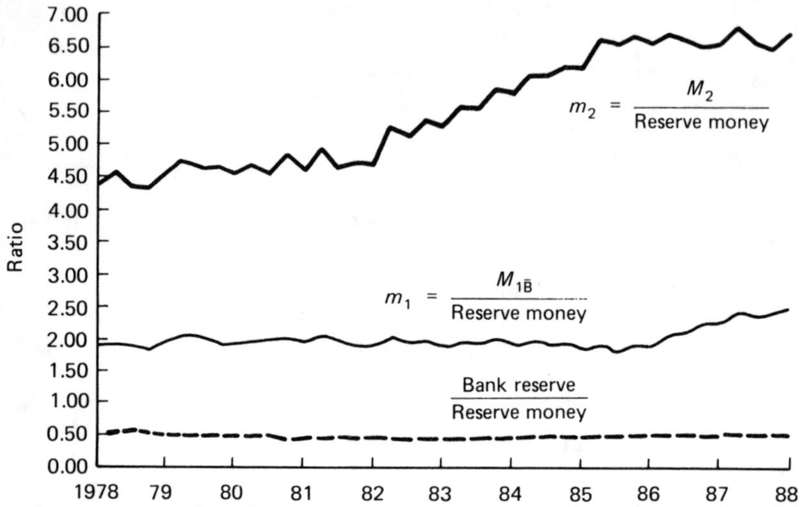

Figure 5.2 Money multipliers, 1978–88 (quarterly data)

famous equation $MV = PT$, which is an identity or a balance sheet approach. The Cambridge School changed the emphasis from the money-supply side to the cash-balance approach, i.e. people keep a certain proportion of their income in money balance. A. Marshall devised the equations:

$$M = kY$$

and

$$M = kY + k'A,$$

where Y = income = PO (price level × output; this is a modified form of Fisher's PT)
k = proportion of income kept in money balance
A = wealth of the people
k' = proportion of wealth held in money balance
M = money

Income velocity, Y/M is the reciprocal of the Marshallian k. Keynes attacked vigorously the notion of income velocity, calling it unstable, and instead proposed 'liquidity preference' as a more stable and clear

Table 5.8 Reserve money and money multipliers, 1978–88 (quarterly data)

	Bank reserves[1] *NT$m*	*Reserve money*[2] *NT$m*	M_{1B} *NT$m*	*Multiplier*[3] *w.r.t.* M_1 $= m_1$	M_2 *NT$m*	*Multiplier*[4] *w.r.t.* M_2 $= m_2$	$\frac{\textit{Bank reserve}}{\textit{Reserve money}}$
1978.1	66 345	127 428	239 444	1.879	560 781	4.401	0.521
1978.2	72 021	135 118	259 701	1.922	620 845	4.595	0.533
1978.3	85 098	150 635	279 957	1.859	654 313	4.344	0.565
1978.4	86 391	164 941	300 213	1.820	714 131	4.330	0.524
1979.1	78 427	155 972	306 014	1.962	714 692	4.582	0.503
1979.2	74 778	152 142	311 815	2.049	719 973	4.732	0.492
1979.3	78 194	156 887	317 616	2.024	726 637	4.632	0.498
1979.4	80 100	168 433	323 417	1.920	782 285	4.644	0.476
1980.1	87 286	178 019	341 778	1.920	811 137	4.556	0.490
1980.2	90 516	183 411	360 140	1.964	859 460	4.686	0.494
1980.3	97 396	192 484	378 501	1.966	877 249	4.558	0.506
1980.4	86 038	196 470	396 862	2.020	953 613	4.854	0.438
1981.1	102 052	210 108	410 537	1.954	964 623	4.591	0.486
1981.2	97 148	207 195	424 211	2.047	1 025 096	4.947	0.469
1981.3	112 498	222 359	437 886	1.969	1 033 154	4.646	0.506
1981.4	112 127	240 426	451 560	1.878	1 131 401	4.706	0.466
1982.1	124 795	248 002	468 040	1.887	1 160 575	4.680	0.503
1982.2	110 672	237 472	484 520	2.040	1 249 129	5.260	0.466
1982.3	118 958	256 432	501 000	1.954	1 306 630	5.095	0.464
1982.4	122 496	260 769	517 480	1.984	1 406 189	5.392	0.470
1983.1	134 997	277 628	525 150	1.892	1 468 679	5.290	0.486
1983.2	130 994	276 520	543 464	1.965	1 549 184	5.602	0.474
1983.3	146 682	293 764	566 201	1.927	1 633 995	5.562	0.499
1983.4	142 846	302 462	612 902	2.026	1 777 608	5.877	0.472

Table 5.8 continued

	Bank reserves[1] *NT$m*	*Reserve money*[2] *NT$m*	M_{1B} *NT$m*	*Multiplier*[3] *w.r.t.* M_1 $= m_1$	M_2 *NT$m*	*Multiplier*[4] *w.r.t.* M_2 $= m_2$	*Bank reserve* / *Reserve money*
1984.1	158 623	315 522	603 620	1.913	1 826 270	5.788	0.503
1984.2	159 657	316 523	633 637	2.002	1 930 076	6.098	0.504
1984.3	173 760	330 299	635 833	1.925	2 008 361	6.080	0.526
1984.4	174 685	342 845	669 619	1.953	2 134 220	6.225	0.510
1985.1	189 129	360 703	665 684	1.846	2 236 273	6.200	0.524
1985.2	184 781	354 292	682 712	1.927	2 355 830	6.650	0.522
1985.3	202 423	378 097	686 110	1.815	2 475 175	6.546	0.535
1985.4	210 506	393 314	751 469	1.911	2 633 142	6.695	0.535
1986.1	230 674	417 571	790 728	1.894	2 739 969	6.562	0.552
1986.2	237 019	427 858	881 234	2.060	2 868 619	6.705	0.554
1986.3	259 166	456 430	966 814	2.118	3 027 275	6.633	0.568
1986.4	275 827	506 873	1 137 863	2.245	3 298 862	6.508	0.544
1987.1	295 606	526 023	1 194 174	2.270	3 461 471	6.580	0.562
1987.2	299 638	539 946	1 318 790	2.442	3 694 582	6.843	0.555
1987.3	329 106	579 393	1 375 371	2.374	3 807 333	6.571	0.568
1987.4	359 163	644 127	1 568 225	2.435	4 175 021	6.482	0.558
1988.1	357 049	635 989	1 576 965	2.480	4 273 317	6.719	0.561

Note: 1. Bank reserves = Cash in vault + Reserve deposit with CBC
2. Reserve money = Bank reserves + Currency in active circulation
3. $m_1 = M_{1B}$/Reserve money
4. $m_2 = M_2$/Reserve money
w.r.t. = with respect to

Source: Economic Research Department, CBC, *Financial Statistics Monthly*, April 1988, p. 63.

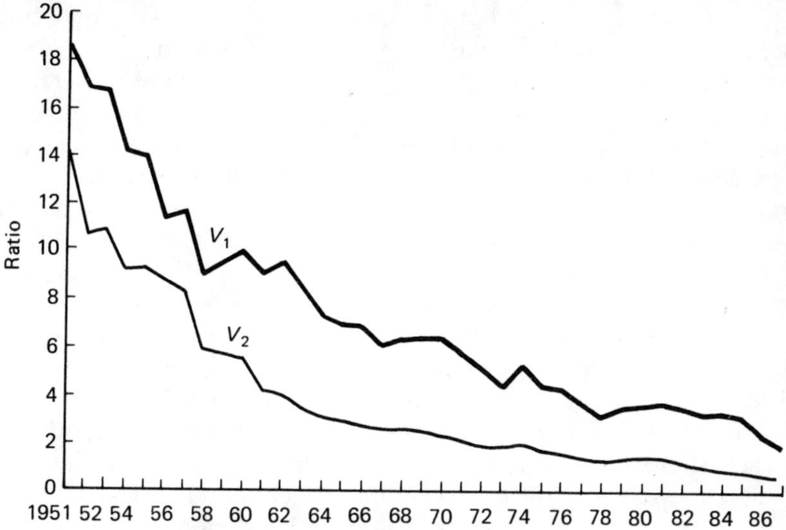

Note: $V_2 = \dfrac{GNP}{M_2}$ $\quad V_1 = \dfrac{\text{GNP}}{M_{1B}}$

Source: DGBAS; Economic Research Department, CBC, *Financial Statistical Monthly*, Taiwan District, ROC.

Figure 5.3 Income velocities of circulation, 1951–87

concept.[18] In fact, liquidity preference is the inverse of income velocity. The Radcliffe Report, following the Keynesian thinking, commented that income velocity was a hazy concept.

Milton Friedman revived the importance of money and income velocity.[19] One of the central points in monetary theory is whether we regard income velocity as stable or not. If V is stable, a change in the money stock can affect economic activity directly and in a predictable manner, and hence monetary policy is effective. Conversely, if we believe V is unstable, an increase or decrease in the money stock can be offset by an opposite change in velocity, and hence monetary policy is ineffective.

Quantity theory of money and income velocity are easily understood by the man in the street. If the money stock or velocity is increased, prices go up. In time of inflation, people tend to spend money faster in order to avoid erosion of the value of money. Hence velocity is closely related to the monetary condition; inflation would increase velocity, while deflation would decrease it.

In theory, the rise or fall of income in cyclical movement would affect income velocity. But in the experience of Taiwan we do not see the income velocity changing in response to the cyclical movement. The periods of high real-growth-rate were (i) 1964–7, averaging annually 10.75 per cent; (ii) 1970–3 (before the first oil crisis) averaging annually 12.55 per cent; and (iii) 1976–8, (before the second oil crisis) averaging annually 12.40 per cent. These three periods can be regarded as upswings of the business cycle. The subsequent periods – (a) 1968–9, averaging annually 9 per cent; (b) 1974–5, averaging annually 2.95 per cent, with the lowest at 1.1 per cent in 1974; and (c) 1979–82, averaging annually 6.1 per cent. These subsequent periods can be regarded as the downswing of the business cycle. However the cyclical movement does not exhibit any effect on the income velocities, V_1 (GNP/M_{1B}) and V_2 (GNP/M_2) (Figure 5.3); instead, the graph shows the declining trend of the income velocities. The two velocities were at a higher level in the earlier period, 1951–60 than in the latter period, 1961–86; they also declined more sharply in the earlier period because in the 1950s and 1960s there was inflation. Thereafter the decline was more gentle. Price stability in the 1980s can also explain the decline of the two velocities.

5.10 SAVINGS AND INVESTMENT RATIOS AND THE FINANCIAL SYSTEM

The savings and investment ratios can be regarded as the link between the financial sector and the real sector, and are crucial to economic growth. The high growth rate of Taiwan's GNP is characterised by the spectacularly large export surplus, a favourable balance of payments, and an increase in international reserves.

The underlying forces are the high savings and investment ratios. The savings ratio (S_1), defined as the ratio of net savings to national income, rose from 5.3 per cent in 1951 to the heights of 35 per cent in 1973 and 1978, fell to 30 per cent in 1985, and rose again to 39 per cent in 1987 (see Table 5.9 and Figure 5.4). The average S_1 ratio in 1970–9 was 30.9 per cent with the standard deviation of 3.8 per cent, and that in 1980–7 was 32.2 per cent, with the standard deviation of 3.9 per cent.

If we relate personal savings to disposable income, the savings ratio (S_2) rose from 5.4 per cent in 1951 to 23.1 per cent in 1973 and fell marginally to 22.8 per cent in 1985. The average S_2 ratio in 1970–9

Table 5.9 Savings ratios, 1951–87 (NT$ million)

	Net Savings (*1*)	*National Income at Factor cost* (*2*)	*Savings Ratio* (S1) % (*1*)÷(*2*)	*Personal Savings* (*3*)	*Disposable Income* (*4*)	*Savings Ratio* (S2) % (*3*)÷(*4*)
1951	552	10 454	5.28	519	9 687	5.36
1952	759	14 568	5.21	330	13 006	2.54
1953	971	19 413	5.00	520	18 381	2.83
1954	671	20 619	3.25	523	19 812	2.64
1955	1 196	24 431	4.90	802	23 200	3.46
1956	1 323	27 748	4.77	986	25 163	3.92
1957	1 898	31 999	5.93	1 173	29 776	3.94
1958	1 789	35 617	5.02	1 655	33 714	4.91
1959	2 056	41 234	4.99	1 712	38 563	4.44
1960	3 852	50 410	7.64	2 871	45 293	6.34
1961	4 555	56 814	8.02	4 010	52 890	7.58
1962	4 660	61 294	7.60	4 534	58 011	7.82
1963	9 416	70 179	13.42	7 230	64 697	11.18
1964	13 461	82 629	16.29	10 151	74 011	13.72
1965	14 928	90 537	16.49	9 400	82 459	11.40
1966	19 171	100 846	19.01	13 734	92 900	14.78
1967	23 322	116 302	20.05	15 481	106 113	14.59
1968	26 435	133 641	19.78	14 934	115 835	12.89
1969	33 496	151 474	22.11	14 114	133 179	10.60
1970	42 062	176 655	23.81	25 060	158 646	15.80
1971	57 309	207 940	27.56	34 553	184 727	18.70
1972	78 346	247 777	31.62	43 277	206 565	20.95
1973	112 179	320 623	34.99	65 877	284 902	23.12
1974	136 012	431 758	31.50	74 329	370 542	20.06
1975	115 326	455 451	25.32	64 495	398 078	16.20
1976	174 855	543 737	32.16	82 429	446 490	18.46
1977	205 927	537 395	32.31	108 759	529 324	20.55
1978	264 281	757 568	34.89	132 895	622 263	21.36
1979	315 544	909 795	34.68	154 652	747 267	20.70
1980	375 117	1 147 818	32.68	170 944	922 843	18.52
1981	418 826	1 376 241	30.43	227 947	1 129 824	20.18
1982	405 781	1 484 510	27.33	246 697	1 224 065	20.15
1983	483 447	1 621 876	29.81	298 616	1 351 243	22.10
1984	571 994	1 823 910	31.36	338 948	1 483 704	22.84
1985	583 019	1 928 950	30.22	356 291	1 561 558	22.82
1986	829 108	2 269 217	36.54	535 380	1 823 955	29.35
1987	990 538	2 529 327	39.16	654 647	2 053 557	31.88

Note: Including personal savings and savings of non-profit institutions.
Source: Directorate-General of Budgeting, Accounting and Statistics (DGBAS). Col. (1) taken from DGBAS. *National Income of the Republic of China*, 1987, p. 73; cols (3) + (4) taken from Council for Economic Planning and Development. *Taiwan Statistical Data Bank*, 1988, pp. 56–58.

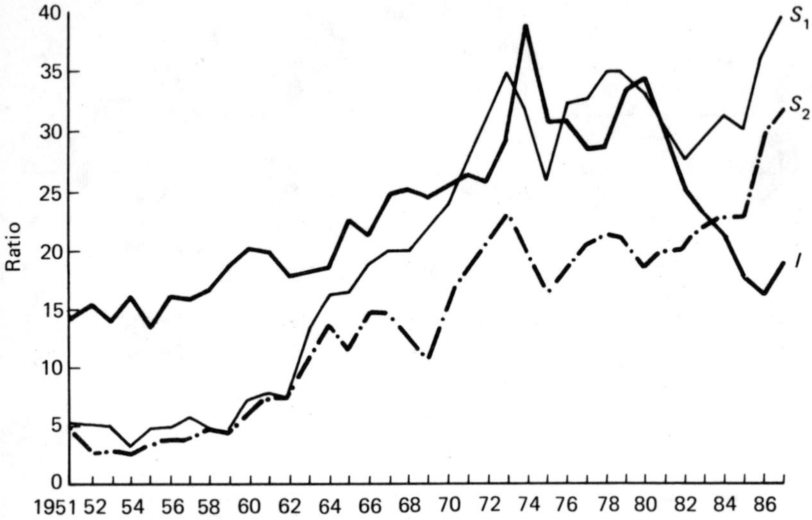

Notes: I = Investment ratio

$$= \frac{\text{Gross domestic capital formation}}{\text{GDP at current market price}}$$

S_1 = Savings ratio (1)

$$= \frac{\text{Net savings}}{\text{National income at factor cost}}$$

S_2 = Savings ratio (2)

$$= \frac{\text{Personal savings}}{\text{Disposable income}}$$

Source: DGBAS, *Taiwan Statistical Data Book*, 1987

Figure 5.4 Investment ratio and savings ratio, 1951–87

was 19.6 per cent with a standard deviation of 2.2 per cent, and that in 1980–7 was 23.5 per cent with a standard deviation of 4.5 per cent. The S_2 ratio was lower than the S_1 ratio by about 7 percentage points.

Table 5.10 presents an international comparison of the savings ratio, investment ratio and investment/savings ratio of NICs, developed countries (the USA, Japan, West Germany, and the UK), Hong Kong and Malaysia. The savings ratio of Taiwan is high compared with all these countries except Singapore. In 1986, the savings ratio of Taiwan was 36 per cent whilst that of Singapore was 40 per cent.

Table 5.10 International comparison of investment, savings and investment/savings ratios*

	1970	*1973*	*1978*	*1983*	*1986*
Taiwan					
(1) Investment ratio, *I*	25.7	29.3	28.5	23.0	18.7
(2) Savings ratio, S_1	23.8	35.0	34.9	29.8	35.8
(3) *I/S* ratio	1.4	1.1	1.1	1.0	0.6
S. Korea					
(1) Investment ratio, *I*	26.4	24.8	29.7	29.9	29.5
(2) Savings ratio, S_1	17.1	22.8	25.2	25.3	32.5
(3) *I/S* ratio	1.5	1.1	1.2	1.2	0.9
Singapore					
(1) Investment ratio, *I*	32.5	34.9	35.7	48.5	37.1
(2) Savings ratio, S_1	18.4	29.0	34.0	45.8	39.9
(3) *I/S* ratio	1.8	1.2	1.1	1.1	0.9
*Hong Kong**					
(1) Investment ratio, *I*	20.6	23.2	27.5	26.2	21.8
Malaysia					
(1) Investment ratio, *I*	16.1	22.5	24.8	33.4	–
(2) Savings ratio, S_1	19.3	26.0	28.8	–	–
(3) *I/S* ratio	0.9	0.9	0.9	–	–
USA					
(1) Investment ratio, *I*	17.4	19.1	19.5	16.8	–
(2) Savings ratio, S_1	8.3	11.2	9.0	2.1	–
(3) *I/S* ratio	2.4	1.9	2.4	9.0	–
Japan					
(1) Investment ratio, *I*	35.5	36.4	30.8	28.5	–
(2) Savings ratio, S_1	30.9	29.1	22.3	18.4	–
(3) *I/S* ratio	1.3	1.4	1.6	1.8	–
West Germany					
(1) Investment ratio, *I*	25.5	23.9	20.8	20.8	–
(2) Savings ratio, S_1	20.1	18.1	13.1	10.4	–
(3) *I/S* ratio	1.4	1.5	1.8	2.3	–
UK					
(1) Investment ratio, *I*	19.0	20.1	18.6	16.5	–
(2) Savings ratio, S_1	14.2	12.3	9.0	6.8	–
(3) *I/S* ratio	1.5	1.8	2.3	2.8	–

Note: * Investment Ratio and Savings Ratio are expressed as percentages of GNP, whilst *I/S* Ratio is simply a relative between investment and savings amounts

Sources: 1. Council for Economic Planning and Development, *Taiwan Statistical Data Book*, 1986.
2. Economic Planning Board, ROK, *Korea Statistical Yearbook*, 1986; and Bank of Korea, *National Income in Korea*, 1982.
3. Ministry of Trade and Industry, Singapore, *Economic Survey of Singapore*, 1986 and various issues.

continued

Table 5.10 sources continued

4. Hong Kong *Monthly Digest of Statistics*, February 1987; * data for national savings are not available.
5. *UN National Accounts Statistics: Main Aggregates and Detailed Tables, 1983* (New York: UN, 1986).

The reason for the high savings ratio in Taiwan is fundamentally related to the hard-working and thrifty nature of the people. The Chinese people by tradition try to work hard in their lifetime and to save as much as they can, not only for their old age but also for their children and grandchildren.

Savings come from three main domestic sources (namely, government saving, corporate saving and private saving) and the foreign source (i.e. foreign borrowing or aid for investment). With an increase in income, private savings had expanded not only in absolute value, but also in the share of net savings, from 40 per cent in 1951 to 66 per cent in 1987 (see Table 5.11). In 1987, private saving constituted 66 per cent of net saving; government saving, 19 per cent; public enterprise saving, 2.7 per cent; and private enterprise saving, 12.1 per cent. Hence corporate savings constituted 14.8 per cent.

The investment ratio, *I*, defined as the ratio of gross domestic capital formation to gross domestic product rose from 14.5 per cent in 1951 to 39.5 per cent in 1974, dropped to 34.3 per cent in 1980 and then declined steadily to its nadir of 16.2 per cent in 1986, (see Table 5.12 and Figure 5.4). However, it rose to 19.3 per cent in 1987. The average investment ratio in 1970–9 was 29.8 per cent with standard deviation of 4.0 per cent and that in 1980–7 was 23.4 per cent with the standard deviation of 5.8 per cent. The most striking and alarming feature is that the investment ratio has been declining rather sharply since 1980. Why has the investment incentive become lower? One plausible explanation is that the high and fluctuating interest rates in the world market in the early 1980s, the reduced growth rate of gross domestic capital formation,[20] the appreciating NT dollars since 1985 and the trade protectionism policy of the developed countries contributed to dampen the investment incentives. Another possible explanation is that investment in the previous period, 1970–9 was exceptionally high, which would naturally reduce the incentive to invest in the subsequent period according to the principle of acceleration. But it is still a puzzle in view of the fact that exports have been booming in the recent years. Vigorous export activity ought to be conducive to investment incentive.

A survey of 1638 big manufacturing firms in 1985 showed that most

Table 5.11 Sources of net savings in Taiwan, 1951–87 (NT$ million)

	1951	*1961*	*1975*	*1980*	*1985*	*1987*
1. Net savings	1 290	8 492	115 614	371 694	583 019	990 538
Government savings, %	35.50	28.17	35.38	31.43	22.61	19.14
Public enterprise savings, %	4.57	13.40	10.73	11.23	10.98	2.63
Private enterprise savings, %	19.69	11.21	–1.89	11.35	5.30	12.13
Household and non-profit organisations savings, %	40.23	47.22	55.78	45.99	61.11	66.09
2. Reserve for capital depreciation	641	4 380	41 071	108 934	210 836	257 225
3. Foreign borrowing for investment	–152	1 111	22 362	23 283	–372 718	–666 839
4. Domestic gross capital formation	1 779	13 983	179 047	503 911	421 137	580 924

Source: DGBAS, *National Income in Taiwan Area*, 1987 (pp. 35 and 72) and various issues.

Table 5.12 Investment ratios, 1951–87

	Gross domestic capital formation[1] *(NT$million)* (1)	*GDP* *(NT$million)* (2)	*Investment ratio* (%) (3)=(1)/(2)	*I/S ratio*[2] (4)
1951	1 779	12 252	14.52	3.22
1952	2 643	17 166	15.40	3.48
1953	3 224	22 863	14.10	3.32
1954	4 041	25 087	16.11	6.02
1955	3 998	29 838	13.40	3.34
1956	5 524	34 219	16.14	4.18
1957	6 355	39 936	15.91	3.35
1958	7 458	44 683	16.69	4.17
1959	9 732	51 525	18.89	4.73
1960	12 618	62 170	20.30	3.28
1961	13 983	69 677	20.07	3.07
1962	13 733	76 762	17.89	2.95
1963	15 950	86 823	18.37	1.69
1964	19 089	101 476	18.81	1.42
1965	25 546	112 089	22.79	1.71
1966	26 736	125 440	21.31	1.40
1967	35 882	145 162	24.72	1.54
1968	42 624	169 153	25.20	1.61
1969	48 219	195 940	24.61	1.44
1970	57 886	225 675	25.65	1.38
1971	69 179	262 247	26.38	1.21
1972	81 082	314 310	25.80	1.04
1973	119 373	407 535	29.29	1.06
1974	215 325	545 024	39.51	1.58
1975	179 047	584 494	30.63	1.55
1976	216 231	701 117	30.84	1.24
1977	232 950	820 473	28.39	1.13
1978	279 671	980 318	28.53	1.06
1979	393 379	1 180 552	33.32	1.25
1980	503 911	1 470 175	34.28	1.34
1981	529 833	1 749 447	30.29	1.27
1982	468 004	1 859 665	25.17	1.15
1983	469 395	2 041 370	22.99	0.97
1984	484 361	2 255 111	21.48	0.85
1985	421 137	2 357 106	17.87	0.72
1986	438 234	2 701 773	16.22	0.53
1987	580 924	3 017 231	19.25	0.59

Notes: [1] Gross domestic capital formation = gross fixed capital formation + increase in stock.
[2] The ratio of gross domestic capital formation to net savings (Table 5.6 column 1).

Source: DGBAS, *Taiwan Statistical Year Book*, 1987, p. 40.

of them reported that their investment in capital equipment in 1985 was less than that in 1984, and that they believed that there were several reasons for the decline of investment incentive:

1. world recession;
2. the changing industrial structure of Taiwan;
3. the possible suspensions of the Regulations for Encouraging Investment;
4. the conservative attitude of financial institutions;
5. exchange control is too strict and the NT dollar is too high in the exchange market;
6. many regulations are not suitable to the current situation;
7. the new Labour Law may be a disturbing factor.

But one factor, which has been overlooked and which people do not like to mention for political reason, is the shadow of China on Taiwan. The antagonism between The People's Republic of China (PRC) and Republic of China (ROC) still exists.

Table 5.7 shows that the investment ratio of Taiwan in 1986, (18.7 per cent) was low compared with South Korea (29.5 per cent), Singapore (37.1 per cent), and Hong Kong (21.8 per cent).

The ratio of gross domestic capital formation to net savings, or *I/S* ratio, showed a high and fluctuating level in 1951–62 (mean = 3.76, and standard deviation = 0.89), a lower and also varying level in 1963–87 (mean = 1.23, and standard deviation = 0.33) (see Table 5.12). This implied that in the first period, investment was almost 3.75 times of domestic saving and foreign capital had to fill in the gap. In the second period, investment exceeded domestic savings by only about 35 per cent, and the economy of Taiwan relied much less upon the inflow of foreign capital to fill in the savings gap. In the current period, savings exceeded domestic investment, so that savings had to flow out to finance foreign investment. The low investment incentive and the sharply declining investment ratio contribute to explain the progressively declining trend of the *I/S* ratio.

As savings funds cannot be effectively invested in the domestic economy, they would naturally be accumulated in the form of international reserves, or else would flow out in the form of foreign investment. The increasing export surplus and consequently the international reserves, can be considered as the statistical expression of the excess of savings funds, not being utilised at home. Resources, which are not invested or utilised at home, are exported. There is in fact a close relationship between the declining investment ratio and the rising export surplus. It is interesting to note in Figure 5.5 that from 1973 to 1986, the export surplus ratio (defined as the ratio of exports minus imports of goods and services to GDP) went up, whilst the investment ratio (gross capital formation/GDP) went down in a convergent movement. Also, the consumption ratio (consumption expenditure/GDP) slid down gradually from 91 per cent in 1952 to 62 per cent in 1986 whereas the savings ratio went up from 5 per cent in 1952 to 35 per cent in 1973 and maintained that high level with some variations until 1987.

Table 5.10 shows that the high and rising savings ratio coupled with the declining investment ratio in the 1980s explains the declining investment/savings ratio in several countries, including Taiwan, South Korea and Singapore. Savings are used to finance investment; without adequate savings, an expanded investment expenditure would cause inflation. Investment is to enhance savings, through an increase in income via the multiplier effect. Investment in machinery and capital equipment is to enhance productivity of the economy and hence income and saving. Therefore savings and investment interact on each other in mutual cause and effect.

Obviously the investment ratio is positively correlated with the savings ratio. In the period, 1951–85 the adjusted coefficient of determination, R^2 is 0.694. The coefficient of the S_1 ratio is 0.468, implying that a change of 1 per cent of the S_1 ratio would be associated with 0.47 per cent change of the I ratio. The t-value is 8.66 implying statistical significance at even the 1 per cent level.[21]

Conversely, if we do the regression equation of S_1 ratio on I ratio, the adjusted coefficient of determination, R^2, remains the same, whilst the coefficient of I ratio is 1.484, with a statistically significant t-value.

However, in 1987, the savings ratio went up to 39.2 per cent, whilst the investment ratio went down to 19.3 per cent (see Tables 5.9 and 5.12). This had upset the correlation considerably.

What is the role of financial institutions in enhancing savings and investment ratios? The liberalisation of the financial system with respect to the deposit rate had encouraged people's savings and induced the flow of savings fund into the banking system. The best illustration was in the late 1940s and early 1950s, when there was hyperinflation during the time of the retreat of the nationalist government from China to Taiwan. The interest rate on time and savings

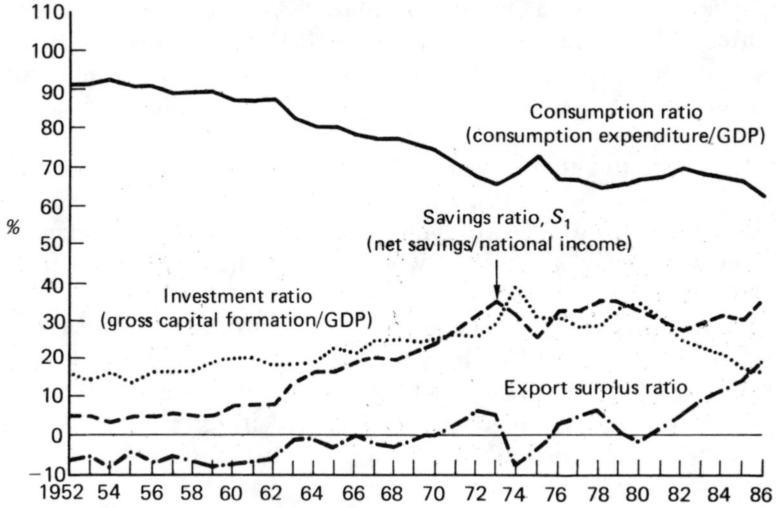

Figure 5.5 Consumption, saving, investment and export surplus ratios

deposits of banks was deliberately kept low by the monetary authority on the hypothesis that the low deposit-rate would be conducive to the low lending-rate, which was essential to investment and rehabilitation of the economy. At that time the low-interest-rate policy was adopted by most of the developing and developed countries alike, on the basis of the Keynesian theory that low interest-rate would induce a bigger volume of investment, through the schedule of marginal efficiency of capital. As a result, savings did not flow adequately into the banking system; instead, it was attracted to the informal money market by the higher rate of interest. The banking system being starved of investible funds was unable to satisfy the demand of investors and so investors had to borrow from the informal money market at high rates of interest. The monetary authority of Taiwan was courageous enough as to embark on a high and realistic interest-rate policy in the early 1950s. Preferential interest rate (PIR) deposit was instituted from the first quarter of 1950 to the first quarter of 1955. Depositors were paid at a high monthly rate of interest to compensate for the high inflation rate and to attract the savings funds back into the banking system, instead of the informal money market. Time, savings and PIR deposits as percentage of money supply rose from 2 per cent in 1950 (first quarter) to about 57 per cent in 1952 (third quarter) and about 53 per cent in 1953 (second quarter). The interest rate on one-month PIR deposit was as high as 7 per cent per month in 1950 (first and second quarter) and then dropped gradually to about 1 per cent in 1955 (first quarter), as the inflation rate was lowered.[22]

It is interesting to note that the high level of time, saving and PIR deposits had the effect of curbing inflation and that as the inflation was gradually slowed down, the necessity of having the PIR deposit, which was in fact a subsidy, was reduced, and finally the special arrangement of the PIR deposit was abolished in 1957.

In the period, 1950–7, the lending rate had to be high because of the high deposit rate. The interest-rate structure was closer to equilibrium than before. This might explain the more effective role of banks as intermediary between savers and investors, and the enhancement to saving and investment, which laid the foundation of economic growth of Taiwan.

However, the so-called liberalisation of the financial system of Taiwan should not be exaggerated. Apart from this short episode of high deposit rate and an attempt to resort to market forces, the banking and financial system had remained under tight and rigid control. As mentioned in Chapter 2, the banking system is dominated by government banks, which are subject to numerous regulations and political hindrance.

Until recently the deposit and lending interest rates of banks had long been regulated by the Central Bank of China. The foreign exchange rate (external monetary policy) too had long been controlled by the Central Bank of China; market forces in terms of demand and supply of foreign exchange did not have a decisive effect on the exchange rate until recently. In short, the financial system was rather rigid.

It is only in the past two or three years that great effort has been really devoted to the policy of 'liberalisation, internationalisation and institutionalisation'. With the freedom of banks to quote their own prime rates as from February/March 1986, and the abolition of exchange control as from 15 July 1987, the financial system has become much liberalised and internationalised. All the old arguments against the rigidity of the system have been dissipated.

In order to understand further the importance of the savings ratio and investment ratio, we can make use of the concept of incremental capital/output ratio and apply Tsiang's condition to take-off as follows (and as shown in Table 5.13):

Table 5.13 The 'take-off' ratio of Taiwan

	S/Y (1)	$I/\Delta Y$ (2)	$\Delta L/L$ (3)	$S/Y - I/\Delta Y \times \Delta L/L$ (4)
1954	4.61	1.723	3.66	–1.70
1955	4.81	1.950	3.51	–2.00
1956	4.83	2.240	3.57	–3.20
1957	5.12	2.220	3.47	–2.50
1958	5.74	2.392	3.56	–2.80
1959	6.42	2.322	3.86	–2.60
1960	6.77	2.463	3.90	–2.80
1961	8.60	2.159	3.81	0.40
1962	11.02	1.902	3.68	4.00
1963	12.87	1.932	3.52	6.10
1964	15.08	2.046	3.10	8.70
1965	17.36	2.092	2.92	11.30
1966	18.51	2.482	2.81	11.50
1967	19.68	2.983	3.19	10.20
1968	21.16	2.854	2.95	12.80
1969	23.06	2.561	2.80	15.90
1970	25.65	2.352	2.73	19.20
1971	28.84	2.178	2.56	23.30
1972	30.40	2.876	1.96	24.80
1973	30.24	3.557	1.93	23.40
1974	31.09	3.441	1.83	24.80
1975	31.29	3.666	1.81	24.70
1976	31.56	3.544	1.82	25.10
1977	32.32	3.182	1.86	26.40
1978	33.41	3.116	1.88	27.50
1979	32.91	3.569	1.96	25.90
1980	31.82	3.903	1.89	24.40
1981	30.90	4.082	1.85	23.40
1982	30.48	3.171	1.77	24.90
1983	30.18	2.777	1.60	25.80
1984	31.47	1.841	1.51	28.70
1985	–	–	–	–
1986	–	–	–	–

Note: S/Y, Percentage of national income saved calculated from five-year moving averages of total net savings and the five-year moving averages of national income.

$I/\Delta Y$, Net annual investment/annual increment of real national income, both in five-year moving averages.

$\Delta L/L$, Annual rate of increase of population calculated from five-year moving averages of population numbers.

Source: S.C. Tsiang, 'Success or Failure in Economic Take-off', a paper represented to the Conference on 'The Problem of Development', held in Buffalo, New York, on 27–29 May, 1988, Table 3; and DGBAS, *Taiwan Statistical Data Book, 1987* and various issues.

$$S/Y - I/\Delta Y \times \Delta L/L$$

Since $I = \Delta K$, $I/\Delta Y$ (or $\Delta K/\Delta Y$) is the incremental capital/output ratio. $\Delta L/L$ is the rate of increase of labour supply, which is assumed, for simplicity's sake, to be related to a certain proportion of population. The idea is to make sure that the increasing population would not seriously upset the capital/labour ratio and the savings ratio.

As shown in Table 5.13, on the basis of five years moving average, the savings ratio, S/Y increased from about 5 per cent in the 1950s to over 30 per cent in the mid-1980s; the incremental capital/output ratio, $I/\Delta Y$ was steady and even declining in 1982–4; and the rate of increase in labour supply also declined in the early 1980s. Hence the take-off ratio (column 4) increased steadily from 6.1 in 1963 to 28.7 in 1984. The economy could grow by its own propelling force; it could generate adequate savings to support the growth of domestic investment; furthermore the expanding manufacturing, and servicing activities could absorb the new supply of labour.[23]

Thus Tsiang concludes that Taiwan 'took off' around 1963 (see Table 5.13). Kuo has the similar view, stating that in the analysis of Taiwan economy, 1961–3 is often used as the demarkation period for Taiwan's economic take-off.[24] She said that in addition to the condition of savings rate, 'the monetary reform was successfully achieved by 1961'. As a matter of fact, the monetary reform was only partially achieved, as the monetary and banking system had not yet been well reformed. Fei, Ranis and Kuo with their theory of labour surplus economy, regard the period before 1968 as labour surplus and that after 1968, as labour scarcity.[25] In that sense, the turning-point with regard to labour condition (what they call labour surplus is tantamount to unemployed plus those underemployed) was at around 1968.

On the criterion of financial development, we may consider that the second half of the 1960s should be the starting period of accelerated growth, because:

1. monetary and banking development began to have a favourable effect on the economy after the rehabilitation of the Central Bank in 1961 as shown in Chapters 3–5;
2. the real GNP growth rate went up from an average of 7.6 per cent in 1960–3 to an average of 10.3 per cent in 1964–70;
3. unemployment rate declined sharply from 6.4 per cent in 1964 to 3

per cent in 1970 and 1971 (full employment)[26] as labour was absorbed predominantly into the manufacturing industry, and at the same time labour was released from the agricultural sector or shifted into the industrial sector, on account of the combined increasing productivity of agriculture and industrialisation;
4. international demand for Taiwan products was very favourable because of the Vietnamese War.

The views of the authors quoted are in fact not in conflict, although there are different emphases. It seems safe to say that the commencing period of accelerated growth was in the second half of 1960s.

To sum up, the monetary system of Taiwan evolved from the hyperinflation background in China. This explains the ultra-conservative attitude in monetary policy, currency issue, bank-reserve requirement, foreign-exchange policy and other monetary matters in subsequent periods.

Monetary growth exceeded income growth, in nominal terms as well as in real terms. The monetisation process during the course of economic development and the high savings ratio contribute to the explanation of this phenomenon.

Generally speaking, there was price stability except in the early 1950s, and in 1974 and 1980/81 (see Table 5.2), the lagged effect of the two oil crises.

Income is the most important determinant of the demand for money. Interest rate and expected change in prices play a minor role. The *T*/*GNP* ratio which is associated with the transaction function of money may contribute to the demand function.

Is money an exogenous or endogenous variable in the economic system of Taiwan? In view of the predominant influence of the trade balance on the money supply, we may treat money as an endogenous variable. The scope of conducting an active monetary policy; in the sense that an increase or decrease of money supply by a deliberate action of the Central Bank would lead to an expansion or contraction of income, is rather limited; hence the endogenous nature of money is not manifest.

The foreign sector (or the balance-of-payments effect) is the most important determinant of money supply.

The D_2/C, D_2/R, and D_1/C ratios are presented in Figure 5.1.

Apparently, the growth in high power money explains most of the growth in money supply.

The money multiplier with respect to M_2 shows a rising trend in the 1980's, because of the rapid increase in M_2; the money multiplier with respect to M_{1B}, however, has been stable.

The income velocities of circulation show a declining trend. They do not exhibit cyclical variation as postulated in theory.

The high savings ratio is conducive to economic growth. It has been estimated that the take-off period of Taiwan was around 1963. There is a close correlation between savings ratio and investment ratio.

The liberalisation of the monetary system is a modern trend.

6 Monetary Policy

6.1 OBJECTIVES OF MONETARY POLICY

The most important objective of monetary policy of Taiwan was to reform currency in order to combat inflation as explained in Chapter 5. To achieve price stability and to stabilise the exchange rate (before 1985) were the main concern of the monetary authority.

As Taiwan suffered from hyperinflation in the 1940s and early 1950s, the monetary policy was to restrict money supply and to have a high-interest-rate policy by introducing temporarily the PIR deposits, as mentioned in Chapter 5. The annual growth rate of M_{1B} was as high as 54.6 per cent in 1952 and the average was 34.2 per cent in 1952–8 (see Chapter 5, Table 5.1). The inflation rate (CPI) was very high in 1948–52 (not shown in Table 5.1), and almost 19 per cent in 1953. The average in 1952–8 was 8.3 per cent which was, however, on a much lower level than in the previous period, 1948–52. Inflation was actually subdued from the 1960s until 1974, when it rose again to the high rate of 47.5 per cent as a result of the first oil crisis, and the world-wide rise in prices. Money supply, M_{1B} was increased to 50.4 per cent in 1973 in response to the demand for money, but was slowed down to the growth rate of 10.5 per cent in 1974 and 28.8 per cent in 1975. The second oil crisis, in 1978–9, did not have much effect on consumer prices; the CPI index rose by only 5.8 per cent in 1978, and 9.8 per cent in 1979, whilst M_{1B} was increased by 37.0 per cent and 7.7 per cent in 1978 and 1979 respectively (see Chapter 5, Table 5.1). Consumer prices have become very stable since 1982, (the CPI index remaining at almost 100), mainly because of the appreciating NT dollars, causing a lower import cost and cost of living. Money supply, M_{1B}, had risen fast in 1986 (+ 51 per cent), and in 1987 (+ 12 per cent in January–May), because the Central Bank of China had attempted to slow down the appreciating NT dollars, by purchasing foreign exchange in the market and issuing money.

Before 1985, the Central Bank attempted to stabilise the exchange rate by pegging it to the US dollar, so that it would not depreciate officially in the 1950s–1970s.[1] There was strict exchange control. Since the New Bank Act 1975, the money and discount market has been established, some non-bank financial institutions have been opened up, and some new financial instruments have been introduced.

This brings us to the third objective of monetary policy, i.e. to stimulate economic development and exports. Loans for export enjoy a specially low interest rate. The Central Bank has made various measures to encourage investment in capital equipments, to encourage foreign investment and hence to stimulate economic growth.

Another important objective of monetary policy was to rehabilitate or reorganise the financial institutions. As explained in Chapter 2, many banks had to retreat from China to Taiwan, some banks had to be reorganised from the old structure of Japanese days, and some new banks had to be established to cope with the current situation.

6.2 INSTRUMENTS OF MONETARY POLICY

As Taiwan cannot effectively use either open-market operation or Central Bank discount-rate policy, because the money and capital markets have not yet been fully developed, the instruments of monetary policy include the following:

1. variation of cash–reserve ratio and liquidity ratio;
2. interest-rate policy with regard to deposit rates and lending rates of banks;
3. selective credit control and allocation of export-refinancing facility to banks;
4. persuasion and directive from the Central Bank.

6.2.1 Variation of cash-reserve and liquidity ratios

Within the legal requirements of minimum and maximum ratios, the Central Bank has the authority to set the *actual* cash-reserve requirement for banks.[2]

The Central Bank changes the cash–reserve ratio occasionally, and this serves as both a prudential and a monetary control function. In view of the fact that the money and capital markets have not yet been fully developed and open-market operation has not yet been successfully implemented as a control device, it seems that the required cash–reserve ratio is meant primarily to ensure the safety of the banking system. Currently, since July 1986, the required ratio for cheque accounts is 23 per cent of deposits; for passbook deposits, 21 per cent; for savings deposits, 8–14 per cent; for time deposits, 10 per cent and for foreign-currency certificates of deposits (CD FC), 7 per cent.

Banks are also required to maintain a minimum liquidity ratio, which is currently 7 per cent of deposits. Liquid assets include excess reserves, net due from banks, Treasury bills, net holding of negotiable certificates of deposit, bankers' acceptances, commercial papers guaranteed by banks or bill finance companies, government bonds, corporate bonds, bank debentures and other securities approved by the Central Bank. The liquidity ratio has not often been changed; its variation is much less than that of the cash–reserve ratio.

It is interesting to note the contrast in reserve requirement between Taiwan and Singapore. In Taiwan, the cash–reserve ratio is much higher than that in Singapore, which is only 6 per cent of deposits. But the liquidity ratio in Taiwan is much lower than that in Singapore, which is 18 per cent of eligible liabilities.[3] The contrast is due mainly to the difference in the financial structures. As the financial system in Singapore is much more developed with an international outlook, the emphasis is on the liquid-assets requirement rather than on a cash–reserve requirement.[4] The reverse is the case in Taiwan. Liquid assets can yield some interest to banks, and the supply of sophisticated liquid assets can be enhanced with the development of money and capital markets. The goal of a banking system is to reduce the cash–reserve ratio, to be supplemented by the liquidity ratio, because cash does not yield any return to banks and the high cash ratio would be a drag to the banking system.

6.2.2 Interest-rate policy

The deposit and lending rates of banks should be considered as the cornerstones of the interest-rate structure of the formal financial system. They are regulated by the Central Bank with the advice of The Bankers' Association of Taiwan. The Central Bank fixes the maximum rates on deposits – currently 6.25 per cent for one-year fixed deposit and 3.75 – 6.25 per cent for savings deposit.

The Central Bank fixes the maximum and minimum lending rates for short, medium and long-term loans,[5] and allows specially low interest rates for loans for export. In the current movement towards financial liberalisation, banks are free to quote their own prime rates, ranging from the lowest of 6.25 per cent for Bank of Taiwan and Taipei City Bank and the highest of 7.50–8.75 per cent for some small and medium business banks as at March 1987.

The Central Bank fixes the interest rates for accommodation to banks, which are in effect a refinancing facility. The lowest rate (4.50 per cent) is for rediscounts, and for export financing. The rate for import financing in foreign exchange is 6.75 per cent; that for accommodation against secured loans is 5.50 per cent; that for temporary accommodation is 9.00 per cent; and for accommodation in foreign currency is 7.50 per cent.

Although there is nominally a central bank rediscount rate, unlike the Bank Rate in the UK and the Federal Reserve Rediscount Rate in the USA, it cannot be said to be the leader of the structure of interest rates and cannot serve effectively on a regulation of money and interest. Hence, in effect, it does not serve the function of the so-called central bank discount rate policy of a developed economy, as a regulator of money and credit.

On reviewing the interest-rate structure, one would have the impression that the Central Bank is the great regulator and that market forces play a less significant role in the determination of interest rates. However, it can be said that the Central Bank often follows the market and that there is much interaction between regulations and market forces. Nevertheless, in the banking tradition of Taiwan, regulations are predominant.

6.2.3 Selective credit control

Selective credit control and allocation of export-refinancing facility to banks are exemplified in section 6.2.2 with respect to special support to exports and other activities.

6.2.4 Persuasion and directive

Persuasion and directive from the Central Bank are effective instruments of monetary policy, first, because banks follow faithfully the direction of the Central Bank in the case of Taiwan, and second because most of the important banks are government-owned or controlled.

6.3 EXCHANGE RATE POLICY

6.3.1 Exchange rate, international reserves and money supply

Exchange-rate policy is the external part of monetary policy, affecting directly trade and production. According to David Hume's theory of specie flow mechanism, a higher exchange rate would encourage imports and discourage exports thus bringing the trade balance (and consequently the balance of payments) back to equilibrium. The experience of the NT dollar in recent years shows that in the short run the appreciating exchange rate did not reduce the trade surplus immediately. Whilst the NT dollar appreciated sharply in 1986–8, the trade surplus continued to surge forward unabated.

The increasing exports in 1985–8 had induced high real income growth. The large export surplus and consequent surplus in the balance of payments caused the international reserves of Taiwan to soar from US$18.6bn in June 1985 to US$76.7bn in February 1988. It should be noted that in Taiwan foreign exchange and gold are concentrated in the hands of the Central Bank, whilst commercial banks and the general public hold very little of them. In other countries, such as the USA, Japan, West Germany, the UK, Singapore, Hong Kong and others, commercial banks hold substantial amounts of foreign exchange. Thus, international comparisons should be made in this respect.

The slow-down in the rate of increase of export surplus and in the accumulation of international reserves in the first quarter of 1988 can be interpreted as the lagged effect of NT dollar appreciation. In fact speculative capital inflow because of anticipation of the rising NT dollar has further enhanced the surplus of the balance payments. This would increase bank liquidity, making banks more willing to lend. Money and credit have therefore increased, and interest rate has been lowered.

M_{1B} was increased from NT$683bn in June 1985 to NT$1584bn in February 1988 the growth rate (compound) being 1.027 per cent per month.[6] In the same period M_2 was increased from NT$2356bn to NT$4235bn, the growth rate being 1.018 per cent per month. The growth rate of M_{1B} was slightly greater than that of M_2.

Consumer price index rose from 103.87 in June 1985 to 105.23 in February 1988 (1981=100) – an increase of only 1.36 percentage points in 32 months. In the same period, wholesale price index declined from 96.36 to 87.58 (1981=100), a decline of 8.78 percentage points in 32 months. Thus price increase was very much slower than monetary (M_{1B} and M_2) increase. In particular, in December 1987, M_{1B} was increased by 6.94 per cent or 83.3 per cent per annum! Yet in December CPI was increased by only 1.2 per cent, and the wholesale price index fell by 0.60 per cent.

The trade surplus and the increasing international reserves would logically cause an increase in money supply. The regression equations

Table 6.1 Regression equations relating international reserves to money supply (M_{1B} and M_2)

Dependent Variable	*Estimated Coefficient for Explanatory Variable*				R^2	*DW*	*Method*
	Constant	*IR*	*ΔIR*	*lnΔIR*			
1. M_{1B} (monthly data; January 1985 – February 1988)	645 875.803 (26.68)	15.081 (46.97)			0.984	1.803	Cochrane – Orcutt two-stage method
2. M_2 (monthly data	10 766 338.822 (27.46)	28.584 (21.31)			0.928	1.697	Cochrane – Orcutt two-stage method
3. ΔM_{1B} (quarterly data; 1985, II–1987, IV)	80.044 (0.004)*		15.248 (4.74)		0.714	3.629	Ordinary least square (OLS) method
4. ΔM_2 (quarterly data)	69 237.438 (2.40)		19.765 (4.28)		0. 671	2.601	OLS
5. $\ln\Delta M_{1B}$ (quarterly data)	0.764 (0.33)*			1.215 (4.36)	0.679	3.272	OLS
6. $\ln\Delta M_2$ (Quarterly data)	9.060 (8.79)			0.351 (2.86)	0.476	2.409	OLS

Notes: 1. Figures in parenthesis are *t*-values.
2. For monthly data, $n = 38$; for quarterly data, $n = 11$.
3. * Statistically insignificant at 5 per cent level; however, for the coefficients of the intercepts, the statistical insignificance can be ignored.
4. Roman numerals denote calendar quarters.

Source: Economic Research Department, Central Bank of China, *Financial Statistics Monthly, Taiwan District*, April 1988 and various issues; CBC, *Financial Statistics, Taiwan District* (compiled in accordance with IFS format) April 1988 and various issues.

(Table 6.1) and Figure 6.1 show that the export surplus has been persistently monetised through the increase in international reserves. In Table 6.1 equations (1) and (2) show the very close correlation between M_{1B} and M_2 on the one hand, and international reserves on the other hand, the R^2 being 0.984 and 0.928 respectively. The *t*-values of the coefficient for the explanatory variable are statistically

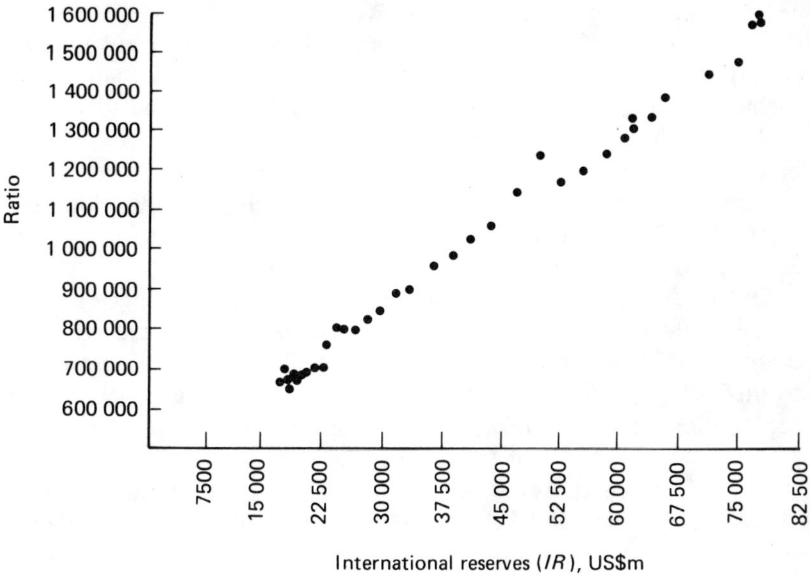

Note: $M_{1B} = 645\ 875.803 + 15.081\ IR$
t-value: (26.68) (46.97)
$R^2 = 0.984$
$D.W. = 1.803$

Figure 6.1 Scattered diagram showing the close relationship between M_{1B} and international reserves, January 1985–February 1988 (monthly data)

significant. The D.W.s are above 1.4 (the minimum standard for number of observation of 38) after the Cochrane–Orcutt two-stage method. Equation (1) shows that an increase of US$1 of international reserves would be associated with an increase of NT$15.1 of M_{1B}; Equation (2) with an increase of NT$28.6 of M_2. As M_2 includes savings funds (time and savings deposits), it is logical that an increase in international reserves would induce a greater increase of M_2 than M_{1B}.

We use quarterly data for the change in M_{1B} and M_2 (i.e. equations for ΔM_{1B} and ΔM_2), because some of the irregular (or negative) monthly changes can be eliminated. All the four equations (3)–(6) have the t-values of the coefficients to be statistically significant, except those for the intercepts of equations (3) and (5), which however can be ignored. Their *D.W.*s are in order, under the ordinary least square (OLS) method. The R^2 for ΔM_{1B} equation and ΔM_2 equation (i.e. equations (3) and (4)) are naturally lower than the R^2 for M_{1B} equation and M_2 equation (i.e. equations (1) and (2)).

With respect to elasticity, equations (5) and (6) show that 1 percentage point increase in international reserves would induce 1.2 percentage points increase in M_{1B} and 0.4 percentage point increase in M_2. The R^2 for equation (6) is lower than those of other equations, as is naturally the case for $\ln\Delta$ equations.

The lending and deposit rates, which are the cornerstones for the interest-rate structure of the banking system, have gone down considerably. The average time-deposit rate of banks has come down from 7.40 per cent in 1985 to 6.25 per cent in early 1988. The secured-loan rate of banks has declined from 9.3 per cent in early 1985 to about 7 per cent (average prime rates of leading banks) in early 1988. Indeed, some banks cannot effectively lend out their deposit fund, and the banking system is so liquid, that some banks have refused to accept large amounts of deposit, in view of the large flow of speculative fund from abroad.

The Central Bank has been trying hard to slow down the appreciation of the NT dollar. In the course of intervention in the foreign-exchange market, the Central Bank has to buy US dollars and to sell NT dollars. Hence new money is issued, consistently increasing the money supply. In order to absorb excess liquidity in the market, the government has to issue large amounts of savings bonds, government securities and Treasury bills.

One important issue is related to the holding of different categories of foreign exchange in the portfolio of international reserves. It was revealed in the Legislative Council in November 1987, that 58 per cent of the international reserves was in cash, of which about 80 per cent was in US dollars, 11 per cent in Deutschsmarks and 8 per cent in Japanese yen. Obviously, the Central Bank suffered heavy loss in holding the depreciating US dollars. It can be suggested that the Central Bank should switch immediately into Japanese yen, Deutschmarks and Swiss francs to some extent as soon as it has acquired US dollars in the overseas markets in the course of intervention. In this way, the portfolio can be gradually diversified into strong currencies. Furthermore, to acquire strong currencies with US dollars would cause these currencies to appreciate, relative to the NT dollar. This would alleviate the undesirable effect of the appreciating NT dollar on Taiwan's exports.

Since questions were raised at the Legislative Council the portfolio of international reserves has been much diversified. In order to support exporters, the Central Bank accepted the future exchange contract for some time in 1986 and 1987. As there was only one-way upward expectation, the Central Bank suffered heavy loss.

6.3.2 Appreciating exchange rate and price change

The huge export surplus and the increase in international reserves have caused money and credit to increase. But in spite of the increase in M_{1B} and M_2, consumer prices and wholesale prices have not yet risen. Consumer prices remain quite stable, whilst the wholesale price index fell steadily from 98 in January 1985 (1981=100) to 87.6 in February 1988. This is because the wholesale prices are much affected by both the import and export prices. The appreciating NT dollar has caused the import prices to be lower. For the sake of maintaining the export-market share, exporters try hard not to increase domestic market-prices. According to the monetary theorists, particularly Milton Friedman, there is a very close correlation between money supply and prices in the long run, which implies that there may be a lagged effect.

The interesting question as to why prices have not gone up yet can be explained in the following manner:

1. the appreciating NT dollar has a deflationary effect, *per se*, on the economy because import prices and cost of living fall as it appreciates;
2. petroleum price is falling and, generally speaking, the world commodity prices have not gone up;
3. the restrictive monetary policy, inclusive of the big issues of savings bonds, and government securities to absorb liquidity, has helped to restrain price increase to some extent;
4. if the money supply is increased persistently, there may be a reburst of inflation after some time. That depends upon the effectiveness of absorbing liquidity in the economy, the world commodity market trend, the saving and investment trend of the people and other factors.

In the 1960s the exchange rate system of Taiwan was under rigid control at the exchange rate of NT$40 per US$. Since 1979, exchange rate has been under managed floating (with strong central bank

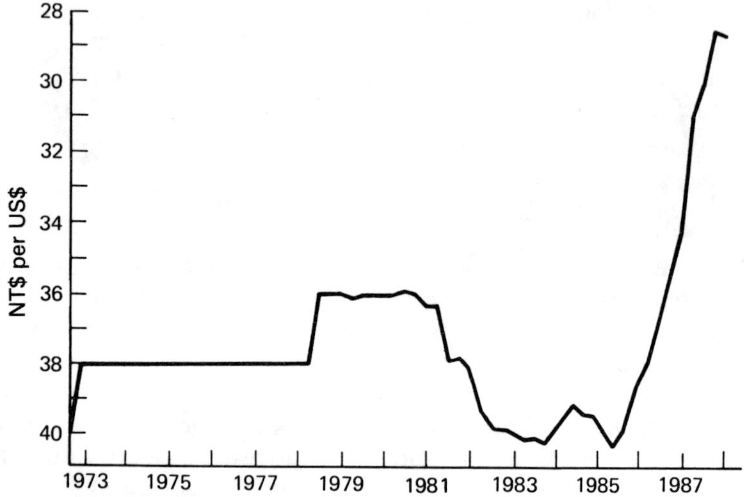

Source: Economic Research. Department, CBC, *Financial Statistics Monthly Taiwan District, ROC*, April 1988.

Figure 6.2 Exchange rate of NT dollars, 1973–88 (first quarter) (quarterly data)

intervention) in line with the policy of financial liberalisation. The exchange rate went up to NT$38 in 1973–8, and then to about NT$36 in 1979–81 (see Figure 6.2). From 1981 to 1986, the exchange rate depreciated to the nadir of NT$40.40 in the third quarter of 1985. Obviously, the NT dollar was much undervalued in this period; consequently, the trade surplus was increased from US1412m in 1981 to US10 621m in 1985, with exports expanding from US22 611m in 1981 to US30 723m in 1985.

A study of the real exchange rate and the price competitive index confirms this view. The real effective exchange rate is defined as the effective exchange rate deflated by the relative price change in foreign and home countries.[7] In 1980 the trade balance was minimum, at US77.5m; and the balance of payments could be said to be close to equilibrium. We take 1980=100, as the base for analysis, and so the effective exchange rate index (EEI) with exports to the major trading partners (the USA, Japan, Canada, Singapore and Hong Kong) is set at 1.000. The EEI shows a decline to 0.949 in the third quarter of 1985 (see Figure 6.3) implying that the NT dollar was undervalued. However, the index turned up to 1.253 in the fourth quarter of 1987 implying that the NT dollar was no longer undervalued or even overvalued.

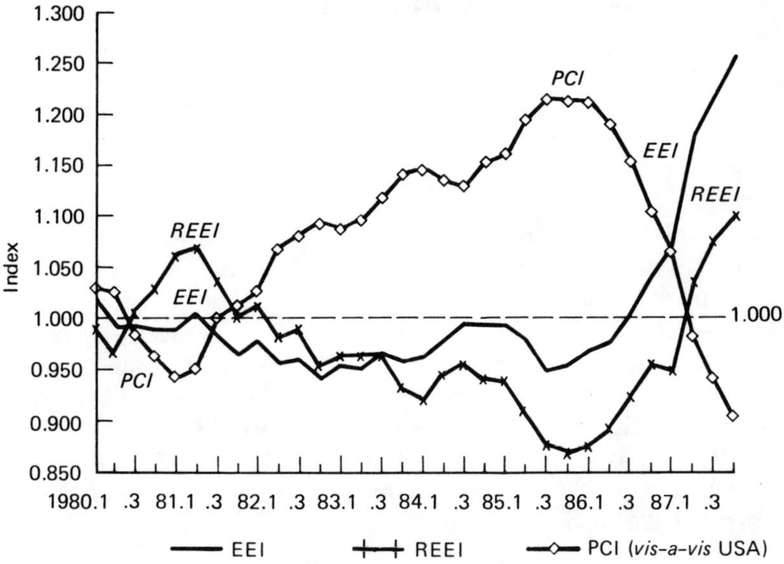

Source: 'The Report on the Courses of the Current Economic Problems and the Appropriate Goverment Policy', no 2, 'The Effect of Exchange Rate Change on Export Trade of Taiwan', Chung-Hua institution for Economic Research, Taipei, no 76, 582.273 dated November 1987 pp. 35–49.

Figure 6.3 Effective exchange rate index, real effective exchange rate index and price competitive index (*vis-à-vis* the USA) of NT dollar

Similarly, if we take 1980 as the basis of the real effective exchange rate index, or REEI in 1980=1.000, we find that the REEI rose in 1981, declined continuously to the nadir of 0.870 in the fourth quarter of 1985,[8] but rose again to 1.102 in the fourth quarter of 1987.

This analysis in real terms shows that the NT dollar was really undervalued at least in the period 1980–5.

Furthermore, the price competitive index, PCI, is used to supplement the analysis. It is defined as the relative price levels of foreign and domestic prices, multiplied by the relative exchange rates of home and foreign countries.[9] The PCI *vis-à-vis* the USA rose from 1.000 in 1980 to 1.213 in the third quarter of 1985 and fell to 0.903 in the fourth quarter of 1987. The loss of price competitiveness on the part of the USA also helps to explain her great trade deficit, and, conversely, the trade surplus of Taiwan.

These indices indicate that the big export surplus in the current period is partly due to the lagged effect of the undervaluation of the NT dollar in the previous period.

The reasons why the appreciation of the NT dollar apparently had no immediate effect on reducing the trade surplus of Taiwan can be ascribed to several factors:

1. as explained above, the PCI increases implying that the increasing price-competitiveness of Taiwan products may partly offset the rising NT dollar;
2. the exchange rates of competitors have risen just as much, or even more such as Japanese yen, Deutschmark, and South Korean won, so that Taiwan's exports to the USA (her major market), Japan, EEC, and other overseas markets would not be priced out;
3. productivity in Taiwan's manufacturing industries has increased in recent years,[10] which partly compensates for the rising NT dollar in order to maintain competitiveness;
4. the exporting firms have to accept a lower profit margin, in order to maintain the market share. As most of the exporting firms in Taiwan are small domestic enterprises, some of the marginal firms have actually gone out of business;
5. the future exchange contracts with the Central Bank may help to alleviate the pressure of the rising exchange rate to the exporters to some extent for some time.

There is in fact a lagged effect of the rising exchange rate on exports. In recent months, export growth has been slower than import growth which is the reverse of the trend in the previous period. It can be anticipated that after some time the effect would be enhanced, and the exchange rate would be stabilised. The crux of the problem is not the exchange rate, but the trade balance, or the balance of payments in the wider perspective. How to correct the trade surplus on the part of Taiwan or, conversely, the trade deficit on the part of the USA is the concern of both countries.

6.4 MAJOR ISSUES OF MONETARY POLICY

Financial liberalisation and internationalisation have been the commonly accepted goal of monetary policy in recent years. The major issue is how fast they should be carried out, so that the monetary system can be effectively reformed without much drawback, and disturbance.

Some economists, notably S. C. Tsiang, advocate that the speed should be fast enough so as to break through the traditional ties, otherwise the old practice may hinder the reform. Specifically, financial liberalisation includes:

1. freeing interest rates from excessive Central Bank regulation;
2. allowing free market forces to react on the exchange rate, instead of merely the Central Bank intervention and control;
3. deregulation of the financial system in a general way so that financial institutions can have more liberty to estimate their own cost and benefit, such as in deciding the deposit rate and lending rate, and in investing their surplus fund at home or abroad. The proposed privatisation of government-owned banks into public companies or the concept of 'government-ownership, but commercial management' can be treated as a sort of deregulation.

Other economists, bankers, and businessmen believe that the speed should not be too fast otherwise drawbacks and abuses may arise because different institutions may not adapt themselves flexibly to the new circumstances on account of the lack of free-market practice in the past and may sometimes speculate against the common good. They believe that financial liberalisation should proceed step by step in a cautious way. If there is any hindrance, it may change its course, or may be slowed-down. Although in the past, both the government and the Central Bank took a rather conservative attitude in avoiding radical changes, they seem to have changed their attitude in the past two or three years.

Liberalisation of the interest rates will be explained in Chapter 7, Section 7.1 below. The issue of government-owned banks is now a hot topic. The offshore banking system has been established. Exchange control is now mainly concerned with the inflow of speculative foreign funds, rather than with the outflow of funds as it was traditionally. In fact, people are encouraged to invest their funds abroad. All these measures indicate that financial liberalisation and internationalisation is proceeding at a high speed.

One important issue of monetary policy is related to the adjustment of exchange rate. It was felt by the USA, the big-trade-deficit country *vis-à-vis* Taiwan, that the NT dollar has been very much undervalued in years since 1981. This problem has been analysed in the previous section.

The current exchange issues are:

1. whether currency adjustment can solve the US trade deficit problem from the standpoint of the USA;
2. whether the NT dollar should appreciate at a fast rate, or at a slower rate from the standpoint of Taiwan.

It is generally agreed among economists throughout the world (i.e. including Taiwan, USA, Japan, and other countries) that depreciation of the US dollar alone cannot solve the problem, unless it is supplemented by increasing productivity of US industries, by reducing the US budget deficit and by various monetary and fiscal measures. Taiwan argues the case further by drawing an analogy with the lowering of tariff rates. When Taiwan lowered the tariff rates recently, the competing countries which benefited most were Japan, West Germany, South Korea, and other EEC countries, but not the USA. By the same reasoning if Taiwan's currency appreciates further, the trade benefit may not come to the USA, because US industries may not gain the market.

Naturally, Taiwan does not like her currency to appreciate, and would not if there were no political and economic pressures from the United States. The crux of the problem of Taiwan is not the appreciation of the exchange rate, but the ways of reducing her large export surplus with the USA in order to appease the USA. The USA threatens to eliminate the Generalised System of Preference (GSP), reduce the textile quota of Taiwan, and take various measures to reduce the imports from Taiwan. One way for Taiwan to do this is to open the door to import more goods from the USA, which Taiwan has in fact been doing. Another way is to diversify the export market, by exporting less to the USA and more to the EEC and other countries. Taiwan has already increased her export share to West Germany and other EEC countries; but similar effort should also be made to increase trade with South-east Asia.

The third way to reduce the export surplus is to encourage outward investment overseas, which can be selective in favour of high-technology industries (such as computer and semiconductor industries) in the USA, Japan, Germany and the UK, and in favour of those industries overseas which can promote trade and economic cooperation with Taiwan. The capital outflow would ease the pressure on the appreciation of exchange rate. Hence the central problem is how to aim at a balance-of-payments equilibrium (or reducing export surplus) in order to adjust the exchange rate.

As a matter of fact, a persistent export surplus is also not favourable to the Taiwan economy, because the increasing international reserves would cause excess liquidity to the financial system and hence inflation in the longer perspective.

When Taiwan lowers tariffs to import more goods, many import-substitution industries would suffer. But, if the exchange rate were to appreciate (which is the alternative policy choice), exporters would suffer, particularly those small industries, which play the predominant role on the export trade of Taiwan. Apparently Taiwan chooses to open the tariff door to encourage imports, rather than to resort to exchange-appreciation. However, circumstances are such that both measures have to be taken simultaneously in the current period.

If currency appreciation is inevitable – given the balance-of-payments position and the pressure from the USA – one related issue is the speed at which the NT dollar should appreciate. Currently, there are two views. One is that the rate of appreciation should be slow, so that industries and exporters can adapt themselves gradually to the circumstances. Many businessmen and bankers hold that view. The other view is that the appreciation rate should be fast enough to avoid people's speculation. In 1985, the Central Bank of Taiwan adjusted the exchange rate upward by only 1 or 2 cents a day. As a result, people speculated with certainty that the exchange rate would go up. A prominent economist, S. C. Tsiang, proposes that the exchange rate should be adjusted upward in one big step to the near-equilibrium position, which people will expect to be stabilised for some time. But, what precisely is the near-equilibrium position? It is a subjective view. The problem is whether an appreciation by big steps would reduce speculation, and hence inflow of hot money or not?

Nevertheless, in 1986 and 1987, the Central Bank adjusted the exchange rate at a faster rate. In particular, the exchange rate was adjusted upward from NT$28.10 per US$ on 5 January 1989 to NT$27.65 on 11 January 1989 – an appreciation of 1.63 per cent within six days.

Part III
Financial Development and Economic Growth

7 Development of the Financial and Real Sectors

7.1 FINANCIAL DEVELOPMENT AND ECONOMIC GROWTH

The Shaw–McKinnon thesis postulates the merit of financial deepening and financial liberalisation in inducing the free play of market forces,[1] so that savings and exports can be encouraged and interest rate and exchange rate can reflect the true market condition. Economic growth can then proceed without so many restrictions and controls, which would otherwise distort the functioning of financial institutions and markets, suppress market signals of capital and labour, and encourage the biased development of capital-intensive industries, inconsistent with factor endowment and comparative advantage. Thus there is a strong link between financial development and economic growth.

Following that thesis, financial development can be measured in terms of financial deepening and financial liberalisation. Indicators of financial deepening (Table 7.1) show that its progress in Taiwan has been very impressive. We select the years 1952, 1961, 1975 and 1987, because 1952 marked the beginning of the published statistics in Taiwan;[2] in 1961 the Central Bank of China resumed full operation in Taiwan; in 1975, the New Bank Act was passed and 1987 was close to the current period. The M_{1B}/GNP ratio (or the Marshallian k, or the inverse of income velocity) rose continuously from 5.93 per cent in 1952 to 50.74 per cent in 1987, with the compound rate of change of 6.33 per cent. This implies that people hold more and more cash balance M_{1B} relative to GNP for transaction purpose.

The M_{1B}/GNP ratio shows the greatest increase from 9.43 per cent in 1952 to 135.08 per cent in 1987, with the compound rate of change of 7.90 per cent. With high income growth, particularly in the 1970s and 1980s, more savings were accumulated and diverted into the banking system as deposits.

If we take regard of the increase in population and the price increase, the per capita, real balances M_{1B} and M_2 exhibit also high

Table 7.1 Indicators of financial deepening, 1952–87 (end of year)

					Compound Rate of Change, % per annum			
	1952	*1961*	*1975*	*1987*	*1952–61*	*1961–75*	*1975–87*	*1952–87*
1. M_{1B}/GNP, %	5.93	11.06	22.58	50.74	7.17	5.23	6.98	6.33
2. M_2/GNP, %	9.43	24.02	56.40	135.08	10.95	6.29	7.55	7.90
3. Per capita, real balance, M_{1B} w.r.t. CPI	962	2 796	14 328	75 752	12.59	12.38	14.89	13.29
4. Per capita, real balance, M_{1B} w.r.t. GNP deflator	–	–	13 923	72 031	–	–	14.68	–
5. Per capita, real balance, M_2 w.r.t. CPI	1 531	6 071	35 782	202 461	16.54	13.51	15.54	14.98
6. Per capita, real balance, M_2 w.r.t. GNP deflator	–	–	34 770	191 766	–	–	15.29	–
7. Banking density (number of banking offices per 10 000 persons)	–	–	0.29	0.46	–	–	3.92	–
8. FI density (number of financial institution offices per 10 000 persons)	–	–	1.52	1.61	–	–	0.48	–

9. Ratio of bank assets to GDP, %	–	31.93	74.05	123.48	–	6.19	4.35	5.34 (1961–87)
10. Ratio of assets of financial institutions to GDP, %	–	37.52	96.65	184.29	–	6.99	5.53	6.31 (1961–87)
11. Relative share of financial sector in GDP, %[1]	0.99	1.73	2.82	2.92	6.40	3.55	0.29	3.14
12. Relative share of financial sector in employed labour's force, %[2]	–	0.14	1.59	2.85	–	18.95	4.98	12.29 (1961–87)

Notes: [1] See Table 7.2.
[2] See Table 7.3.

Source: Central Bank of China, R.O.C. Economic Research Department, *Financial Statistics Monthly*, June 1988; Council for Economic Planning and Development, R.O.C., *Taiwan Statistical Data Book*, 1987; DGBAS, *Quarterly National Economic Trends, Taiwan Area R.O.C.*, May 1988.

growth rates, parallel to the growth of nominal money balances. The per capita, real balance M_{1B}, on the assumption of constant (1981) CPI, rose from NT$962m in 1952 to NT$75 752m in 1987, with the growth rate of 13.29 per cent. As expected, the growth rate for the period, 1975–87, after the passing of the New Bank Act 1975, was the most marked, being 14.89 per cent. The per capita, real balance, M_2 on the assumption of constant (1981) consumer prices rose from NT$1531m in 1952 to NT$202 461m in 1987, with a growth rate of 14.98 per cent.

Similarly, if we use the GNP deflator as an adjustment of the per capita, real balances, the result would be similar as shown in Table 7.1.

Banking density in terms of number of banking offices per 10 000 persons was increased from 0.29 in 1975 to 0.46 in 1987, with the rate of change of 3.92 per cent. The broader definition of financial institution density, in terms of number of FI offices (including trust and investment companies, credit cooperatives, credit departments of Farmers' Associations and Fishery Associations, and Postal Savings Banks) increased marginally from 1.52 in 1975 to 1.61 in 1987.

The ratio of bank assets to GDP was increased from 31.93 per cent in 1961 to 123.48 per cent in 1987, with the annual rate of change of 5.34 per cent. The ratio of the assets of financial institutions to GDP was increased from 37.52 per cent in 1961 to 184.29 per cent in 1987, with the annual rate of change of 6.31 per cent.

The contribution of finance, insurance and real estate to GDP in terms of value added was increased from 1 per cent in 1952 to 2.92 per cent in 1987, with the annual rate of change of 3.14 per cent (see Tables 7.1 and 7.2). The value-added of that sector was increased from NT$133m in 1951 to NT$88 003m, with a growth rate of 19.77 per cent per annum (Table 7.2).

To take a broad category in economic structure, we would note clearly in Table 7.2 that:

1. the service sector had remained steady at about 44 per cent of GDP, in the course of industrialisation or economic transformation;
2. the industrial sector rose from about 24 per cent of GDP in 1951 to about 52 per cent in 1987,
3. conversely the agricultural sector declined from 23 per cent to 5 per cent in that long period.[3]

	1951	1961	1975	1987	Annual Growth Rates, % 1951–61	1961–75	1975–87	1951–87
1. Agriculture, hunting, forestry and fishing	3 980 (23.47)	19 225 (27.59)	74 875 (12.81)	158 814 (5.27)	17.06	10.20	6.47	10.78
2. Industry	2 925 (23.86)	20 546 (29.49)	268 058 (45.86)	1 566 956 (51.99)	21.52	20.14	15.85	19.07
2.1 Mining and quarrying	173 (1.41)	1 416 (2.03)	7 266 (1.24)	15 229 (0.51)	23.40	12.39	6.36	13.24
2.2 Manufacturing	2 122 (17.31)	15 158 (21.75)	214 314 (36.67)	1 310 506 (43.48)	21.73	20.83	16.29	19.54
2.3 Electricity, gas, water and sanitary services	147 (1.20)	1 269 (1.82)	15 446 (2.64)	115 772 (3.84)	24.06	19.54	18.28	20.35
2.4 Construction	483 (3.94)	2 703 (3.88)	31 032 (5.31)	125 449 (4.16)	18.79	19.05	12.35	16.70
3. Services	5 447 (44.43)	30 919 (44.37)	254 152 (43.48)	1 338 950 (44.43)	18.96	16.24	14.85	16.52
3.1 Wholesale and retail trade	1 775 (14.48)	11 510 (16.52)	78 668 (13.46)	429 063 (14.24)	20.56	14.72	15.18	16.47
3.2 Transport, storage and communication	528 (4.31)	3 719 (5.34)	35 363 (6.05)	180 851 (6.00)	21.56	17.45	14.57	17.60
3.3 Finance, insurance and real estate*	133 (1.08)	1 202 (1.73)	16 471 (2.82)	88 003 (2.92)	24.62	20.56	14.99	19.77
3.4 Housing	1 018 (8.30)	4 526 (6.50)	34 369 (5.88)	166 908 (5.54)	16.09	15.58	14.08	15.22
3.5 Government services	1 269 (10.35)	7 546 (10.83)	57 741 (9.88)	268 662 (8.91)	19.52	15.65	13.67	16.04
3.6 Other services	724 (5.91)	2 416 (3.47)	31 540 (5.40)	205 463 (6.82)	12.81	20.14	16.90	16.99
Less: Imputed bank service charge	93 (0.76)	1 013 (1.45)	12 591 (2.15)	50 851 (1.69)	26.97	19.72	12.34	19.14
Gross domestic product (GDP)	12 259 (100)	69 677 (100)	584 494 (100)	3 013 869 (100)	18.98	16.41	14.65	16.52

Note: * The share (in terms of value added) of real estate in that group is very small, e.g. in 1975 and 1986 it was only 2 per cent and 6.75 per cent respectively.
Figures in parenthesis are percentages.

Source: DGBAS, *Quarterly National Economic Trends, Taiwan Area*, May 1988, pp. 38–9.

The number of employed persons in financing, insurance, real estate and business services increased from 4000 in 1961 to 229 000 in 1987 (see Table 7.3) or from 0.14 per cent of total employed labour force in 1961 to 2.85 per cent in 1987. The growth rate in terms of number of employed persons was thus 16.84 per cent per annum from 1961 to 1987.

Likewise, as a reflection of the industrialisation, employment in the agricultural sector declined, whilst that in the industrial sector and in the service sector (to a lesser extent) rose (Table 7.3).

The progress of financial deepening is very impressive. The growth rates in the early period, 1952–61 appeared to be high, because of the initial stage at a low level. If we consider the period of modern banking, 1975–1986, the progress has been well maintained.

In terms of the aforesaid indicators, or in quantitative terms, the financial development seems to be parallel to economic growth. But with respect to organisation or management, there is much room for improvement. First, the payment system is inefficient, because people are not encouraged to use cheque accounts,[4] as there are so many returned cheques. Instead, payment is usually made through the Postal Remittance and Savings System, whereby a person receiving a postal order has to go to the nearest postal bank to receive the money, or a person has to go to the postal bank to instruct payment to the payee. Much time is lost to individuals with small accounts and ultimately to the community as a whole.

Another defect of the banking system is that it is a common practice to use a seal, instead of signature, to open an account, to draw money, to lend or to borrow money. This poses not only a great risk of forgery, but also a possibility that the person who has entrusted the seal to another person, may not know his liability in lending or borrowing money. For example, in the Tenth Credit Corporation Case the culprit, Chua, used the seals of many employees of his enterprise to make money transactions. This abuse is well-known in the market, but banks interviewed explain that their staff is used to examining the truthfulness of a seal, but not that of a handwritten signature. That is not really a correct explanation. Given time, the staff can be trained to examine signature. It is only the lack of inertia to change.

The bureaucracy of government-owned banks on account of strict regulations is a drag on the banking system. Moreover, political interference in bank management has caused inefficiency in government banks.[5]

Table 7.3 Number of employed persons by industry in Taiwan, 1961–87 (average of the year)

	1961	1975	1987	Growth rates, % 1961–75	1975–87	1961–87
1. Agriculture, hunting, forestry and fishing	1 640 (56.69)	1 681 (30.45)	1 226 (15.28)	0.18	– 2.60	– 1.11
2. Industry	472 (16.32)	1 927 (34.90)	3 430 (42.76)	10.57	4.92	7.93
2.1 Mining and quarrying	54 (1.87)	62 (1.12)	31 (0.39)	0.99	– 5.61	– 2.11
2.2 Manufacturing	347 (11.99)	1 518 (27.50)	2 810 (35.03)	11.12	5.27	8.38
2.3 Electricity, gas and water	6 (0.21)	23 (0.42)	35 (0.44)	10.07	3.56	7.02
2.4 Construction	65 (2.25)	325 (5.89)	554 (6.91)	12.18	4.54	8.59
3. Services	781 (27.00)	1 913 (34.65)	3 367 (41.97)	6.61	4.82	5.78
3.1 Commerce	312 (10.78)	775 (14.04)	1 435 (17.89)	6.72	5.27	6.04
3.2 Transport, storage and communication	89 (3.08)	314 (5.69)	429 (5.35)	9.42	2.63	6.24
3.3 Financing, insurance, real estate and business services[1]	4 (0.14)	88 (1.59)	229 (2.85)	24.71	8.30	16.84
3.4 Public administration, social and personal services	376 (13.00)	736 (13.33)	1 275 (15.89)	4.91	4.69	4.81
Total employed labour force	2 893 (100)	5 521 (100)	8 022 (100)	4.72	3.16	4.00

Notes: 1. Business services constitute quite a big proportion of employed persons in the finance group.
Figures in parenthesis are percentages.

Source: DGBAS, *Yearbook of Manpower Statistics, Taiwan Area*, published in June 1988, pp. 36–8 and previous issues.

Government banks have to turn over their profit or surplus to the Treasury of the Ministry of Finance every year. They are not in a position to plough back the profit into reserves for future expansion. Hence, they cannot expand effectively. In contrast, as an example the International Commercial Bank of China, having been turned into a private bank in 1971, has enjoyed a much faster rate of progress than the government banks.

All these points indicate that the financial system needs radical reform. The financial system, along with the reduction of import tariff and the other relaxations of control, has been very much liberalised with respect to the exchange rate and interest rate.

If we study carefully the economic structure and compare the growth of various sectors (Tables 7.2 and 7.3) we will find that the share of the financial sector (denoted by the group of finance, insurance and real estate) in GDP is rather small (2.9 per cent in 1987), whilst the share of manufacturing is large (43.5 per cent in 1987). This is because of the nature of the economy and of the fact that Taiwan is not yet well developed in international banking business. As an international comparison, in South Korea in 1985 'finance, insurance, real estate and business services' contributed 11.5 per cent to GDP, and manufacturing contributed 30.74 per cent (Table 7.4). In sharp contrast, 'financial and business services' constituted 23.2 per cent of GDP in Singapore in 1986, whilst manufacturing constituted only 27.2 per cent. (Table 7.5). Perhaps Singapore is an extreme case, as it is an international port, as well as a financial centre in South-east Asia.

However, the growth rate of the financial sector in Taiwan appeared to be very similar to that of manufacturing – about 20 per cent in 1951–87, and 15–16 per cent in the period, 1975–87 (see Table 7.2).

With respect to the employment of labour force, the financial sector took only 2.9 per cent of labour force in 1987 whilst the manufacturing sector took 35.0 per cent and the commercial sector, took 17.9 per cent (see Table 7.3). Apparently, the finance sector requires skilled personnel. The growth rate of the financial sector was greater than that of the manufacturing sector and that of the commercial sector in all periods.

7.2 LAND REFORM AND INDUSTRIALISATION

The model for economic growth in Taiwan can be simplified as shown in Figure 7.1.

Table 7.4 Contribution to GDP by various industry sectors in S. Korea (at constant 1980 prices: billion won)

	1980	*1985*
1. Agriculture, hunting forestry and fishing	5 524.7 (14.57)	7 890.2 (14.28)
2. Industry:		
Mining and quarrying	520.0 (1.37)	792.9 (0.15)
Manufacturing	11 214.3 (29.58)	16 805.0 (30.74)
Electricity, gas and water	786.2 (2.07)	1 697.6 (3.10)
Construction	3 149.8 (8.31)	4 749.2 (8.69)
3. Services:		
Wholesale and retail trade, restaurants and hotels	4 967.5 (13.10)	7 107.4 (13.00)
Transport, storage and communication	2 915.4 (7.69)	4 170.2 (7.63)
Finance, insurance, real estate and business services	4 171.7 (11.00)	6 313.0 (11.55)
Community, social and personal services	1 192.5 (3.15)	1 700.4 (3.11)
Producers of government services	2 823.6 (7.45)	3 167.0 (5.79)
Producers of private non-profit services to households	705.3 (1.86)	1 010.5 (1.85)
Less imputed bank service charge	1 191.4 (3.14)	2 199.7 (4.02)
Gross domestic product (GDP)	37 914.9 (100.00)	54 674.4 (100.00)

Source: National Bureau of Statistics, Economic Planning Board, R.O.K., *Korea Statistical Yearbook, 1986*; Economic Planning Board, R.O.K., *Monthly Statistics of Korea*, Second quarter of 1986.

The land reform, 1949–53 laid the foundation of industrialisation in the subsequent periods, 1960s–1980s.[6] Land was equitably distributed. It was carried out in three stages:

1. Rent reduction programme, 1949. Previously rent was as high as 50–70 per cent of the total annual yield of the main crop. It was then reduced to 37.5 per cent. Instead of oral agreement between landlords and tenants, which enabled the landlords to evict tenants easily with a short notice, all the lease contracts had to be in written form and the tenure should not be less than six years and was also renewable.

Table 7.5 Gross domestic product by industry in Singapore (at current factor cost, S$ million)

	1960	*1970*	*1980*	*1984*	*1985*	*1986*
1. Agriculture and fishing	74.90	133.30	314.50	335.50	295.30	250.00
	(3.73)	(2.51)	(1.35)	(0.92)	(0.84)	(0.71)
2. Industries:	363.10	1601.70	9292.60	14909.00	13554.30	13438.30
	(18.29)	(30.11)	(39.93)	(40.79)	(38.49)	(38.20)
Quarrying	6.10	19.60	80.30	125.30	104.90	80.10
	(0.31)	(0.37)	(0.35)	(0.34)	(0.30)	(0.23)
Manufacturing	235.60	1047.90	7088.40	9362.90	8683.20	9558.00
	(11.87)	(19.70)	(30.46)	(25.62)	(24.66)	(27.17)
Utilities	49.70	148.10	529.00	730.47	750.80	800.70
	(2.50)	(2.78)	(2.27)	(2.00)	(2.13)	(2.28)
Construction	71.70	386.10	1594.90	4690.10	4015.40	2999.50
	(3.61)	(7.26)	(6.85)	(12.83)	(11.40)	(8.53)
3. Services:	1580.40	3695.10	15075.70	24134.60	24563.90	24821.30
	(79.61)	(69.46)	(64.78)	(66.03)	(69.75)	(70.55)
Commerce	712.50	1608.30	5532.40	7091.80	6752.40	6706.20
	(35.89)	(30.23)	(23.77)	(19.40)	(19.17)	(19.06)
Transport and communications	282.80	595.00	3415.00	5102.00	5134.80	5530.60
	(14.24)	(11.18)	(14.67)	(13.96)	(14.58)	(15.72)
Financial and business services	224.50	757.40	3855.30	7796.20	8134.60	8143.10
	(11.31)	(14.24)	(16.57)	(21.33)	(23.10)	(23.15)
Other services	360.60	734.40	2273.00	4144.60	4542.10	4441.40
	(18.16)	(13.80)	(9.77)	(11.34)	(12.90)	(12.62)
Less imputed bank service charge	33.10	110.20	1410.90	2827.40	3196.50	3329.10
	(1.67)	(2.07)	(6.06)	(7.74)	(9.08)	(9.46)
GDP	1985.30	5319.90	23271.9	36551.7	35217.0	35180.5
	(100.00)	(100.00)	(100.00)	(100.00)	(100.00)	(100.00)

Source: Ministry of Trade and Industry, Singapore, *Economic Survey of Singapore* 1986, p. 88.

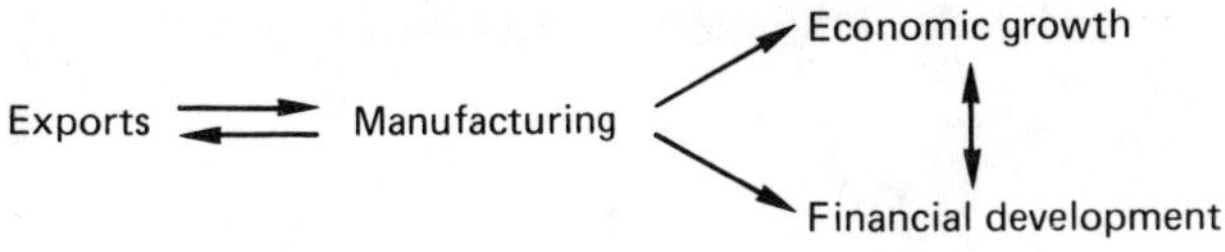

Figure 7.1 Exports, manufacturing, economic growth and financial development

2. Sale of public farmland, 1948–53. As a heritage from Japanese rule, about 25 per cent of farm land was owned by the government. The Taiwan Provincial Government sold the public farmland to farmers, preferably to the present tenant cultivators, and farmhands. The sale price was equivalent to 2.5 times the total annual yield of the main crop. The purchasers had to pay by equal instalments in ten years with payment of interest. From 1948 to 1953, about 63 000 hectares of public farmland were sold to 121 953 farming families.[7]
3. Land-to-the-tiller programme 1953. In order to carry out further this programme in accordance with the Principles of Dr Sun Yat Sen, the Government acquired farmland from landlords on the following guidelines:

   (a) The land price was equivalent to 2.5 times the annual total yield of the main crop of that land.
   (b) Landlords were compensated with 70 per cent of the purchase price in land-bonds (or commodity bonds) to be redeemed in kind, the balance of 30 per cent was paid with stocks of public enterprises.
   (c) A landlords was allowed to retain 3 hectares of paddy field or 6 hectares of dry land. All land in excess of this had to be compulsorily sold to the government for resale to existing tenant-farmers, who paid off in twenty equal semi-annual instalments in 10 years. The programme was completed in the same year, 1953. In this programme, 143 568 hectares of privately tenanted farmland were purchased from 106 049 landlords by the government and were resold to 194 823 farm families.

As a consequence of the land reform, and also for the sake of financing the government purchase of land from the landlords, four big public enterprises (namely, paper, cement, mining and agro-industries) were converted into private enterprises in 1955.

The success of the land reform was due to many political, and economic factors:

1. There was no problem of 'vested interest' in this reform, unlike the condition in China which had thwarted the effort for many years before the war. When the National Government reoccupied Taiwan, the officials who executed the reform programme came mainly from China with the government and were not landlords, whilst the landlords were local Taiwanese.[8] Hence the officials were faithful in carrying out the land reform.
2. The support of the Farmers' Association, which had been well organised to communicate with the government, and to support all measures of the Reform.[9]
3. The strategy of acquiring land from the landlords, by means of taxation measures in the first instance. A few years before the land reform, taxation on land was increased heavily, particularly for absentee landlords. At the same time, the public enterprises, which were virtually government monopolies, made good profit. So when the government offered those shares to the landlords in exchange for their land, the offer was accepted without much resistance because after all the return to land was then rather small.

The favourable effect of the land reform on economic development was tremendous, which can be summarised as shown in Figure 7.2 and as follows:

1. Farmers' incentive to work and to invest in the land was very much enhanced. Efficiency and productivity on farming was increased at a high rate, so that supply of food and raw materials was boosted to support industrial development. Furthermore, the rising income in the rural area, had provided a good market for industrial goods.

2. Because of the increasing agricultural productivity, surplus labour was released from the farms and diverted to industries helping the industrialisation programme.

There is a remarkable phenomenon of rural industrialisation in Taiwan and industries and farming are intermixed throughout the island. It is a favourable phenomenon that industries are spread throughout the island, even in the countryside,[10] instead of concen-

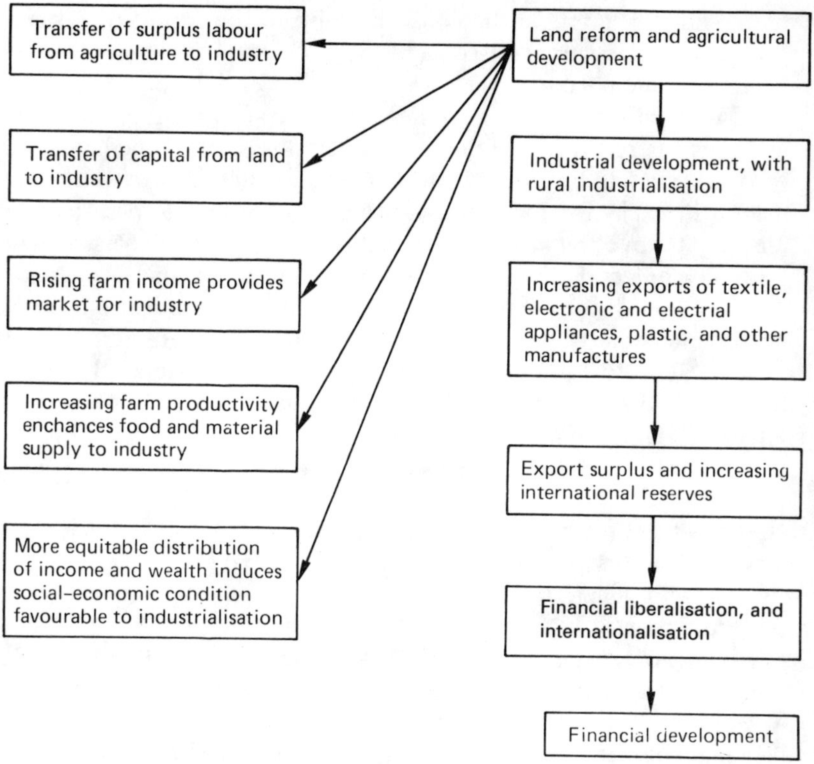

Figure 7.2 Effect of land reform on economic development

trating in a few big cities (such as Manila, Bangkok and Jakarta) as in other countries. The industrial spread helps the farming community as well as the industries, because farmers or farm labourers can get odd jobs in near-by factories and their farming income can therefore be supplemented by side-income from industries. The industries benefit, because they can draw labour supply from the nearby countryside and are less restricted to the location than in big cities. The reasons for this spread are manifold, including the fast and convenient transportation system, the historical development of industries, and the economic advantage of developing heavy industries in Kaohsiung, the big international port in the south, and light industries throughout the island.

3. The increasing agricultural productivity contributed not only to

the feeding of people in the cities, but also to the export of agricultural products. Sugar and rice were the major export commodities in the 1950s, when Taiwan was short of foreign exchange.

4. The land reform had also the effect of transferring capital from land to industry.[11] Prior to the reform, landlords sat on the land, and were only keen to buy more land. Since they sold their excess holding of land in exchange for industrial shares, they began to turn their attention to investment in industries. Some of them sold the shares of the public enterprises later, and reinvested in other manufactures.

5. The land reform contributed to the more equal distribution of income and wealth, because farmers' income has been increasing.[12] Prior to the reform in 1949, only 39 per cent of farmers tilled their own land, 36 per cent were full-tenants and 25 per cent were part-tenants.[13] After the reform the ratios were 78, 12 and 10 respectively in 1971, and 82, 6 and 12 respectively in 1985.

Agricultural reform and industrialisation are like the two legs of a person. The first step forward was in fact taken by agricultural reform, although industrialisation seems to gain the limelight in modern time.

It is of no exaggeration to say that agriculture together with US Economic Aid financed the industrialisation in the early phase. The US Aid helped to combat inflation and to finance the serious foreign-exchange gap. It amounted to US$1444m over the critical period of 1951–65, or US$10 per capita per annum. The US Aid imports constituted about 30 per cent of total imports in 1951–61.[14] The model of development is shown in Figure 7.1. All the favourable factors of land reform such as transferring labour and capital to industry, rising rural income to provide market for industry, increasing farm productivity to enhance food and material supply to industry and more equitable distribution of income and wealth are in fact the classical theory of the relationship between agriculture and industry.[15] In the case of Taiwan, one particularly good phenomenon is what is called rural industrialisation, or the spread of industries to the rural area. This would solve a lot of social-economic problems, such as the avoidance of concentration of population in big cities, enhancing farmers' income with odd jobs in industries, factory workers helping with work on a farm during the harvest season, etc.

In the 1950s and early 1960s, as Taiwan was still an agricultural economy, the main production was rice and sugar. Rice was important for home-consumption as well as for export. The agricultural reform was crucial in that period, because Taiwan was short of supply in many commodities and there was a high rate of inflation in 1949–53. The increase in productivity of rice helped to stabilise cost of living to a large extent, and to curb inflation.

The export of rice and sugar constituted over 90 per cent of total exports. There was a big trade deficit,[16] and a big foreign-exchange gap, according to the theory of developing economy.

7.3 IMPORT-SUBSTITUTION AND EXPORT-ORIENTATED STRATEGY

It has been a common mistaken belief, among many economists, that Taiwan had adopted a solely export-oriented strategy since the 1960s. But in fact she has had an import-substitution policy since 1949 and has never abandoned that policy. At the same time, she has adopted many effective measures for encouraging exports such as low interest-rate for export loans (monetary measures); import-duty remission for exports,[17] business income tax and stamp-duty remissions for export sale, (fiscal measures);[18] the establishment of three Export Processing Zones at Nantze, Kaohsiung and Taichung, and other facilities.

What is called the export-orientation policy of Taiwan is historically and inherently based on the import substitution policy. Let us discuss this in historical perspective. For the sake of conserving scarce foreign exchange, the primary function of industrialisation was to develop infant industries, to substitute for imports. Thus light consumer-goods industries, such as textiles, shoes, sugar, cement, fertiliser, plywood, paper, glass, etc. which were labour-intensive, were started first. In this first 'Import-Substitution Period', in the 1950s, the main features of government policy include (a) a protective tariff system, (b) import restrictions in quota and various ways, (c) multiple exchange rates and allocation of foreign exchange for imports. This period also saw the land reform, agricultural development and the privatisation of four big government enterprises.

In the second 'Import-Substitution Period' in the 1960s, the emphasis was turned to intermediate goods requiring more skill and capital and producing a higher value-added. The emerging industries include the petrochemical industry, plastics industry, artificial and integrated fibre industry, electronic and electrical industry, iron and steel industry, motor vehicle assembly, and shipbuilding and repairing industry.

When those industries had been established and the domestic market had become saturated, entrepreneurs had to find export markets as an outlet for their products. Meanwhile, the government embarked on an export-orientation policy in various ways. Thus this period coincided with the export-expansion episode in the 1960s–80s. The strong export industries, such as textile, plastics, electronic and electrical, and chemical industries were originally set up with the aim of import-substitution.

The evidence of import protection is shown in Table 7.6. The nominal tariff rate declined from 56 per cent in 1974 to 39 per cent in 1979 and to 13 per cent in 1988. As it is an average unweighted tariff rates for various import items, it is not very appropriate to regard it as the general level of tariff rate, nor to have an international comparison.

The ratio of tariff revenue to import value declined from 14 per cent in 1971 to 12 per cent in 1979 and to 5 per cent in 1988. This ratio should also be interpreted in great care. If the import duty is high, imports can be effectively reduced, and therefore the tariff revenue would be reduced.

Nevertheless, the two ratios have declined, particularly in 1987 and 1988 under strong pressure from the USA. With regard to the degree of protection of the import-substitution industries, it was found that the aforesaid emerging industries had high effective tariff rates in 1964–79.[19] Some of these industries have become strong export industries, such as textiles, plastics, electronic and electrical goods and the petro-chemical industries.

Import-substitution and export-orientation policies have in fact been simultaneously pursued since the 1960s, although it can be said that greater and greater incentives have been provided for encouraging exports. As the infant industries have grown up in strength, the emphasis was shifted from import-substitution to export-orientation. An estimate of the export incentives was made by Liang Kuo-Shu and Liang Hou Ching-Ing, by way of interest subsidy, and various tax concessions from 1956 to 1978. The height of export subsidy occurred in 1971, when there was a subsidy of NT$5.71 for every US dollar of exports. Thereafter the subsidy declined to NT$2.49 in 1978, and is expected to be lower still in the current period of 1989 with large export surplus.[20]

Since 1955, numerous measures have been taken to encourage exports. The Regulations for Rebate of Taxes on Export Products 1955, and the Statute for the Encouragement of Investment 1960 (see

Table 7.6 Nominal tariff rate and the ratio of tariff revenue to imports, 1971–88 (shown as percentages)

Year	*Nominal tariff rate*[1]	*Ratio of tariff revenue to imports CIF*
1971	–	14.14
1972	–	12.12
1973	–	12.64
1974	55.65	11.74
1975	52.69	9.88
1976	49.13	11.42
1977	46.17	10.41
1978	43.58	11.27
1979	39.14	11.62
1980	31.17	9.00
1981	31.17	7.46
1982	31.04	7.61
1983	31.04	7.60
1984	30.81	7.72
1985	26.46	7.89
1986	22.83	7.67
1987	19.37	7.25
1988	12.60	5.00*

Notes: [1] Estimated by taking the average unweighted tariff rates of various items
* estimated (possibly 4.6–6.0)
Source: *Annual Custom Report of China*, ROC

notes 17 and 18) played the key role in fiscal measures for tax concession. Under the latter statute, a new approved industrial establishment was given a five-year holiday from the starting date of operation, and exemption from import duties on machinery and equipment. The China External Trade Development Council was founded in July 1970 to promote exports and to do market research. A levy of 0.0625 per cent was raised on exporters' revenue as United Funds for Promotion and Extension of Exports.[21]

The Programme for Improvement of Foreign Exchange and Trade Control in 1958 which aimed at reducing the strict control on foreign exchange allocation was also a promotion of exports, as the simplified and low exchange rate was favourable to the export trade. Three Export Processing Zones were established in 1966, and so was the Hsin-Chu Science-Based Industrial Park in September 1980. The

Foreigners' Investment Ordinance and the Overseas Chinese Investment Ordinance were enacted in May 1980. Investment and trade go together.[22] Indeed, in the later phase of industrialisation, export promotion and development strategy, (now aiming at high technology) are interwoven.

Monetary measures included low interest-rates for export loans, and favourable Central Bank allocation of credit for exports, as discussed above.

If we take a historical review of the whole world, we find that most of the countries were industrialised through import-substitution strategy, notably Germany in the nineteenth century, Japan right through the Tokugawa Period and Meiji Period until recently, the USA, Canada, and Australia in the nineteenth and early twentieth century. The only exceptions may be Hong Kong, and Singapore where the home markets are so small that it would not be feasible to adopt the protection policy. The reason for adopting the import-substitution policy is mainly based on the infant industry argument. In the early phase of industrialisation, it would be very difficult for new industries in developing countries to compete with international giants, and therefore protection for the home market is necessary. It would be easier to start with light consumer manufactures, because they require less capital and skill. Later on, as the country acquires more technical skill, she can manufacture more sophisticated goods. This is typically the case of Taiwan.

The common argument in favour of export-oriented policy as expounded in current literature is that (a) the export market is world-wide and big, whilst the home market is small and limited, and (b) open competition in the overseas market strengthens efficiency and productivity of industries.[23] Empirical studies in many countries show that export-orientation countries have progressed much faster than those with high tariff wall and trade protection, e.g. Hong Kong, Singapore, Taiwan, Korea, Israel, Sweden, and Switzerland versus Latin America, Central America, and some Asian countries. This may be true, but those advocators of export policy seem to overlook the following salient facts:

1. The export market is much more difficult to penetrate than the home market, mainly because export business is subject to the tariff and non-tariff barriers of the importing countries. The risk is much greater than that in the home market, which can enjoy all

sorts of protection and subsidy from the home government. This argument would carry more weight in the early stage of development.

2. All the export economies started industries for import-substitution. When their industries have been established on the basis of the home market, they can then expand their production by exporting.
3. Apart from historical development, an analysis of a cross-section of the current state shows that most of the industrial countries also have big home markets as their basis, e.g. the USA, Canada, and the Soviet Union. Even Japan, depending so much upon exports, also has a large home market of 122 million people.

The interesting question is why some countries can shift from import-substitution to export-orientation, and why other countries cannot do so, and their industries become weakened by sheltering behind the tariff wall. Generally speaking, the factors for the shift can be enumerated as follows:

1. qualities of the people such as a capacity for hard work, thrift, and a high level of education;
2. political and economic stability;
3. free, enterprising spirit of the people, so that they are prepared to venture into new fields;
4. favourable international demand for their export products;
5. appropriate government policies, including particularly monetary and fiscal policies, which are to harmonise with the free, enterprising spirit of individuals.

Taiwan is unusually well-placed in these respects. The people's spirit of free enterprise is further enhanced by the fact that when the Nationalist Government retreated from China to Taiwan in 1948–9, and international politics was adverse to Taiwan, people in Taiwan felt rather insecure and thought that they must work very hard in order to survive. This fighting spirit urged people forward to overcome difficulties. This also explains why in Taiwan there were as many as 70 000 small manufacturing and exporting firms; why economic growth is characterised by small enterprises,[24] and why small firms contributed the major part of exports.

The high export growth of Taiwan is also the result of favourable international demand condition, particularly the demand from the USA. In 1985 about 48 per cent of Taiwan's exports went to the USA, 11.3 per cent to Japan, 2.6 per cent to West Germany, and 2.1 per cent to the UK. The major part of her exports go to developed countries, rather than to developing countries. Her main exports consist of (a) textile and textile related products, (b) electronic and electrical machinery and apparatus, (c) plastics articles, and (d) machinery and metal manufactures. The favourable international demand condition is the consequence of many factors, including mainly (i) the rising wages of the developed countries, (ii) the declining labour productivity of some US industries; (iii) the changing industrial structures of some developed countries, thus importing light manufactures (such as textile, garment and shoes) from Taiwan,[25] and (iv) the undervaluation of the Taiwan currency in 1980–6.

The appropriateness of monetary policy has been discussed in this chapter. The finance of manufactures and exports was supplemented by the informal money market. The relationship between manufacturing and export growth can be depicted in Figure 7.2 as shown in Section 7.2. Manufacturing production and exports react on each other to promote economic growth, and financial development. Economic and financial growth progress side by side, and reinforce each other.

The whole growth model can then be conceptualised in Figure 7.3. As Taiwan was originally an agricultural economy, we take agricultural development as the basis and so it is presented at the base line in the model. Land reform or agricultural development started to accelerate the growth movement. As industrialisation is under way, industrial development progresses faster than agricultural development and financial development. Financial development lags behind industrial development because of the rigidity and inward-looking of the financial system. Liberalisation and internationalisation would help to accelerate financial growth. It is hoped that in future financial development will be parallel to industrial development.

7.4 MANUFACTURING AND EXPORT GROWTH

In the export-led economy of Taiwan, manufacturing growth and export growth go hand-in-hand as has been shown in Figure 7.1. The progress of industrialisation can be gauged in terms of the composi-

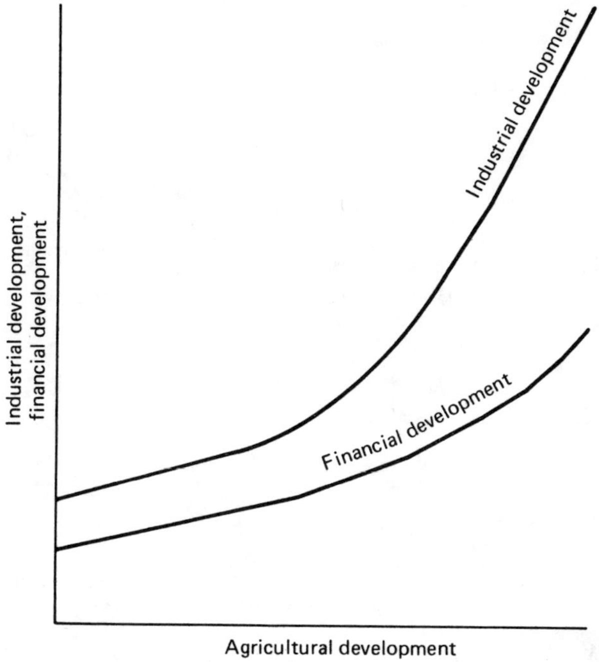

Figure 7.3 The relationship between agricultural, industrial and financial development

tion of exports. In 1952, agricultural products (mainly rice) constituted 22.1 per cent of total exports; processed agricultural products (mainly sugar) 69.8 per cent; and industrial products, only 8.1 per cent. By 1965, the corresponding percentages were changed to 23.6 per cent, 30.4 per cent and 46.0 per cent respectively. Industrial products constituted about half of exports in the first half of the 1960s, which can be considered as the turning-point in the changing structure of the economy. Since the second half of the 1960s, the percentage of industrial products has been increasing very rapidly, so much so that in 1987, those corresponding percentages stood at 1.2 per cent, 4.9 per cent and 93.9 per cent respectively.

The composition of industrial products has also undergone some changes. In the early stages of industrialisation, Taiwan exported only textiles, garments, shoes and other light manufactures. In the 1970s and 1980s, she exported more and more electronic and electrical machinery and apparatus, plastic articles and machinery and metal

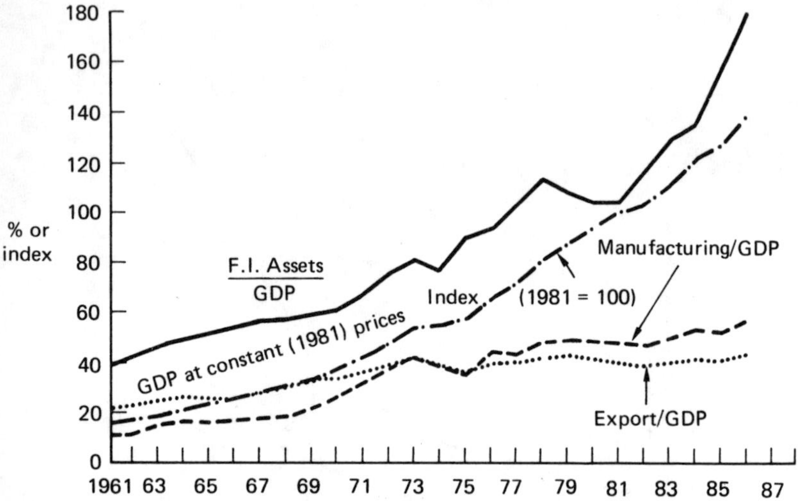

Source: *Taiwan Statistical Data Book*, 1986.

Figure 7.4 Real GDP index and ratios of exports, manufacturing and assets of financial institutions to GDP

manufactures. In particular, Taiwan's exports of computers and parts, electronic and other sophisticated products are now world-known.

In the early stages, Taiwan competed with developing countries, in the developed countries (e.g. in USA, Japan and EEC). Later on, she also competed with developed countries in skill-intensive products.

Undoubtedly the role of finance in manufacturing and in exports is crucial. Nevertheless, one should not gain the impression from Figure 7.4 that financial development is faster than manufacturing and export growth, because after 1975, as more financial institutions and markets were set up, and more financial instruments were introduced, the ratio of financial assets to GDP was increased at a fast rate, and yet there remain many shortcomings in the finance sector, which are discussed in Chapter 8.

The agricultural reform contributed to the earnings of foreign exchange and to the reduction of the exchange gap.

When industrialisation had got under way after 1965, exports of textile, shoes, and other sundry goods began to replace rice, sugar and other food products. Later, manufacturing exports had become more sophisticated; more and more electronic and electrical goods, microcomputers, plastic goods and other skill-intensive manufactures were being exported.

Thus export deficit has turned into export surplus since 1971, and the export surplus had increased to US$19.0bn in 1987 (almost 20 per cent of GNP). The international reserves rose to US$76.7bn in December 1987, but declined to US$70.3bn in June 1988.

Under such favourable conditions, financial liberalisation and internationalisation have been accelerated, which will further enhance financial development.

In reviewing the historical development, one comes to the general conclusion that the first step was actually taken at the agricultural reform, which started the chain of favourable progress. The idea can be captured in Figure 7.3, showing that (a) agricultural development preceded and supported industrial development in the early phase; (b) industrial development was accelerated after 1965, and (c) financial development lags behind industrial development. Perhaps, after the current phase of financial liberalisation and internationalisation, financial development may be expected to speed up.

8 Liberalisation and Reform of the Financial System

8.1 LIBERALISATION OF INTEREST RATE

The liberalisation of interest rate had gone through several legislations, as follows:

1. The First Amendment of the Bank Act, Article 33, on 1 September 1947, stated that the maximum interest rates for deposits and lending of banks have to be determined jointly by the associations of banks and financial institutions and the Central Bank. (Bank of Taiwan was then the acting authority.)
2. On 19 December 1947, the 'Regulations for the Control of Interest Rate' were promulgated, which stated that the deposit rate of banks should not exceed the lending rate, and which authorised the Central Bank to determine the maximum lending rate.
3. An Amendment to the Bank Act in 1971 stated that the Central Bank had the power to determine the maximum interest rates for various types of deposits, and that the range (maximum and minimum) of lending rate should be proposed by the Association of Banks and approved by the Central Bank.
4. The New Bank Act, Article 41, promulgated on 4 July 1975, restated the aforesaid Amendment.
5. On 7 November 1980, the Central Bank announced 'the Major points of Consideration of Interest Rates of Banks', which stated that (i) the Association of Banks could, in consideration of the money-market condition, propose to the Central Bank a range of deposit rates, although the maximum deposit rate was still determined by the Central Bank; and (ii) the Association of Banks could propose to the Central Bank a range of lending rates for the latter's approval; the range was to be widened to allow flexibility in operation. Moreover, interest rates in the money market and NCDs (Negotiable Certificate of Deposits) are not subject to the limitation of the maximum deposit rate.
6. On 1 March 1985, ten leading banks, including the Bank of

> Taiwan, Taipei City Bank, China International Commercial Bank, announced their prime rates, which are the basic lending rates, and which are determined by banks individually according to their own position and market condition. This so-called 'basic lending-rate system' was followed by other banks in September 1987.

Thus, as from March 1985, the lending rate has been completely free, although the maximum deposit rate is still controlled by the Central Bank. Subject to market forces, there is much flexibility in the interest rate system of banks. Besides, with the establishment of the three bill finance companies in 1976–8 and the development of the money market, business enterprises can conveniently obtain finance from the money market and very often the interest rate in the money market is below the lending rate of banks and other financial institution. With the abolition of exchange control, the financial system of Taiwan has become much more internationalised. All the former comments on the rigidity of the financial system have disappeared.

Shirley W. Y. Kuo, the Minister of Finance, has shown that the liberalisation of interest rate was in fact actively pursued in two stages – the first stage in 1980–1, with the announcement of 'the Major Points of Consideration of Interest Rates of Banks', and the second in November 1984.[1] The first stage cannot claim much success because within a given range of lending rates, banks tend to lend at the upper limit. The second stage was also to widen the range of lending rates. With the increasing liquidity of the banking system, the lending rate fell gradually so that the difference between the actual lending rate and the upper limit of the lending rate set by the Central Bank was considerably widened. This has culminated in the establishment of the basic lending-rate system, which is determined by market forces.

The New Bank Act 1989 was passed, which liberalised further the financial system. Banks' ceiling and floor limits on deposit and lending rates, in accordance with the Central Bank Act 1975, have been abolished. Instead, both local and foreign banks are allowed to set their own deposit and lending rates freely according to their funding cost.

The Act also allows establishment of private banking institutions and permits foreign banks to open savings account, take longer-term loans and do trust business.

Thus the market-oriented financial system is expected to inspire competition and efficiency in the system.

8.2 LIBERALISATION OF FOREIGN EXCHANGE

It would be useful to review the historical development of the exchange rate system. In the 1950s when Taiwan was very short of foreign exchange, the NT dollar was pegged to the US dollar at an unrealistically high exchange rate. In 1953, the exchange rate was about NT$14 to US$1. The Foreign Exchange Certificate System was then introduced, whereby exporters who gained the foreign exchange could sell the foreign exchange certificate to importers at free market rate. Taiwan adopted a complicated multiple-exchange-rate system, with different exchange rates for different types of imports (essential and non-essential goods) and with requirement for exporters to surrender certain portions of foreign-exchange proceeds to the authorities at official rates. There were a black market and all sorts of abuses.

The Programme for Improvement of Foreign Exchange and Trade Control was promulgated in April 1958. The overvalued currency was devalued and the multiple-exchange-rate structure was replaced by a dual-rate structure, i.e. the basic official exchange rate and the exchange certificate rate. Export proceeds and inward remittances were granted the exchange certificates, which were transferable and represented full import rights. Market demand and supply determined the exchange-certificate rate, which was stabilised at NT$40 per US$1 by August 1958.

The basic official exchange rate and the exchange-certificate rate were finally merged at that level in June 1961, giving rise to a single unitary-exchange rate, which not only simplified the administration of exchange control but also assured exporters of a sound economic calculation.

Since 1961, the NT dollar was in fact pegged to the US dollar around the level of 40. The Central Bank administers the exchange rate tightly under its control. Because of the huge export surplus, market forces have been exerting an upward pressure on the exchange rate in 1985–8, and the exchange rate has been floating, under the management of the Central Bank. Indeed, management of the exchange rate is associated with that of money supply.

On 15 July 1987, exchange control on current account of the balance of payments (such as transactions for goods and services) was completely abolished; exchange control on capital account is limited only to large transactions of over US$5m. People are free to invest in foreign securities and to remit money abroad, if the amounts do not exceed US$5m in one year. Nevertheless, remittance of money into Taiwan is still subject to control, and may not exceed US$50 000 for fear of the inflow of 'hot money'. The control over inward remittance is ironically opposite to the control over outward remittance, as in the past forty years.

In terms of the order of liberalisation, it is a correct policy to liberalise the current account of the balance of payments before the capital account. In fact, the latter is the most difficult task as it can only be undertaken when the economy has been stabilised and progressing.

8.3 ORDER AND SPEED OF LIBERALISATION

Liberalisation of the financial system has to go along with the liberalisation of the real sector, including trade and investment; and the order of liberalisation has to be studied carefully. It seems that the equilibrium (or close to equilibrium) balance of payments, budget balance, and price stability are the important preconditions for the liberalisation of the financial system, including notably the interest rate and foreign exchange. Reduction of tariff and non-tariff barriers is usually taken as one of the first steps towards liberalisation. Relaxation of exchange control over the capital account of the balance of payments is regarded as the final step, as experienced in many countries, such as Singapore, Japan and the USA. Thus the order and speed of liberalisation would be important determinants of success or failure.

Liberalisation of the regulations with respect to the opening of new domestic banks, security houses, branches of foreign banks, and the latter's scope of lending and accepting deposits has been discussed in various sections. With the establishment of new security houses since May 1988, the stock market of Taiwan has been booming to a dangerous extent!

8.4 A CONSIDERATION OF THE REFORM OF FINANCIAL INSTITUTIONS

8.4.1 Banks

One of the current major issues is how to reform the government-owned banks in order to increase their efficiency. If it is not feasible to maintain the present form of ownership and management, what steps should be taken to convert government-owned banks into private enterprises?

It has been recognised that privatisation of government banks may help to inspire a spirit of free enterprise and hence efficiency into the banking system, as we learn that privatisation of four public enterprises in 1955 had helped to promote industrialisation. However, it is also argued, particularly by some government officials, that so far, some of the private banks in Taiwan have not generally performed well, e.g. the trouble of the Overseas Chinese Bank.[2] Likewise, the trust and investment companies with private capital organisation and free enterprise had great trouble with the fundamental weakness of being linked to certain families. There is the worry that privatisation of government-owned banks may not be able to achieve its desired goal.

Current thinking in government circles is along the following lines. First, new laws and regulations should be promulgated for the administration of government banks, so that they can enjoy independence or liberty in management without the restraint of political factors. Their boards of directors should have full power in exercising control over the banks, and should take full responsibility. The directors and supervisors should have special knowledge of banking and finance and a certain portion of directors should be those persons who have been promoted from experienced bank executives.[3] Banks should be independent in appointing or dismissing officers, and should not have to follow the rules of the civil service. The system of rotation of appointment of the chairman of the board of directors, general manager and deputy general manager has to be considered carefully and needs to be changed.[4] Under the current system their tenure of appointment is limited to three years, but can be extended, if necessary, to another three years. As the tenure is rather short, leading figures of the banks cannot adopt a long-term policy. The lack of continuity of policy can cause a bank to become less efficient. All these new ideas of change have been discussed in meetings of the Executive Yuan, Economic Reform Committee and reported in the Research Report of the Finance Division, vol. III, November 1985, pp. 7–22.

Second, many economists and government officials tend to believe in the principle of 'government ownership, and private enterprise management'. As the shares of those banks are owned by central, provincial or municipal government, they are related to the legislative councils of the three levels of people's representatives. If the shares are to be sold on the stock exchange to the general public, such a resolution may meet opposition from the legislative councils, because that would be equivalent to requesting those people's representatives to abandon their existing right to control the banks. Thus a practical and feasible way is to maintain government holding of the shares, but to free the management from all sorts of government regulations. In other words, the bank would be run as a commercial bank in the private sector, and would be controlled by an independent board of directors, although the shares are owned by the government. Once the government has appointed the board of directors, it would not interfere in the running operation of the bank. However, if the bank did not perform well, the government would be able to reorganise the board of directors.

Another possibility which could be considered is to convert government-owned banks into public companies, and to sell a part of the shares to the general public, with the government retaining a controlling share. This would follow the Singapore example, i.e. the Development Bank of Singapore.

In this way, the bank could operate as a free enterprise, with the government retaining control by appointing the Chairman of the board, and a few directors. It has been argued that this would be a practical way, because, for example, Chang Hwa Commercial Bank already has private ownership of 43.75 per cent of its shares; Hua Nam Commercial Bank, 41.86 per cent; and First Commercial Bank, 25.50 per cent. If the government sold out only a small portion of each bank to the general public, the bank could be converted into a private one, i.e. one with more than half its shares in the hands of the general public.

In the officially declared policy of financial liberalisation and privatisation, this proposal appears to be appealing to the authority. Whether the government banks would eventually follow the principle of 'government ownership, and private enterprise management' or would be converted into private banks by the government selling off some shares will be seen in future.

Another related issue is how to strengthen the private banks, so that they can operate efficiently in the free market without causing crisis. A common weakness of private banks in Asia is that the organisation is on a family basis. The management is closely held by family members. Lending is mainly to their own related business, which often speculates in the property market or the share market. If the related businesses collapses, that can cause a shock to, or even the downfall of, those banks. Such cases have happened in Thailand, Hong Kong, Singapore, Philippines and other countries.[5] In Taiwan too, some private commercial banks (e.g. Overseas Chinese Commercial Bank, see Chapter 2, Table 2.1) also have strong family links. In order to prevent such pitfalls, the Economic Reform Committee proposes to amend the Bank Act so that one shareholder or his family cannot hold more than a certain percentage of the shares of the bank. However, in practice, there are some ways to by-pass the law and it is rather difficult to distinguish between 'a family' and a group of related persons.

The government is not inclined to issue new licences for private banks, on the ground that some of them have not performed well and have had some trouble in recent years.

Is it likely that there may be joint ventures between local and foreign financial institutions in commercial banking? To date, such ventures have not developed. But in view of the openness of the economy and the changing attitude towards internationalisation, such a possibility should not be ruled out. In manufacturing, there are many joint ventures between local and foreign enterprises (e.g. the car-assembly industry). A joint venture in commercial banking may help to introduce new management techniques and overseas connections which would enhance efficiency and internationalisation in the banking industry.

As the banking system has been, by tradition, rather rigid and inward-looking, bank officers are naturally not well-trained in foreign exchange, and other international business. Computerisation of the banking system has to be carried out more effectively, according to the comments of Japanese and American bankers. Training of bank officers in international business and in new management technique is fundamental for the reform of the banking system.

8.4.2 Investment and Trust Companies

Perhaps the weakest spots in the financial system are the investment and trust companies which had had a lot of trouble in recent years, mainly from speculative activity, linked to family business. The government has been trying hard to discourage family organisation, but in vain. Seven out of eight trust and investment companies are controlled by certain families.[6] Probably the only exception is the China United Trust and Investment Corporation, which after some reorganisation, has become truly a joint stock company, not controlled by one family. The Central Investment Company, which is the investment arm of Kuomingtang, has some shares in it.

The Economic Reform Committee proposed to amend the existing 'Regulations Governing Management of Investment and Trust Companies' (see Article 101 of the Bank Act).[7] Among various amendments the Committee proposed that directors and supervisors of investment and trust companies should not be allowed to have a vested interest in their own family business. Other proposed amendments included limiting clean overdraft (i.e. without collateral), and permitted lending to service industries, as well as the present practice of lending only to productive industries.

The government's original intention in establishing the eight investment and trust companies was to let them provide long-term credit to business, but to discourage them from providing short-term commercial credit, because the latter can be well served by commercial banks. In other words, the investment and trust companies are intended to play a complementary role in the credit structure, instead of competing with banks. Thus they are not allowed to accept demand deposits.

Prior to August 1983, they were allowed to accept only fixed deposits of over six months; since then, they have been allowed to accept trust funds for fixed periods of six months or less and also trust funds for unspecified periods. They are supposed to lend with a maturity period of over one year; in practice, they usually lend for 13 months.

When the China Development Corporation was set up in 1959, it was hoped that it would provide venture capital for business, grant long-term loans, and do corporate finance business, like a merchant bank. Unfortunately those objectives were not fulfilled.

Basically, the monetary authorities were not prepared to issue more licences for banks, but wanted to see more investment and trust companies to provide long-term credit to business. Hence seven companies were established in 1971–2. Unfortunately, they were more interested in short-term credit business and property market business than in providing long-term loans. They did very little corporate finance or fee-based business. As they cannot accept demand deposit, their charge for funds is higher than that of the banks; they have to lend to marginal borrowers, taking more risk. Since the collapse of the stock market in 1980–1, most of the investment and trust companies have been in difficulty. The decline of domestic interest rates in 1986 and 1987 and the low interest rate in the money market have added difficulty to the companies with respect to collecting deposits.

The investment and trust companies are like the finance companies in Singapore, Malaysia and South-east Asia in the sense that they finance housing loans and hire purchase of motor vehicles and other consumer durables. But the missing link in the financial structure is the lack of merchant banks, which deal in corporate finance, underwriting of new shares, merging and takeover of companies and other fee-based activities, as in the UK, Germany, Hong Kong, Singapore and other countries. Taiwan may consider strengthening the China Development Corporation in that direction, and also establishing a few merchant banks. There are about 70 000 small and medium business firms in Taiwan. They need to issue new capital or to borrow on long term in the capital market. Merchant banks can play a great role in this respect for stimulating further economic growth.

8.4.3 Credit Cooperatives

The credit cooperatives – notably the Tenth Credit Co-operative in 1985 – have had several crises in recent years. As a matter of fact the Credit Cooperative Act has been promulgated for more than forty years; some of the regulations are not appropriate to present conditions and need to be amended.[8]

It has been suggested that there should be an independent Credit Cooperative Act so that there is a clear distinction of responsibility and control by the Ministry of Finance, and the provincial and municipal governments. Deposits should be effectively collected from the local regions for financing trade and investment in the region. The merit of credit cooperatives, and also of the credit departments of Farmers' and Fishery Associations are that the management is close to the local people and knows the borrowers well enough. The principle of credit cooperatives is 'one member, one vote', and they are therefore very democratic organisations. Unfortunately, in the past, some families with local influence happened to control the credit cooperatives – this again falls victim to the family linkage. Public opinion should be aroused and the Credit Cooperative Act should be amended in order to eradicate this pitfall.

The credit departments of the Farmers' and Fishery Associations have performed a useful function of grass-root finance. The Farmers' Association was well-established in the time of the Japanese Occupation. The provision of rural credit through the Farmers' Association can be said to be much more effective than other agricultural countries in South-east Asia, such as Malaysia, Indonesia, Philippines and Thailand.

8.4.4 Insurance Companies

Insurance companies are not well-developed in Taiwan. In order to promote greater efficiency, the government is considering granting a few licences to foreign insurance companies. Thus the insurance business would be open to international competition.

The concept of having a more efficient system of payment by more popular use of cheques, instead of going through the Post Savings System has been discussed. To do away with the practice of using seals on cheques and on documents for lending and borrowing, instead of using personal signature should be considered as a step towards the reform of the financial system as already explained.

8.5 A CONSIDERATION OF STRENGTHENING THE CAPITAL MARKET

The stock market of Taiwan is rather volatile and many researchers have commented that it is more speculative than other stock markets. One reason is that it is a small market, relative to the stock markets in New York, London and Tokyo, and is therefore more easily cornered by some big groups of speculators. Another reason is that in recent years, the Taiwan economy has been in a very liquid state, with excess cash balance, consequent upon the huge export surplus and with the inflow of foreign funds in anticipation of the appreciation of the NT dollars. A third reason is that some officers or administrators in the Stock Exchange of Taiwan are also engaged in self-investment or speculation in shares, causing abuses and 'insider trading'.

The stock price index soared up from 2341 (1966=100) on 5 January 1988 to 8790 on 24 September 1988, an increase of 3.75 times within nine months![9] On 25 September, in view of the abnormally rising price, the Ministry of Finance announced the resumption of the capital gain tax on shares, which was within the integrated-income-tax schedule. That tax had been introduced in 1974 but was suspended in 1976, because the government wanted to encourage people to invest in shares. The announcement of the resumption of that tax sparked off the fall of the stock market – a fall of 33 per cent within twenty-two working days to its nadir of 5881 on 26 October 1988, with insignificant transactions.

As a result, there were demonstrations by investors protesting against the government, and the government had to concede to some extent by allowing a wider tax-exemption margin – from NT$3m to NT$10m – and a reduction of the tax on share contract from 0.3 per cent to 0.15 per cent of the transaction amount.

It can be argued that the sharp fall in the stock market was inevitable in view of the overvaluation of stock prices. The announcement of the resumption of capital-gain tax on shares served only as a sparking point.

In order to strengthen the capital market, so that savings can effectively flow into the productive channel, the regulations of the Stock Exchange of Taiwan must be amended and faithfully enforced; the aforesaid abuses, 'insider trading', and other shortcomings should be eliminated.

Furthermore, Taiwan needs to develop more financial instruments, or to introduce new ones, so that investors can have more channels to place their savings. The recent attempt to privatise some public enterprises, thereby issuing new shares in the market is a step in that direction. Since the recent liberalisation of securities companies, the number of securities companies has grown to about sixty-two.

9 Summary and Conclusions

The hard-working spirit and thriftiness of the people in Taiwan are the key human factors in successfully exploiting the favourable geographical position of Taiwan. The high savings ratio and the emphasis on education, technical training, and research play an important role of her 'economic take-off'.

Taiwan's model of development is characterised with respect to growth with equity and with price stability. The struggle for survival resulting from their difficult political and international circumstances strengthened the strong determination of the people. This in turn nurtured a good supply of entrepreneurs, which have been a factor of growth.

Within about thirty-eight years, Taiwan has been transformed from an agricultural economy to an industrial one. Monetary and fiscal policies and various government measures play a crucial role in this transformation. Structural change in financial institutions, and gradual financial liberalisation and deepening have contributed to economic growth. The future trend of growth would be towards high-technology industries, service, banking and financial sectors. In this perspective, the monetary and financial development should be reviewed along with economic growth.

With the transformation, there has been a change from international isolation in 1950–71, to international recognition, as the world has been amazed at Taiwan's miracle of growth.

The breakthrough was from economic success of high growth to international recognition of excellent performance. In international politics, many countries are trying to have more economic, social and cultural communication with Taiwan. Indeed, Taiwan has regained considerably her international status.

In reviewing the development, one should note two forces at work – government control *versus* market forces. There has been a shift from rigid control to liberalisation, e.g. in interest rate, foreign-exchange rate, and the privatisation of public enterprises and more recently of government-owned banks. In other words, Taiwan is relying more and more on market forces, instead of on rigid control as in the past. This shift from rigidity to flexibility should enhance efficiency in the systems, and promote a better allocation of resources.

Another vital change is that Taiwan has been shifting from inward-looking development strategy to an outward-looking one. This applies to both the real sector and the financial one. Import tariff and non-tariff barriers have been progressively reduced. The restrictive regulations on foreign banks have been continuously reduced, more foreign banks have been admitted, and the offshore banking system has been in operation since 1984. All these are consequences of the policy of internationalisation and liberalisation.

Currently, there is a determined attempt to shift the industrial structure from labour-intensive industries such as textiles, garments and sundry goods to capital- and skill-intensive industries such as electronics, computer, semiconductor and engineering industries.

There is also an attempt to reduce pollution, even though this may retard industrial growth. The Environment Protection Bureau has been set up. There is a plan to build four incinerators for the city of Taipei. Other measures are being taken to combat pollution in the air, rivers and the land. Banks are being encouraged to lend more funds to high-technology industries and to help to finance the installation of anti-pollution devices.

There is a trade-off between high growth and pollution control, because any device for reducing pollution means additional cost to industry and agriculture. In the past, the high growth rate of the manufacturing industry was in fact achieved at the expense of the quality of life of the people. Now, as the people and government are increasingly aware of the hazards of pollution, it can be expected that the growth rate of Taiwan will be reduced to some extent by having to deal with the pollution problem.

The future growth prospect depends much upon political stability. The death of the late President Chiang Ching Kuo in January 1988 ended the period of 'strong leadership' politics. The new era ushers in 'democracy' politics, or collective leadership. For the sake of fostering democracy, or respect to the general will of the people, new measures have been introduced, such as the abolishment of the Martial Law, the amendment of the Security Act, the New Labour Law, allowing trade unions to be organised and acknowledging that workers have the right to strike, if necessary, etc.

Consequently, there may be stronger labour demand, culminating in more strikes, official and unofficial, in the coming years. The enforced industrial peace under martial law for many years had contributed much to the speculator growth, but may now face a challenge; labour unrest may hinder economic development.

Those measures which allow more liberty for the people and workers are certainly a big step forward towards democracy. The worry is their backfire on the economic scene. Whether we should take an optimistic view with respect to the former, or a pessimistic view with respect to the latter depends upon political, social and economic factors. Only time can answer those complicated questions with conflicting forces at work.

It is not the objective of this book to analyse the problems of development. Our emphasis is on money, banking and finance.

The banking structure in Taiwan consists of three groups of banks:

1. those which moved from Mainland China to Taiwan;
2. those which were a legacy of the Japanese Occupation;
3. new rising banks after the War.

The rehabilitation of the Central Bank of China in 1961 and the Bank Act 1975 opened a new epoch of modern banking, with the rapid development of the money and capital markets and the establishment of the off-shore banking units.

The domestic banks are dominated by the government-owned banks. The characteristic features of domestic banks, foreign banks, medium and small business banks are analysed with respect to their assets and liabilities, and their growth rates of deposits, loans and aggregate assets. Because of the difficult political and economic circumstances, and its long tradition, the banking system was inward-looking and rather rigid in the 1950s and 1960s. More foreign banks were admitted in the late 1970s and 1980s in order to promote efficiency and competition in the banking business, thus inducing internationalisation of banking. In the amended Bank Act 1989 the restriction on foreign banks was much reduced, with respect to savings deposits, long-term loans, security business, credit-card business and others. Foreign banks are now allowed to open one branch in Kaohsiung.

Investment and trust companies and credit cooperatives should be considered as the weakest spot in the financial system, with several crises in the recent years. There is a need to establish some merchant banks to help the issue of new capital and to do corporate finance.

The 'grass-root' financial institutions – that is, the credit cooperatives, credit departments of the Farmers' and Fishery Associations – play a role in collecting deposits and in lending to small business enterprises in different regions. The finance of agriculture or the provision of rural credit can be said to be much more effective than in many other developing countries. The offshore banking system, which was started in 1984, is growing at a fast rate, although it is still rather inward-looking.

The insurance companies are not yet well developed partly because Asian people have not developed the habit of taking out life insurance policies. The insurance business has been rather protected. Recently along with the government policy of internationalisation and liberalisation, the insurance business has been (and is still being) gradually opened to international companies. American companies, in particular, are interested in entering the Taiwan market.

The informal money market denotes the unsatisfied demand for funds and the underdevelopment of the banking and financial system. Yet it has a role to play in financing small enterprises, although at a higher interest rate. As the financial system is progressively developed, and as the interest rate is low in the current period, the informal money market is gradually losing its importance as shown in Chapter 3, Tables 3.4, and 3.5.

Deposits have grown much faster than loans in recent years signifying that the banking system is in rather a liquid state, because of the big inflow of foreign funds, consequent upon the export surplus. This may also be considered as a reflection of low investment incentive, as the demand for loans for the sake of investment is not up to expectation.

The fast-growing deposit, lending and other banking statistics signify a growing economy, but with much financial instability in view of the crises of some trust and investment companies and a private bank. There was evidently a shift from an inward-looking and rigid banking system to a more outward-looking and flexible one; a shift from banking protectionism to a more competitive and open banking system; a change towards privatisation of government-owned banks; and a change in the portfolio of banks, which now hold more government securities and money-market instruments, in consequence of the development of money and capital markets.

The currency reform was promulgated in June 1949, with the issue of New Taiwan currency. Reserve requirement of deposit money banks is categorised into different types of deposits – cheque deposit, demand deposit, savings deposits and time deposit. However, in practice the average cash-reserve ratio of banks is about 13 per cent. The required liquid asset ratio is 7 per cent, but the actual one is about 30 per cent, showing excess liquidity.

By and large, monetary growth exceeded nominal income growth. If we deflate the monetary growth with the consumer price index, the 'real' monetary growth also exceeded 'real' income growth.

There is however no pressure on price increase. As the economy is 'monetised' and capital is accumulated, more money is required for transaction, and money can be issued to some extent without causing inflation. The demand for money balance is in conformity with a theoretical model and is a function of (i) national income; (ii) interest rate; (iii) expected change in prices, and (iv) the trade/GNP ratio.

The most important determinant of money supply is the external sector (net foreign assets); the change in net claims on the private sector and government sector is the secondary factor. The money multiplier with respect to M_{1B} has been quite stable; and that with respect to M_2 has been rising, because of the increasing time and savings deposits. The ratio of bank reserves to reserve money has also been quite stable. The income velocities of circulation have been declining, mainly because of the reduction of the inflation rate.

The high savings and investment ratios contributed much to the economic growth and financial development. They are high as compared with the developed and developing countries. It is, however, a paradox that in spite of thc strong export activity, the investment incentive has been low since 1980. This will pose a danger in future that investment will not be adequate to sustain the growing economy.

As the money and capital markets have not yet been fully developed, Taiwan resorts to the instruments of (i) variation of cash-reserve ratio and liquidity ratio, (ii) interest-rate policy with regard to deposit rates and lending rates of banks, (iii) selective credit control and allocation of export-refinancing facilities, and (iv) persuasion and directives. The monetary policy of Taiwan was directed mainly toward stabilising prices and exchange rates. It also helped to stimulate economic development and exports.

Taiwan adopts a conservative attitude in foreign-exchange-rate policy, being the external part of monetary policy. The consistently large export surplus has caused a high inflow of foreign funds, and a pressure on the appreciating NT dollars; international reserves have soared and the banking system becomes very liquid. The appreciating NT dollar has not immediately reduced the trade balance; there is evidently a time-lag.

Although money supply, M_{1B} and M_2 rose in 1985–8, consumer prices were quite stable and wholesale prices even declined. The appreciating currency, by itself, would have a deflationary effect on the economy via the reduction of import prices.

In the 1950s, the NT dollar was pegged to the US dollar at an unrealistically high rate. There was a complicated multiple-exchange-rate system, with the foreign-exchange-certificate system, before the Programme for Improvement of Foreign Exchange and Trade Control in April 1958. Thus before July 1978 the exchange-rate system was a kind of adjustable peg-rate system. The appreciation or depreciation of the NT dollar against other currencies followed that of the US dollar, but did not reflect the changes in Taiwan's balance of payments, and the pursuit of internal policy objective was sometimes offset by external disturbances. To avoid that problem, the NT dollar ceased to be pegged to the US dollar in July 1978; the so-called 'managed-floating-rate system' was adopted and the foreign-exchange market has been gradually developed.

The foreign-exchange market was officially established in February 1979; only those 'appointed banks' were allowed to sell or buy foreign exchange under some restrictions which were gradually lifted. Practically all commercial banks are allowed to participate in the foreign exchange market, and branches of foreign banks are also allowed to participate in the Foreign Exchange Centre to determine the spot rate of the US dollar.[1] With the New Bank Act, 1989, financial liberalisation has been further accelerated.

Historically, land reform and agricultural development formed the basis of industrialisation. With high rates of manufacturing and export growth, and with increasing export surplus and international reserves, the financial institutions and markets follow the rising tide of development. Financial liberalisation and internationalisation are now persistently pursued; the major issue is whether such a policy should be carried out at a fast rate, or at a slower rate for easier adjustment. Another current issue is how to transform the government-owned banks, so that they may become more efficient in operation. There is a need to reform the financial system, with respect to banks, investment and trust companies, credit cooperatives, insurance companies, system of payment, etc.

The issue of land bonds to finance acquisition of land from the landlords in the land reform, agricultural finance through the Farmers' Associations and credit cooperatives, finance of medium and small business, export finance with specially low interest rates, and currently finance of high-technology industries and pollution-control equipments . . . all these measures connote the role of finance in economic development. Thus, the rapid development of financial institutions, markets and instruments is the result of the increasing role of finance.

Apart from the appropriate monetary–fiscal policies and development strategy one must not forget that the international demand condition was favourable to Taiwan, although Taiwan suffered from international diplomatic isolation. The Vietnamese War stimulated the growth of the textiles, plastics and petro-chemical industries, which formed the backbone of the industrialisation of Taiwan. International demand continues to be favourable to Taiwan in the 1970s and 1980s, particularly in the US market; the declining labour productivity in the US industries also contributes to this trend.

It can be expected that in the near future the financial system of Taiwan will be more liberalised, flexible, and outward-looking.

Notes

1 Introduction

1. Estimated on the basis of factor costs of constant (1981) prices, adjusted with changes in terms of trade. See Directorate-General of Budgeting, Accounting, and Statistics (DGBAS), *National Income in Taiwan Area*, December 1987, pp. 14–15.
2. The average annual growth rate of population was at a high level of 3.4 per cent in the period 1951–66; it declined to 2.3 per cent in 1967–79 and to 1.5 per cent in 1980–7. In 1987, it was only 1.1 per cent. See DGBAS, *Taiwan Statistical Data Book*, 1987, p. 4.
3. See DGBAS, *Monthly Statistics of the Republic of China*, no 267, March 1988, p. 11.
4. The Gini coefficient declined from 0.558 in 1953 to 0.360 in 1964 and to the lowest of 0.303 in 1980. After that, it went up to 0.317 in 1985 and 0.322 in 1986, implying a reverse trend towards more unequal distribution of income in the 1980s, particularly in 1984–6. See Shirley W. Y. Kuo, 'Achievement of Growth with Equity', a paper presented to the Conference on Economic Development Experience of Taiwan, held in Taipei, 8–10 June, 1988; and DGBAS, *The Survey Report of Personal Income Distribution* in 1986, October 1987, p. 13.
5. See Simon Kuznets, 'Economic Growth and Income Inequality', *American Economic Review*, 45 (March 1955), pp. 1–28.
6. Income elasticity of demand for food is usually less than unity. Hence increase of real income per capita would not increase the expenditure for food in the same proportion. There is a great tendency for the relative contribution of agriculture to national products to decline through long-run process of economic development and for farmers' income to lag behind national income. See Hsieh and Lee, *Agricultural Development and Its Contributions to Economic Growth in Taiwan*, pp. 4–5.
7. E. S. Shaw, *Financial Deepening in Economic Development* (New York: Oxford University Press, 1973); R. I. McKinnon, *Money and Capital in Economic Development* (Washington: Brookings Institution, 1973) and R. I. McKinnon (ed.) *Money and Finance in Economic Growth and Development* (New York: Marcel Dekker, 1976).
8. See Sheng-Yi Lee, *Trade and Investment Relations Between Taiwan and Asian Countries* Chung-Hua Institution for Economic Research (CHIER) Economic Monograph Series, no 16, July 1986, pp. 61–2.
9. Taiwan had a savings gap and foreign exchange gap in the early 1950s.
10. D. H. Robertson, *Essays in Money and Interest* (selected, with a memoir by Sir John Hicks) (London: Collins, 1966).
11. See R. M. Solow, 'A Contribution to the Theory of Economic Growth', *Quarterly Journal of Economics*, 62 (November 1958) pp. 65–94.
12. See S. C. Tsiang, 'Success or Failure in Economic Take-off', a paper presented to the Conference on 'The Problem of Development' at

Buffalo, New York, 27–29 May, 1988; and 'A Model of Economic Growth in Rostovian Stages', *Economica*, 32 (October 1964) pp. 619–48.

13. Quoted from Tsiang's Conference paper (see note 12).

2 Historical Review of the Banking System

1. The international situation turned abruptly unfavourable to Taiwan as there was an imminent risk that the People's Republic of China might take over all the assets of Bank of China in oversea countries. So legislation was hurriedly passed in Taiwan, so that the government shares were 'sold' to private hands, the Bank thereby becoming a private enterprise, and not a government one. The biggest shareholder is Central Investment Company, an investment arm of the KMT Party. Some few shares are still nominally in the hands of some people in mainland China – information from the International Commercial Bank of China. After the reorganisation, there was a split among the overseas branches of Bank of China. Some such as those in the USA and Bangkok, remained faithful to Taiwan, and therefore changed their name to branches of International Commercial Bank of China. Others turned to PRC, and maintained the old name of branches of the Bank of China, such as those in Hong Kong and Singapore. Bank of China maintains its Head Office at Beijing, PRC.
2. See Land Bank of Taiwan, *Thirty-Five Years of the Land Bank of Taiwan* Sept. 1981; *Annual Reports of the Land Bank of Taiwan*, 1982–6; and Tseng Hsiao *Fifty Years of Land Reform in the Republic of China* (Memoirs), Dec 1980.
3. See Bank of Communication of China, *Seventy-Five Years*, 1982.
4. See Bank of Taiwan, *Thirty Years*, pp. 1–16 and 67–76.
5. See Taiwan Cooperative Bank, *Thirty Years*, pp. 2–6.
6. See First Commercial Bank of Taiwan, *Eighty Years*, pp. 1–16, particularly the Table of Evolution on p. 15.
7. See The Medium Business Bank of Taiwan, *Annual Report 1983*, 'History and Organisation', p. 10.
8. See Wing-San Yuan, 'The Bank Interest Rates in Taiwan from Liberalisation to 1961', *Bank of Taiwan*, *Quarterly Journal*, June 1984.
9. See also the Central Bank of China, Taipei, Taiwan, *Financial Institutions in Taiwan*, February 1984.
10. Some of the deposits are also redeposited to Bank of Communication, Farmers' Bank of China, Cooperative Bank of Taiwan, and Medium and Small Business Bank of Taiwan to extend credit to customers, particularly rural credit and small business.
11. Hong Kong and Shanghai Banking Corporation was originally registered in London. After the Second World War it changed the registration to Hong Kong. The chairman of the Board of Directors, and most of the directors and senior officers are British. Therefore we classify it as a British bank.
12. An interview with Daiichi Kangyo Bank gives me this impression.
13. In recent years, Australia has also adopted the policy of economic and financial liberalisation. Banks start to branch out in overseas countries.

3 The Present Structure of the Financial System

1. See Central Trust of China, *Fifty Years*.
2. In fact, the Land Bank of Taiwan, and the Cooperative Bank of Taiwan also provide rural credit. All commercial banks provide short-term export-and-import credit although the Export–Import Bank is entrusted with the task of providing long-term credit.
3. See Central Bank of China, *Financial Institutions in Taiwan*, February 1984, pp. 19–21; and *Annual Report of the Financial Institutions*, 1984.
4. There is no regulation in Taiwan against accepting deposits from employees. In Singapore and Hong Kong, there is no such practice; in Japan, there is.
5. The term 'unorganised money market' used by the Central Bank is rather misleading as the market is in fact organised. In our view, it would be better to use the term 'informal money market', which means the same thing. Interest rates in the informal money market have been systematically compiled by the Central Bank of Taiwan and the Bank of Taiwan – see, for example, the Central Bank of China, *Financial Statistics Monthly*, June 1986, p. 104 and Wing-San Yuan, 'The Bank Interest Rates in Taiwan from Liberation to 1961', *Bank of Taiwan Quarterly Journal*, June 1984.
6. According to the US Aid programme, a counter-fund was created whereby the Taiwan government had to contribute Taiwan currency to the fund, equivalent to US Aid amount. The fund was to finance imports, investments and other approved activities.
7. In fact, the US Aid ended in 1965. Subsequent statistical figures in that column are only to show the lending of the government agencies.
8. There are five major groups of illegal activities: (i) smuggling; (ii) illegal slaughtering of pigs, cattle and sheep; (iii) illegal excavations of sand and stone from river-beds; (iv) black market transaction of foreign exchange and gold, and (v) others such as gambling, drug-dealing, prostitution, underground cabarets etc.

   It was estimated by a direct method that in 1981, the underground economy was about 14.4 per cent of GNP – see 'The Underground Economy and National Income Statistics', by four researchers in DGBAS, namely, Chua, Gia, Lu and Leng, Working Paper, p. 213. However, another research study, Chien Chuan-Ding, 'An Estimate of the Underground Economy', *Monthly Journal of the City Bank of Taipei*, vol. 14, no 5, May 1983 and 'A Study of the Underground Economy of Taiwan', *Quarterly Journal of the Bank of Taiwan*, vol. 32, no 4, December 1981, used an indirect method and came to the conclusion that the underground economy was as much as about 30 per cent! Perhaps that figure was exaggerated; the indirect method was rather arbitrary.
9. From 1961 to 1986, the annual growth rates of manufacturing and 'finance, insurance and real estate' were 18.91 per cent and 18.56 per cent respectively (see Chapter 7, Table 7.2 below). However, real estate should be excluded from the latter group in order to have a more accurate comparison.

10. See R. I. McKinnon, *Money and Capital in Economic Development* (Washington: Brookings Institution, 1973); E. S. Shaw, *Financial Deepening in Economic Development* (New York: Oxford University Press, 1973); R. I. McKinnon (ed.) *Money and Finance in Economic Growth and Development* (New York: Marcel Dekker, 1976); and 'Symposium on Finance in Developing Countries', *Journal of Development Studies*, January 1977, pp. 1–43; and J. G. Gurley and E. S. Shaw, *Money in a Theory of Finance* (Washington: Brookings Institution, 1960).
11. Figures 3.2 and 3.3 are adapted or modified from Tsiang's model – see S. C. Tsiang, 'Fashions and Misconceptions in Monetary Policy and their Influences on Financial and Banking Policies', *Zeitschrift fiir die gesamte Staatswissenschaft*, December 1979, pp. 587–9. Shou-Hsiang Liu followed the same model in his paper 'The Financial Intermediation Role under Dual Financial System' which was presented to the Conference on the Financial Development in Taiwan on 23–25 December 1984, and subsequently published as *Proceedings*, by the Academia Sinica, Taipei, pp. 319–332. Liu analyses the informal money market in terms of (a) intermediation function, (b) risk premium and (c) anti-intermediation function.

4 Assets and Liabilities of Financial Institutions

1. The Central Bank of China, after its rehabilitation in Taiwan in 1961, started to publish banking statistics. Statistical data before 1961 were not properly compiled or presented. Therefore, all bank statistics in this book start from 1961.
2. For example, at the end of 1986, out of the total assets/liabilities of NT$566bn, NT$285bn (50.4 per cent) were redeposited in the Central Bank, NT$274bn (48.4 per cent were redeposited in the four government banks (Bank of Communications, Land Bank of Taiwan, Farmers' Bank of China, and Medium Business Bank of Taiwan), NT$1.3bn (0.2 per cent) were invested in government securities; and only NT$3.6bn (0.6 per cent) were lent out to government enterprises.
3. For statutory reserve requirement, see Note 5 below.
4. The Government started issuing Treasury bills in 1973. Bankers' acceptance and negotiable certificates of deposits were introduced in 1975. After the promulgation of the 'Regulations Governing the Dealers of Short-Term Negotiable Instruments,' three bill finance companies were established in 1976–8 as mentioned above.
5. As from June 1982, the statutory requirement is as follows:

Cheque account	23 per cent
Passbook deposits	21 per cent
Savings deposits:	
Passbook	14 per cent
Time	8 per cent
Time deposit	10 per cent

See *Financial Statistics Monthly*, June 1986, p. 60. In Table 4.7 the cash/deposit ratio is the ratio of the sum of cash (item 1) plus deposit with Central Bank (item 2) to total deposit (item 11).

6. For an analysis of foreign banks in Taiwan, see Lee Sheng-Yi, 'A Study of Foreign Banks in Taiwan', (in Chinese), in the Proceeding of the Conference on 'Change in Financial Environment and the Appropriate Strategy', held in Taipei, on 8 March 1987.
7. Branches of foreign banks have to draw some capital funds from their head offices abroad. The statutory requirement is US$2m minimum.
8. For the relevant statistics, see CBC, *Financial Statistics Monthly*, May 1988 and various issues.
9. One foreign bank interviewed explained that their head-office directed them to suspend lending for the time being. They complained that there was not adequate protection for creditors under the laws in Taiwan.
10. See S. Y. Lee and Y. C. Jao, *Financial Structures and Monetary Policies in Southeast Asia*, pp. 149–71 and 173–97.
11. However, the textile industry (which should not be regarded as strategic industry) gains a substantial share, according to the Annual Report of the Bank of Communication.
12. See Central Bank of China, *Annual Reports of Operation of Various Financial Institutions in Taiwan*, 1979–86.

5 Monetary System

1. See G. C. Pan, *The Analysis of the Inflation in Taiwan in the Early Recovery Period* (Central Bank of China, n.d.), and Chang Kia-Ngau, *The Inflationary Spiral: The Experience in China, 1939–1950* (London: Chapman & Hall, 1958).
2. See Bank of Taiwan, *Thirty Years*, May 1976, pp. 25–33.
3. After October 1948 (the collapse of the Gold Yuan Notes), the exchange rate between OTD and NC became flexible.
4. As in May 1987, the international reserves of Taiwan rose to US$65bn, whereas the gross currency issue was NT$292bn.
5. In the Currency Board System of Malaya and Singapore, the currency reserve was said to be '100 per cent', meaning 100 per cent reserve in gold and convertible foreign exchange. The present Currency Board of Singapore still maintains such a reserve. See Lee Sheng-Yi, *Monetary and Banking Development of Singapore and Malaysia* (Singapore University Press, 1986) (2nd edn.)
6. It should be noted that in some countries, such as Singapore and Malaysia, there is no distinction between demand and time and savings deposits with respect to reserve requirement. The USA and some other countries, however have such a distinction.
7. For monetary control, the emphasis is on banks. In the previous period, 1948–75, banks were categorised into commercial banks, savings banks and industrial banks for the sake of regulating reserve requirement. For the change in actual reserve requirements from 1948 to the present, see Central Bank of China, *Financial Statistics Monthly, Taiwan District*, August 1987, Table 12.

8. See A. Marshall, *Money, Credit and Commerce* (London: Macmillan, 1924). Marshall has a monetary equation, which has long been forgotten, but his simplier equation ($M = kY$) is equally well-known:

$$M = kY + k'A$$

where A = wealth of the people
k' = proportion of wealth held in cash balance
Y = income
k = proportion of income held in cash balance
M = money

9. See H. A. Latané, 'Income Velocity and Interest Rates: A Pragmatic Approach', *Review of Economics and Statistics*, November 1960; 'Cash Balance and the Interest Rate – A Pragmatic Approach', *Review of Economics and Statistics*, November 1954.
10. Radcliffe Report, *Committee on the Working of the Monetary System*, Cmnd. 827, August 1959, para. 392.
11. For a theoretical analysis of the concept of Trade/GNP, see S. C. Tsiang, 'The Monetary Theoretical Foundation of the Modern Monetary Approach to the Balance of Payments', p. 326.
12. In Singapore, the income elasticity of the demand for M_1 and M_2 in real terms in 1968–82 (quarterly data) was 0.962 and 0.950 respectively. See Sheng-Yi, *The Monetary and Banking Development of Singapore and Malaysia*.
13. See Sheng-Yi, *Monetary and Banking Development*, p. 189 for Singapore and p. 228 for Malaysia. The interest rate variable in the money demand function in Malaysia also exhibits a poor performance.
14. From end 1985 to June 1988, the certificate of deposits (which was introduced only in October 1985) was increased dramatically from NT$26.8bn to NT$946.1bn in December 1987, but was reduced to NT$651.5bn in June 1988; savings bond (which was introduced in December 1985) was increased from NT$3.7bn to NT$189.0bn; and Treasury bill-*B* (which was increased sharply in 1983 and 1984) *declined* from NT$74.0bn to NT$31.7bn in August 1987, but increased to NT$86.1bn in June 1988. In the corresponding period foreign assets of Central Bank increased from NT$936.1bn to NT$2173.4bn. See Central Bank of China, *Financial Statistics Monthly*, July 1988, pp. 13–16, 'Assets and Liabilities of the Central Bank of China'.
15. See Milton Friedman and Anna Jacob Schwartz, *A Monetary History of the United States, 1867–1960* (New Jersey: Princeton University Press, 1963) Appendix B.
16. See Harry G. Johnson, *Macroeconomics and Monetary Theory* (London: Gray-Mills, 1971) pp. 136–7.
17. See J. Abrendorf and S. Kanesathasan, 'Variations in Money Multipliers and their Implications for Central Banking', *IMF Staff/Papers* (vol. VIII) 1960, pp. 126–49.
18. See J. M. Keynes, *General Theory of Employment, Interest and Money* (London: Macmillan, 1947) ch. 13 and 14.

19. Milton Friedman, 'The Quantity Theory of Money: A Restatement', in Milton Friedman (ed.) *Studies in the Quantity Theory of Money* Chicago: University of Chicago Press, 1956).
20. The annual growth rate of gross domestic capital formation at current prices (see Table 5.9) from 1970 to 1979 was 21.12 per cent, whilst that from 1980–7 was 2.1 per cent. A similar conclusion was drawn in the Chung Hua Institution for Economic Research (CHIER) Report, 'A Study of the Investment Incentive in Taiwan', presented to the Ministry of Economic Affairs, Bureau of Industries, in January 1985, which stated that the growth rate of the gross domestic capital formation declined from 16.8 per cent in 1964–73, to 8.2 per cent in 1974–83 and to 0.4 per cent in 1982–4 (see p. 12 of Report).
21. 1. Regression of investment ratio, I, on savings ratio, S_1, in 1951–5:

$$I = 13.854 + 0.468\ S_1$$
t-value: (11.31) (8.66)

R^2 adjusted = 0.694
$DW = 0.821$

2. Regression of savings ratio, S_1 on investment ratio, I in 1951–85:

$$S_1 = -14.568 + 1.484\ I$$
t-value: (−3.56) (8.66)

R^2 adjusted = 0.694
$DW = 0.628$

22. For a full discussion, see S. C. Tsiang, 'Monetary Policy in Taiwan'. See also Shirley W. Y. Kuo, *The Taiwan Economy in Transition*, pp. 289–93; and Kowie Chang (ed.), *Economic Development in Taiwan*, pp. 466–9.
23. This is what Fei and Ranis call 'Critical Minimum Effort analysis'; see John C. H. Fei and Gustav Ranis, *Development of Labour Surplus Economy: Theory and Policy* (Homewood, Illinois: Richard D. Irwin, 1965).
24. Quoted from Shirley W. Y. Kuo, *The Taiwan Economy in Transition*, p. 6.
25. See Fei and Ranis, *Development of Labour Surplus Economy*; and Fei, Ranis and Kuo, *Growth with Equity; the Taiwan Case*.
26. See Kuo, *The Taiwan Economy in Transition*, p. 56, Figure 4.1.

6 Monetary Policy

1. There was a black market of foreign exchange until recently, because of exchange control.
2. See, for example, Central Bank of China, *Financial Statistics Monthly*, March 1987, p. 64 for cash–reserve ratio requirement, and p. 66 for liquidity ratio requirement.
3. They include (a) all deposits of Singapore non-bank residents; (b)

borrowing from banks in Singapore less all claims against banks in Singapore, (c) Singapore dollar certificates of deposit issued less holdings of S$CDs and (d) non-resident, non-bank deposits in both Singapore dollars and foreign currencies.

4. The liquid–asset ratio in Singapore has also remained unchanged at 20 per cent from 1961 to 1988; however in 1989 it was changed to 18 per cent.
5. Before 1981, there was also a difference in the interest rates between secured and unsecured loans.
6. According to Taiwan statistics, M_{1B} = currency in active circulation + cheque account + passbook deposits + passbook savings deposits of banks. See Central Bank of China, *Financial Statistics Monthly, Taiwan District*, April 1988.
7. Effective exchange rate index (EEI) = $\sum_{j=1}^{n} \frac{e_{cj}}{e_{bj}} \times w_j$

where e_{cj} = current period exchange rate of NT$ *vis-à-vis* a foreign currency, *j*.
e_{bj} = base period (1980) exchange rate of NT$ *vis-à-vis* a foreign currency, *j*.
w_j = the pattern of weights of the major trading partners.

In other words, EEI = movement of exchange rates of NT$ *vis-à-vis* the currencies of the major trading partners, weighted by Taiwan's exports to these partners. For a statistical analysis of the EEI, REEI and PCI, see 'The Report on the Courses of the Current Economic Problems and the Appropriate Government Policy', no. 2, 'The Effect of Exchange Rate Change on Trade of Taiwan', Chung Hua Institution for Economic Research, Taipei, no 76, 582.273 dated November 1987, pp. 35–49.

8. Real Effective Exchange Rate Index (REEI)

$$\sum_{j=1}^{n} p_{cj} \times W_j = \text{EEI} \div \frac{\sum_{j=1}^{n} \frac{p_{cj}}{p_{bj}} \times W_j}{\frac{p_{cd}}{p_{bd}}}$$

where p_{cj} and p_{bj} = current and base period prices of a foreign country, *j*, respectively.
p_{cd} and p_{bd} = current and base period prices of the domestic country, i.e. Taiwan.

In other words, REEI = EEI, deflated by the relative price changes of foreign and home countries.

9. Price Competitive Index (PCI) = $\frac{P_{it}}{P_{dt}} \cdot \frac{e_{dt}}{e_{it}}$

where P_{it} = the price index of i country at period, *t*.
P_{dt} = the price index of the home country, Taiwan, at period, *t*.
e_{dt} = the exchange rate index of NT$ at period, *t*.
e_{it} = the exchange rate index of *i* currency in terms of US$ at period, *t*.

In other words, PCI = relative price change of the foreign and home prices relative to exchange rate movement of the home and foreign countries.

If PCI goes up, exports would be favourable. Again, we take 1980 = 1.000 as the starting-point.

10. The index of labour productivity increased from 100 in 1981 to 123.78 in 1985, 138.49 in 1986, and 149.27 in the third quarter, 1987. The index of unit labour costs increased at a much lower rate from 100 in 1981 to 108.96 in 1985, 105.55 in 1986 and 101.76 in the third quarter, 1987. This shows Taiwan has been successful in increasing labour productivity, and reducing the rise in unit labour cost to counteract the adverse effect of the appreciating NT dollar. See DGBAS, *Quarterly National Economic Trends, Taiwan Area*, no 39, November 1987, p. 20.

7 Development of the Financial and Real Sectors

1. See E. S. Shaw, *Financial Deepening in Economic Development* (New York: Oxford University Press, 1973); R. I. McKinnon, *Money and Capital in Economic Development* (Washington: Brookings Institution, 1973); R. I. McKinnon (ed.) *Money and Finance in Economic Growth and Development* (New York: Marcel Dekker, 1976); and 'Symposium on Finance in Developing Countries', *Journal of Development Studies*, January 1977, pp. 1–43.
2. The monetary statistics in satisfactory forms started to be published in 1951 or 1952, whilst the banking statistics in consistent form started to be available in 1961.
3. A similar picture was presented by several scholars. See, for example Ramon H. Myers, 'The Economic Development of the Republic of China on Taiwan, 1965–1981', in Lawrence J. Lau, (ed.) *Models of Development*, pp. 20–1.
4. If a person desires to open a cheque account with a bank, there is quite a complicated procedure and a guarantor is required.
5. In Taiwan, there are three levels of so-called people's representatives – the central, provincial and municipal representatives of people's assemblies. All of them may sometimes interfere with the administration of government banks, such as borrowing money or requesting some special favour.
6. For a historical and critical review of the agricultural reform, see Yu-Kang Mao (Counsellor for the Council of Agriculture, Executive Yuan), 'Role of Agriculture in Economic Development in Taiwan', a paper presented to the Conference on Economic Development in the Republic of China on Taiwan, held at Taipei on 22–27 July 1987, pp. 27–32; Tseng Hsiao, *50 Years Land Reform in Republic of China* (in Chinese) which covered the land reform in both mainland China and Taiwan; and *Thirty-Five Years of the Land Bank of Taiwan* (in Chinese), September 1981.
7. See Mao, 'Role of Agriculture', p. 28.
8. In contrast, in the old days in Mainland China, some of the government officials were themselves landlords, and hence for their own self-interest,

they were reluctant to carry out the land-reform by distributing the land to the poor tenant-farmers. This explained why in spite of the outcry for land-reform for years, the programme could not be effectively carried out.

9. Under Japanese rule, the Farmers' Association had been organised in order to produce rice and sugar for export to Japan. After the reoccupation of Taiwan, the government encouraged the organisation of the Farmers' Association, in order to support the Land Reform, and to improve the credit and marketing system of farming.
10. However, it can be said that the western side of the Island is better developed, with more industries, than the eastern side.
11. For an analysis of the flow of capital funds from agriculture to industry in 1911–60, see T. H. Lee, *The Flow of Capital Fund Between Agriculture and Industries in Taiwan*. Dr Lee is now the President of the Republic of China (Taiwan).
12. The Gini coefficient declined from 0.558 in 1953 to 0.461 in 1961 and to 0.317 in 1985; and the ratio of the income share of the richest 20 per cent to that of the poorest 20 per cent declined from 20.5 per cent in 1953 to 11.6 per cent in 1961 and to 4.5 per cent in 1985 (see Shirley W. Y. Kuo, 'Economic Development in the Republic of China', Conference on Economic Development in the Republic of China on Taiwan, held at Taipei on 22–7 July 1987). However, this does not imply that the land reform had such a strong effect, although it was undoubtedly one of the contributing factors.
13. See Yung Wei, 'Planning for Growth, Equality and Democracy: the Non-Economic Factors in ROC's Development Process', Conference on Economic Development in the Republic of China on Taiwan, on 22–7 July 1987.
14. See Liang Kuo-Shu and Liang Hou Ching-Ing 'Trade Strategy and the Exchange Rate Policies in Taiwan', in Wontack Hong and Lawrence B. Krause (eds), *Trade and Growth of the Advanced Developing Countries in the Pacific Basin* (Papers and Proceedings of the Eleventh Pacific Trade and Development Conference) (Seoul: Korea Development Institute, 1981) pp. 151–2.
15. For the contribution of agriculture to economic growth of Taiwan, see Teng-Hui Lee and Yueh-Eh Chen, *Growth Rates of Taiwan Agriculture, 1911–1972*; and S. C. Hsieh and T. H. Lee, *Agricultural Development and its Contributions to Economic Growth in Taiwan*.
16. Taiwan had a trade deficit from 1952 to 1970, averaging US$87.6m per year. The trade balance became positive after 1971. As a result of the first oil crisis, the deficit was US$1327m in 1974, and US$643m in 1975. Thereafter the export surplus progressively increased, particularly in 1984–7. In July 1987, it reached US$65bn (see *Taiwan Statistical Data Book*, 1987).
17. The Regulations for Rebate of Taxes on Export Products were promulgated in July 1955, providing for the rebate of import duty, defence surtax and commodity tax in order to encourage processing of imported materials for exports.
18. As from 1961, export sale was exempted from business income tax and

stamp duty – see the Statute for the Encouragement of Investment (dated 10 September 1960) Articles 16 and 19.

19. For an analysis of the effective tariff rates, see Keh-Nan Sun, 'Tariff Protection and Structural Change in Taiwan', Chung-Hua Institution for Economic Research, *Economic Paper*, no 8, August 1982, pp. 48 and 151.
20. See Liang Kuo-Shu and Liang Hou Ching-Ing, 'Trade Strategy and Exchange Rate Policies'.
21. The rate was reduced to 0.04 per cent during the period of recession from July 1974 to August 1975.
22. See for example, Sheng-Yi Lee, *Trade and Investment Relationships between Taiwan ROC and Asean Countries*, CHIER Economic Monograph Series, no 16, Chung-Hua Institution for Economic Research, Taipei, 1986, pp. 79–80.
23. See, for example, Bela Balassa, 'Export and Economic Growth: Further Evidence', *Journal of Development Economics*, vol. 5, 1978, pp. 181–9; Bela Balassa, 'Exports, Policy Choices, and Economic Growth in Developing Countries after the 1973 Oil Shock', *Journal of Development Economics*, vol. 18, 1985, pp. 23–35; Gershon, Feder, 'On Exports and Economic Growth', *Journal of Development Economics*, vol. 12, 1983, pp. 59–73; Heller, Peter, and Porter, Richard, 'Exports and Growth: An Empirical Investigation', *Journal of Development Economics*, vol. 5, 1978, pp. 191–3.
24. In contrast, South Korea's development strategy is to help big trading houses as conglomerates so that they can have world wide connection and can compete effectively in international market. This follows the Japanese *Zaibatsu* (before the War) and Groups (after the War).
25. As the industrial structures of the USA, Japan and Germany shift upward to skill-and-capital-intensive manufactures, a strong import demand develops for light consumer manufactures. However, in recent years, the industrial structure of Taiwan has also been shifted upward, as she exports computers, and parts, electronic and other skill-intensive goods. By and large, Taiwan exports labour-intensive manufactures to developed countries.

8 Liberalisation and Reform of the Financial System

1. See Shirley W. Y. Kuo, 'The Liberalisation of Interest Rate and Foreign Exchange in Taiwan', a memorial speech in Taipei on 13 August 1988, in honour of the late Professor Ta-Chung Liu.
2. Some private banks have progressed satisfactorily e.g. the Chinese International Commercial Bank.
3. It was recognised that many bank directors knew very little about banking. On the other hand, bank executives, who had worked in the banks for many years, had no chance of being promoted to directorship, because of the existing regulations.
4. The purpose of the rotation system is to prevent corruption and abuses, as an executive is not allowed to stay in one particular post for too long a time.

5. For a detailed discussion, see S. Y. Lee and Y. C. Jao, *Financial Structures and Monetary Policies in South East Asia*.
6. For example, the Chua family once controlled the Cathay Investment and Trust Company. When the case of Tenth Credit Co-operative blew up in 1985, there was a run on the Company.
7. See the Committee of Economic Reform Report, pp. 49–57.
8. For a discussion of the Credit Cooperative Act, and the suggested amendment, see Wang Wing Yun, *The Grass Root Finance of Taiwan – the Past, Present and Future*, (Taiwan: Research and Training Centre of Grass Root Finance, 1981).
9. See Taiwan Stock Exchange Statistics.

9 Summary and Conclusions

1. Hitherto, only five major appointed domestic banks have been allowed to participate in the Foreign Exchange Centre to determine the spot rate.

Bibliography

OFFICIAL SOURCES

ANNUAL REPORTS of various banks, investment and trust companies and other financial institutions.

BANK OF COMMUNICATION OF CHINA, *Eighty Years of the Bank of Communication of China*, March 1987 (in Chinese).

BANK OF TAIWAN, *Thirty Years of the Bank of Taiwan*, May 1976 (in Chinese).

CENTRAL BANK OF CHINA, *Balance of Payments, Taiwan District* (compiled in accordance with IFS format) 1981–present.

CENTRAL BANK OF CHINA, Economic Research Department, *Flow of Funds in Taiwan District* (1965–87).

CENTRAL BANK OF CHINA, Economic Research Department, *Financial Statistics Monthly, Taiwan District.*

CENTRAL BANK OF CHINA, *Financial Statistics, Taiwan District* (compiled in accordance with IFS format) 1981–present.

CENTRAL BANK OF CHINA, Economic Research Department, *A Supplement to Financial Statistics Monthly, Taiwan District*, 3rd edn, October 1987.

CENTRAL BANK OF CHINA, Financial Institution Supervision Department, *Annual Reports of Business Operation of Financial Institutions in Taiwan* (in Chinese); and *Statistical Statements of Financial Institutions in Taiwan* (restricted).

CENTRAL TRUST OF CHINA, *Fifty Years of the Central Trust of China*, October 1985.

DIRECTORATE-GENERAL OF BUDGETING, ACCOUNTING AND STATISTICS, *National Income of Taiwan*, 1987 and various issues.

DIRECTORATE-GENERAL OF BUDGETING, ACCOUNTING AND STATISTICS, *Report of Survey of Personal Income Distribution*, 1987 and various issues.

FARMERS' BANK OF CHINA, *Fifty Years of the Farmers' Bank of China*, April 1983 (in Chinese).

FIRST COMMERCIAL BANK OF TAIWAN, *Eighty Years of the First Commercial Bank of Taiwan*, November 1979 (in Chinese).

HSIAO, DR TSENG, *Fifty Years of Land Reform in the Republic of China* (Memoirs), Research on Land Administration of China, December 1980 (in Chinese).

LAND BANK OF CHINA, *Thirty-five Years of the Land Bank of China*, September 1981 (in Chinese).

Report of the Executive Yuan, Economic Reform Committee (Chapter 3, Banking and Finance Study) November 1985 (in Chinese).

TAIWAN COOPERATIVE BANK, *Thirty Years of the Taiwan Cooperative Bank*, October 1976 (in Chinese).

BOOKS AND ARTICLES

CHANG, CHI-CHENG, Governor of the Central Bank of China, 'Financial Liberalisations in the Republic of China', an address to the First Annual Pacific Basin Finance Conference in Taipei on 13 March 1989.

CHANG, KOWIE (ed.) *Economic Development in Taiwan* (Taipei: Chung Chung Book Co., 1968).

CHENG, CHAO-CHEN, *Land Reform in Taiwan* (Taipei: China Publishing, 1961).

CHIU, PAUL C. H., 'The Short-term Money Demand Function of Taiwan', in Kuo-Shu Liang and Ta-Ho Lin (eds) *Essays on Money and Finance* (in honour of the 80th birthday of Professor Lin Wai Farn) (Taipei, 1984) (in Chinese).

CHOW, GREGORY, 'On the Long-run and Short-run Demand for Money', *Journal of Political Economy*, April 1966, pp. 111–31.

FEI, JOHN C. H.; RANIS, GUSTAV AND KUO, SHIRLEY W. Y., *Growth with Equity: The Taiwan Case* (a World Bank Research Publication) (Oxford: Oxford University Press, 1979).

GALENSON, WALTER (ed.) *Economic Growth and Structural Change in Taiwan: The Post-war Experience of the Republic of China* (New York: Cornell University Press, 1979).

GOLD, B. THOMAS, *State and Society in the Taiwan Miracle* (New York: M. E. Sharpe, 1986).

HO, SAMUEL P. S., *Economic Development in Taiwan, 1860–1970* (New Haven: Yale University Press, 1978).

HSIEH, S. C. and LEE, T. H., *Agricultural Development and its Contributions to Economic Growth in Taiwan* (Input–Output and Productivity Analysis of Taiwan Agricultural Development), Chinese–American Joint Commission on Rural Reconstruction, Economic Digest Series, no. 17 (Taipei, April 1966).

HSING, MO-HUAN, 'Economic Calculation in Relation to Economic Policy', *Industry of Free China*, October 1954 (Taipei) (in Chinese).

HSING, MO-HUAN, *Taiwan: Industrialization and Trade Policies* (Oxford: Oxford University Press, 1971).

HSING, MO-HUAN, 'Further Observations in the Growth and Structural Shifts of the Taiwan Economy: Re-examination and Extension of Professor Simon Kuznet's Studies', *Academia Economic Papers* (Taipei) (in Chinese).

HSING, MO-HUAN, 'Could the Taiwan Economy have Performed Better?: An Appraisal of Economic Policies Adopted by the Government since the 1950s', a lecture delivered in the Chung-Hua Institution for Economic Research, Taipei.

KOO, ANTHONY Y. C., *The Role of Land Reform in Economic Development: A Case Study of Taiwan* (New York: Praeger, 1968).

KUO, SHIRLEY W. Y.; RANIS, GUSTAV, AND FEI, JOHN C. H.., *The Taiwan Success Story: Rapid Growth with Improved Distribution in the Republic of China, 1952–78* (Boulder, Colorado: Westview, 1981).

KUO, SHIRLEY W. Y., *The Taiwan Economy in Transition* (Boulder, Colorado: Westview, 1983).

KUO, SHIRLEY W. Y., (Minister of Finance) 'Liberalisation of the Financial Market in Taiwan in the 1980s', Keynote address at the First Annual Pacific Basin Finance Conference in Taipei on 14 March 1989.

LAU, LAWRENCE J. (ed.) *Models of Development* (A Comparative Study of Economic Growth in South Korea and Taiwan) (San Francisco: Institute for Contemporary Studies Press, 1986).

LEE, T. H., *The Flow of Capital Funds between Agriculture and Industries in Taiwan*, Ph.D. thesis presented to the Cornell University, USA, 1969.

LEE, T. H., *Intersectoral Capital Flow in the Economic Development of Taiwan, 1895–1960* (Ithaca, New York: Cornell University Press, 1971).

LEE, TENG-HUI and CHEN, YUEH-EH, *Growth Rates of Taiwan Agriculture, 1911–1972*, Chinese-American Joint Commission on Rural Reconstruction, Economic Digest Series, no 21 (Taipei, January 1975).

LIANG, MING-YIH; CHEN, KUN-MING, and LIU, SHOU-HSIANG, 'The Demand for Money in Taiwan Revisited' (in Chinese), in Chung Hua Institution for Economic Research, Taipei (CHIER) Economic Papers no 11, September 1982.

LIANG, MING-YIH, 'The Involuntary Demand for Money and the Case of the Missing Money', Institute of Economics, Academia Sinica, Monograph Series no 17, April 1980.

LIN, C. Y., *Industrialization in Taiwan, 1946–72* (New York: Praeger, 1973).

LIU, PAUL K. C., 'Economic Development and Population in Taiwan since 1895: An Overview', in *Essays on the Population of Taiwan* (Taipei: Academia Sinica, Graduate Institute of Economics, 1973).

Proceedings of the Conference on Experiences and Lessons of Economic Development in Taiwan, 18–20 December 1981 (Taipei: Institute of Economics, Academia Sinica).

Proceedings of the Conference on Inflation in East Asian Countries, 20–22 May 1983, CHIER Conference Series no 2.

Proceedings of the Conference on Economic Development in the Republic of China on Taiwan, 22–27 July 1987, CHIER Conference Series, no 7.

SHENG-YI, LEE, *Monetary and Banking Development of Singapore and Malaysia* (Singapore: Singapore University Press, 1986) revised edn.

SHENG-YI, LEE and JAO, Y. C., *Financial Structures and Monetary Policies of South-East Asia* (London: Macmillan, 1982).

SUN, CHEN, 'The Trend of Economic Development and Productivity in Taiwan', *Academia Economic Papers*, The Institute of Economics, Academia Sinica, Taipei, 1976.

TSIANG, S. C., 'The Monetary Theoretical Foundation of the Modern Monetary Approach to the Balance of Payments', *Oxford Economic Papers*, vol. 29, no 3, November 1977.

TSIANG, S. C., 'Monetary Policy in Taiwan', a paper presented to the Conference on Experiences and Lessons Of Economic Development in Taiwan at Taipei on 18–20 December 1981 and later published in Academia Economic Papers, by the Institute of Economics, Academia Sinica, Taipei, pp. 254–7.

TSIANG, S. C., 'Success or Failure in Economic Take-off', a paper presented to the Conference on 'The Problem of Development', held in Buffalo, New York, on 27–29 May 1988.

YU, TZONG-SHIAN, 'The Impact of Monetary and Fiscal Actions on a Trade-oriented Economy', Central Bank Macroeconomic Modelling in Pacific Basin Countries, *Proceedings of the First Pacific Basin Central Bank Conference in Econometric Modelling* (Federal Reserve Bank of San Francisco, 1976) pp. 211–22.

YU, TZONG-SHIAN and LEE, K.C., 'A Trade-oriented Econometric Model of Taiwan, 1961–81', in *Proceedings of the Conference on Pacific Area Economic Models of Project LINK* (Institute of Economics, Academia Sinica, 1983) pp. 511–36.

Index